THE HEBREW SCRIPTURES

Saint Mary's Press
Christian Brothers Publications
Winona, Minnesota

THE HEBREW SCRIPTURES

The Biblical Story
of God's Promise to Israel and Us

by
Mary Reed Newland

Mary Reed Newland
committed much of her life
to the needy.
For this reason,
her family wishes to dedicate
this, her final project,
in her honor to those
who suffer for lack of shelter,
nourishment, and
human dignity.

Nihil Obstat: Rev. Msgr. William T. Magee
Censor Deputatus
12 September 1989
Imprimatur: †Most Rev. John G. Vlazny, DD
Bishop of Winona
12 September 1989

The publishing team included Stephan Nagel, development editor and designer; Barbara Allaire and Carl Koch, FSC, consulting editors; Rosemary Broughton and Joseph Stoutzenberger, consultants; Susan Baranczyk, manuscript editor; Diana Witt, indexer; Eve Marie Dieterman, Benjamin Nagel, and Penny Koehler, photo researchers; and Evy Abrahamson, illustrator and design consultant.

The acknowledgments continue on page 261.

Printed in the United States of America

Printing: 6 5

Year: 1996 95

ISBN 0-88489-231-X

Contents

1

Why Read
the Hebrew Scriptures?
Key Questions
About This Course

THE first question that students of the Scriptures must ask is, Why read the first part of the Bible, formerly known as the Old Testament? The many good answers can be stated briefly as follows:

The roots of faith

The roots of Christian faith are found in the Hebrew Scriptures. Abraham, the early ancestor of the Israelites, has long been called the father of the Christian faith as well as of the Jewish faith. Similarly, recent church documents compare the Christian Church to a branch grafted onto the "good olive tree" of Judaism. So Christians cannot fully understand their faith without knowing these scriptures.

The background to the Good News

The Hebrew Scriptures tell the story of Jesus' people and the religious traditions he loved and practiced. These writings formed the background for his teaching. Likewise, the writers of the Gospels quoted the Hebrew Scriptures over three hundred times. So we miss the meaning of many gospel references if we have not read the scriptures that preceded them.

A portrait of us

Our own adventures with God are mirrored in the story of ancient Israel. The Hebrew Scriptures give us numerous tales of people like ourselves—their wisdom and folly, courage and fears, great deeds and sins.

A plan for the future

Current efforts to save the world with power and force seem to be wearing thin; today may be the time to take seriously the words of the saving God that are found in the Bible. The way to peace, God says, is to practice justice and mercy. As people of the Bible, Christians are called to do this wherever they are in the world, for whoever is in need.

Facing page: At the Jewish festival called *Simchas Torah,* Israelis celebrate the Hebrew Scriptures by carrying the writings in procession while singing and dancing.

The source of Western wisdom

The Bible is the most important book in Western history—the primary source for many of the world's literary, philosophical, and theological works. Its wisdom continues to shape our Western view of the world, of life, and of human nature.

The living word

Viewing the Hebrew Scriptures as classic literature does not fully explain why people have continued to read them for centuries, searching them for hope and wisdom and using them for prayer. The best testimony to their inspired revelation is the countless readers over thousands of years who have found the presence of God in them.

Why Read This Book in Addition to the Bible?

Reading the Bible itself is certainly the most important element of this course. Textbooks about the Bible will never offer the same powerful experience that the living word of God does.

Then why use a textbook at all? Why not simply read the Bible? The reason is that a guided tour of the Bible will help you find your way through its great stories and make the connections between its various parts. This course covers all the books of the Hebrew Scriptures, and you will be asked to read parts of each one. Your reading will be limited to essential passages—for example, a great story, a marvelous poem, a profound prayer, or a wise teaching. In addition, the commentary provided in this book will help you do the following:

- bypass material that is not necessary to understanding a particular story, a book, or the Scriptures as a whole
- become familiar with terms and names that are important to the biblical message
- understand how a specific passage relates to the larger story or book in which it is found

You will be expected to do a lot of reading in this course, but with both this book and the Bible, you have the help you need to make the course a success. The two other necessary ingredients, you yourself must bring:

1. *A willingness to think through the course material:* This book contains many questions and activities to help you,

Recall the first biblical story you can remember hearing. Write a paragraph telling how old you were, who told the story, and the circumstances in which it was told. Retell that biblical story in writing.

but you must choose to spend time reading, reflecting, and praying with the Bible.

2. *A willingness to discuss the course material:* Many opportunities for class discussion will be offered in this course, but you must take advantage of them. This might mean talking about your own feelings of faith in a personal way, even expressing religious doubts you experience. Sharing such thoughts can make you uncomfortable, but honesty is a necessary component in a religion course intended to help you establish an honest relationship with God.

Special study aids

Some special study aids included in this book will help you become comfortable with the Scriptures:

1. *Key terms:* A basic vocabulary of terms will help you in your scriptural study and prayer. All special terms and phrases are printed in **boldfaced** type. When you see these terms, make a special attempt to understand and remember them.

2. *Pronunciations:* Pronunciations are given in the index, on pages 250–260. Look up the correct pronunciation whenever you find a new name—before you guess at pronouncing it. The first attempt to pronounce a word is the pronunciation that tends to stay in the mind. Try to get it right the first time.

3. *Personal reflection activities:* In the margins of this book you will find suggestions for personal reflection. These are short exercises or questions directly related to the ideas being examined. Your teacher may use these activities to start classroom discussions. Or they may be used as homework assignments. Even when they are not assigned by the teacher, do the activities yourself to help your understanding of the material in this course.

Special note on the term *Hebrew Scriptures*

A good way to start this course is to break the habit of calling the Hebrew Scriptures "the Old Testament." Calling something old can imply that it is worn-out or outdated. Imagine referring to the U.S. Constitution as "the Old Constitution." That is what the term *Old Testament* sounds like to Jewish believers.

The Bible is filled with the living presence of God. From here on, try to use the title *Hebrew Scriptures* for the first part of it.

You can make this course a success by thinking through the material and sharing your ideas in class discussions.

Where Do the Hebrew Scriptures Come From?

The Bible comes from the Jews. Even the authors of the New Testament, with the exception of Saint Luke, were probably Jews who had become Christians. This is fortunate for us because more gifted storytellers do not exist, and the Hebrew Scriptures are largely books of stories—the stories of Jesus' people.

The forty-six books of the Hebrew Scriptures come from many different times and authors.

- Some books were originally **oral traditions**—that is, unwritten, memorized versions of Israel's history and laws. As long as four thousand years ago, elders recited these stories around the campfires at night and at the great celebrations when the Israelite tribes gathered to remember God's goodness.
- About the time of David, the histories of the kings probably became the first written documents.
- Later, some of the men who spoke for God (**prophets**) and others who taught about human and divine wisdom (**sages**) wrote their own works, and for those who did not, secretaries and disciples recorded their oracles and sayings.
- Finally, editors combined these written records with the oral traditions.

The resulting books, written on scrolls, became the Jews' most precious possessions.

A Historical Sketch of Ancient Israel

As the notes above suggest, the Hebrew Scriptures are so much a part of Jewish history that they cannot be separated from it. We will be referring to this history throughout the course, and you will need to become familiar with the key events as soon as possible. The following is a description of the key events, many of which may be familiar to you:

The founders and the Promise

The history and the religion of the Israelites began with Abraham. Abraham was a wandering herdsman, or **nomad**, who lived in the region of Iraq around 1850 B.C.E. According to the Book of Genesis, God made an agreement with Abraham. God promised to make Abraham's descendants

The standard practice in educational publications is to use the abbreviations B.C.E. (before the common era) and C.E. (of the common era) in place of the traditional abbreviations B.C. and A.D.

The Treasured Scrolls

The books of the Hebrew Scriptures were first written in the Hebrew language on sheets of goatskin or sheepskin called *parchment*. These leather sheets were sewn together to make one continuous strip. Each end of the strip was fastened to a dowel, and each book was rolled up from both ends to make a *scroll*.

This parchment scroll containing scriptural writings is from fifteenth-century Germany, but it is constructed like those used by the ancient Israelites.

a blessing to the world and to give them the land of Canaan, later known as Palestine. The Promise, as this is called, was that Abraham's descendants would reveal the one God to the world. Christians believe that this Promise reached its fulfillment in the coming of Christ.

Abraham's descendants and their families inherited the Promise. His son Isaac and grandson Jacob, like Abraham, would be called the **patriarchs,** or founders, and their wives, the **matriarchs** of the Jewish faith.

The Israelites and the Covenant

At the close of the Book of Genesis, the descendants of Abraham are living in Egypt, having traveled there from Canaan in order to survive a famine. Yet as the Book of Exodus opens, we find them enslaved by the Egyptians. Practically nothing is known about the hundreds of years—commonly dated from 1700 to 1250 B.C.E.—that the Israelites spent in Egypt.

Moses, the main character in the story of the Exodus, was one of the greatest religious leaders in history. About

1250 B.C.E., the understanding that one God was above all other gods came to Moses with the revelation of God's name—*Yahweh,* meaning "I am the One who is always present."

After a dramatic encounter between Moses and God on Mount Sinai, a **covenant,** or agreement, between Yahweh and the Israelites was confirmed. The Israelites' part of the Covenant was to keep the Ten Commandments, which God had presented to Moses. God's part was to make the Israelites "the people of God" and to be with them as long as they kept the Covenant. Once again, God promised that they would be given the land of Canaan.

The nation and the Temple

After Moses' time, the Israelites entered Canaan. Over the next centuries—about 1200 to 1000 B.C.E.—they fought against the people who lived in that region. In these battles the Israelites were led by military leaders called **judges.** During this time, the Israelites abandoned their nomadic ways for the more settled agricultural life that was native to the region.

Around 1000 B.C.E., Israel became recognized as a nation, with David as its anointed king and Jerusalem as its capital city. David's son Solomon built the Temple in Jerusalem, and it became the principal place of worship for the nation. As both a political and a religious capital, Jerusalem became a great and holy city.

The kings and the prophets

After Solomon's death, in 931 B.C.E., the nation broke in two, with the kingdom of Israel in the north and the kingdom of Judah in the south. Heavy taxes and forced service in both kingdoms created hardships for the people. In addition, the kings often practiced **idolatry,** the worship of idols or other physical objects.

Prophets spoke out against both kingdoms' injustices to the people and infidelity to God. They questioned the behavior of the kings and called them and their people back to the Covenant. Yet the kingdoms continued to oppress the poor and worship pagan gods until eventually both kingdoms were crushed by powerful conquerors. The Assyrians obliterated the northern kingdom of Israel in 722 B.C.E. and took its people into exile. In 587 B.C.E., the Babylonians destroyed Judah, including the city of Jerusalem, and took its people to Babylon as captives.

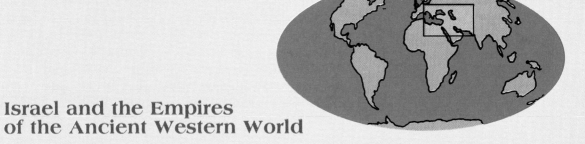

Israel and the Empires of the Ancient Western World

Rome ruled Israel beginning in 63 B.C.E. and destroyed the Temple in Jerusalem in 70 C.E. In 135 C.E., the Romans forbade all Jews to enter Jerusalem.

Alexander the Great conquered the Persian Empire in 330 B.C.E. The Greek rulers of Egypt and Syria, successors of Alexander, controlled Israel for over two hundred and fifty years.

Persia replaced Babylon as ruler of the Near East in 538 B.C.E.

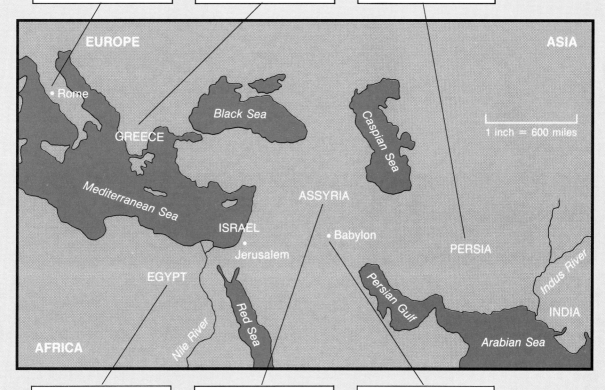

From 2000 to 1200 B.C.E., Egypt frequently dominated the land known as Canaan.

Assyria destroyed the capital of the kingdom called Israel in 722 B.C.E.

Babylon destroyed Jerusalem in 587 B.C.E. and took many of its citizens into exile.

The Babylonian exile and the Jewish Dispersion

While the people were exiled in Babylon, still other prophets encouraged them to repent of their sins and turn back to God. During this time the prophet known as Second Isaiah proclaimed that God was the one and only God. **Monotheism**, the belief in one God, was now the revelation of this people to the world, their blessing to the nations.

After fifty years in Babylon, the exiles were released from captivity by the conquering Persians and allowed to return home. Judah, no longer a politically independent kingdom, had become a district within the Persian Empire, and the returned exiles became known as **Jews,** from the word *Judah.* They rebuilt the Temple and restored Jerusalem, which became the religious capital for the Jews who had resettled all over the world—that is, the Jews of **the Dispersion.**

Because most Jews exiled in Babylon had dropped the Hebrew language from daily use in favor of the Aramaic spoken by their captors, Hebrew took on special status in literary writing and worship. The Jewish leaders began collecting and reflecting on their ancestral writings in Hebrew, and by about 400 B.C.E. the major books of what would become the Hebrew Scriptures were completed.

The people of Israel and the word of God

The Persian Empire was conquered in 330 B.C.E. by the armies of Alexander the Great, making the Greeks overlords of the Jews for nearly three hundred years. The Greeks were followed by the Romans, who captured Jerusalem in 63 B.C.E. Although tolerant of other cultures and religions, the Romans severely punished the people for revolts. Ultimately, a Jewish revolt led to the Roman destruction of Jerusalem and the second Temple in 70 C.E. The surviving Jews fled to Africa, Asia, and Europe. The Jewish Dispersion became the central fact of Jewish history.

The Dispersion, sometimes called *the Diaspora,* stressed the need for an official set of scriptures to guide Jewish religious life. These writings ensured the Jews' sense of identity as a people set apart and bound by the Covenant with God. This identity helped keep the Jews separate from the cultures around them and from the worship of other gods.

By the end of the first century C.E., final editing had defined the Hebrew Scriptures. In 90 C.E., Jewish religious leaders met to agree on the *canon*—that is, the books that would carry special authority as the primary source and guide for religious practice. In translations, this canon became known as the Bible, literally meaning "the books."

The Jews have spent much of their history as exiles—in Egypt, in Babylon, and in their Dispersion. *Above:* Present-day refugees from Indochina resettle in Portland, Oregon. Like the Jews of biblical times, these people struggle to keep their identity in a foreign culture.

What Are the Hebrew Scriptures?

Letters from Home

Imagine what a letter from home might mean to a group of refugees. Even a brief note in their own language would be treasured as a source of deep joy. The Hebrew Scriptures were like that for the Jews of the Dispersion. They were words from their families, from their homeland, and from their ancestors. They told the Jews in their own language how best to live a faithful life in unfamiliar surroundings. Most important, the Scriptures told them that their people still loved them and that the God of their people would be with them always.

All Types of Writing

The Hebrew Scriptures include many types of writing: stories, legends, histories, oracles, conversations, letters, novels, lists, biographies, laws, speeches, poems, proverbs, and prayers. These writings have been assembled and edited into forty-six books that Christians group in the following major sections:

- the Pentateuch
- the historical books
- the wisdom books
- the prophetic books

In this course, the historical books and the prophetic books are combined for purposes of discussion. For example, chapter 7 discusses the books about the prophets Amos, Hosea, Micah, and First Isaiah along with the Second Book of Kings, a historical book, because those prophets spoke to those kings and their people. All the books included in chapter 7 tell us about the decline and destruction of the northern kingdom of Israel.

The Pentateuch

The heart of Israel's story is told in the first five books of the Bible, called the **Pentateuch,** which means "five books." The Jews refer to these books as the **Torah,** a Hebrew word that means "instruction" but is sometimes translated as "the Law." In the Jewish faith, these books are the primary scriptural authority in matters of belief and practice.

The Pentateuch's opening stories about the Creation, Adam and Eve, Cain and Abel, Noah, and the Tower of Babel

List five experiences you have had of being a stranger or of being *with* strangers: for example, moving to a new city or trying to communicate with a foreigner. Next to each experience, list the emotions you felt.

show us God as a loving Creator and reveal the effects of disobedience. Following these stories are the tales of the patriarchs and the matriarchs—Abraham and Sarah, Isaac and Rebekah, Jacob and Rachel, Joseph, and Moses. Next we are told of Israel's slavery in Egypt, its escape, the Covenant at Mount Sinai, and the forty years in the wilderness, ending on the eve of Israel's entry into the Promised Land. The Pentateuch is called the religious masterpiece of the Hebrew Scriptures, and its five books are Genesis, Exodus, Leviticus, Numbers, and Deuteronomy.

The historical books

The historical books tell of Israel's conquest of the land of Canaan—including stories of Joshua, of the judges, and of Israel's first kings (Saul, David, and Solomon). These books also describe the breakup of the nation Israel, the reigns of the later kings, and the prophets' attempts to warn those kings of coming disaster.

In spite of the prophets' warnings, the kings disobey, disaster comes, and exile follows. Fifty years later, a remnant of the people return to Jerusalem, rebuild the Temple, and struggle again with foreign powers and their own weaknesses. Through it all, Israel's prophets remind the people of their Covenant with God and of their call to be a blessing to all the nations of the world. In addition to Joshua and Judges, most versions of the Bible include among the historical books Samuel, Kings, Ruth, Esther, Ezra, Nehemiah, Chronicles, Tobit, Judith, and Maccabees.

The wisdom books

The wisdom books are usually listed as Job, Psalms, Proverbs, Ecclesiastes, Song of Songs, Wisdom, and Sirach.

- The *Book of Job* explores the problem of good versus evil. Job demands a reason from God for the calamities that overcome him, and God answers in a speech of matchless splendor.
- The *Book of Psalms* is a collection of religious songs once attributed solely to David but now to a number of authors. Some psalms were written for liturgical occasions, others for private prayer.
- The *Book of Proverbs* is a collection of writings filled with practical advice about living ordinary life in the spirit of godliness.
- The author of the *Book of Ecclesiastes* was a questioner who, in the end, saw that life was a mystery for which he had no answers. It is wise to live life as well as possible and to enjoy it, he decided.

The Four Writers of the Pentateuch

Many people wrote the books of the Hebrew Scriptures, but the authorship of the Pentateuch has particularly interested scriptural scholars. Modern literary analysts have developed the theory that four documents, which no longer exist in their original form, were combined to form the Torah. We will refer to these documents in our discussion of the Pentateuch.

Although the writers of these documents will be referred to as individual persons, scholars cannot identify them as such. Many scholars prefer to talk about the four *sources* or *traditions* of the Torah rather than the four *authors*.

The Yahwist

The earliest source for the Torah is called the Yahwist because the writer used the Hebrew name *Yahweh* for God. The Yahwist's writings show an obvious interest in the tribe of Judah. Scholars suggest that the writer lived in the tenth century B.C.E., during the time that the united nation of Israel was ruled from Jerusalem. The Yahwist might have been a historian whose task was to put into writing the songs and legends recited at court and at religious festivals.

The Elohist

The name *Elohist* comes from this writer's Hebrew name for God: *Elohim*. After the northern tribes split away from Judah and became the kingdom of Israel, in the ninth century B.C.E., the Elohist rewrote the traditional stories. Just as the Yahwist gave prominence to the people and events in Judah, the Elohist featured heroes from the northern tribes.

The Yahwist and the Elohist can be compared in these terms: If the South had won the Civil War and the United States was split into two American nations, today we would have two distinct histories of prewar events. They would be similar but with differences reflecting the views of the North and of the South.

The Deuteronomists

The oral traditions of the Deuteronomists were different from those of the Yahwist and the Elohist. Scriptural scholars think that this source stemmed from the priestly circles in the northern kingdom and often refer to the source in the plural. The Deuteronomists' primary concern was to update the religious laws from Moses' time.

The Deuteronomists' writings began sometime around the eighth century B.C.E. In addition to the Book of Deuteronomy, they contributed the Books of Joshua, Judges, Samuel, and Kings.

The Priestly Writer

About the time of the Babylonian exile, in 587 B.C.E., the Priestly Writer supplied the final document used in creating the Pentateuch. This document emphasizes elements of the traditional stories that were of special interest to priests: the Covenant, the Temple, and ritual. This author might also have been an editor, weaving the earlier accounts by the Yahwist and the Elohist into the final form of the Torah.

By the time of the Priestly Writer, sacrifices at the Temple had been replaced by assemblies in exile, at which the Scriptures were read, discussed, and prayed over. This writer emphasized the power of God's word in the first verses of the Bible, in which God creates the world, calling each element into existence.

- The *Song of Songs* is a collection of love songs in the form of dialog, the speakers being bride, bridegroom, and attendants.
- The *Book of Wisdom* was meant to strengthen the faith of Israel and spoke for the first time in Israel's history about life after death.
- The *Book of Sirach* was written to show that true wisdom had been revealed by God to Israel.

The prophetic books

The early prophets—such as Samuel and Nathan, Elijah and Elisha—are known for their life stories rather than for their recorded words. Often called the **nonwriting prophets,** they appear in the historical books.

The **writing prophets** are divided into three groups, which are named in reference to the exile in Babylon.

- The *pre-exilic prophets* are Hosea and Amos (who spoke to the northern kingdom of Israel) and Jeremiah, Isaiah, Obadiah, Micah, Nahum, Habakkuk, and Zephaniah (all of whom spoke to the southern kingdom of Judah).
- The *exilic prophets* are Ezekiel (who went to Babylon with the deportees), Second Isaiah, and the unknown author of the Book of Lamentations.
- The *postexilic prophets* include Haggai, Zechariah, Malachi, Third Isaiah, Joel, and Baruch.

Containing some of the most powerful religious writing in the world, the prophetic books tell us about men who loved Israel and who warned it that to depart from fidelity to God would lead not only to moral blindness but to destruction as a nation—which is what happened. In Christian versions of the Bible, the Books of Jonah and Daniel are included with the prophetic writings. Isaiah, Jeremiah, and Ezekiel are called **major prophets** because their books are long, and the others are called **minor prophets** because their books are short.

Other Questions About the Hebrew Scriptures

As soon as you start reading the Hebrew Scriptures, other important questions will arise:

- Are the biblical stories historically true?
- Why do the Scriptures contain contradictory versions of some stories?
- Why is the God of the Hebrew Scriptures often angry, vengeful, and ruthless?

- What about the sins of the biblical heroes?
- What is the meaning of the claim that the Scriptures are inspired?

Historical Truth in the Biblical Stories

Widespread scientific study since the beginning of the last century has revealed much about the peoples and cultures of biblical times. Now we know that the Bible was written by people whose knowledge was limited, which means that it contains errors in dating, mapping, and other historical facts.

Initially, this realization caused dismay within the Christian churches, all of which view the Bible as a fundamental source of truth. For its part, the Catholic church severely restricted scriptural study for fear that people would lose their faith. In 1943, however, Pope Pius XII wrote an *encyclical,* or letter, that encouraged scriptural research and even new translations of the Bible. The church could relax its former policy because archaeology, language studies, and historical research had helped it realize that *historical* truth is not the Bible's major concern. The concern of the biblical writers was *religious* truth, and the history they wrote about was the story of God's loving presence in the world.

Such a history tells a different story than do other histories because its focus is God, not nature or humanity. For example, the story of the Creation is told in a naive, nonhistorical way, without any mention of evolution. Yet what it says is something that Christians believe to be true: God did make the world and all that is in it, and it is good. The point is *that* God made it, not *how* God made it.

Such a history also focuses on events of religious, not political or military, significance. The life of Moses and the Israelites' escape from Egypt, for example, were unknown to the rest of the world and are not even mentioned in most history books. Yet the Exodus is the central event of Israel's story and therefore of the Christian story.

Today the church teaches that the Scriptures are true in all matters related to religious faith. As the leaders of the Second Vatican Council put it, ". . . The books of Scripture, firmly, faithfully and without error, teach that truth which God, for the sake of our salvation, wished to see confided to the sacred Scriptures." In other words, the church wants us to focus on the religious truths in the Bible, not on the less significant details. Christians learned long ago to do this with Jesus' parables. For example, whether or not a Samaritan

Standard history books tell a lot about Egypt and its pharaohs but almost nothing about the Israelites. *Above:* The Nile River provided ancient Egypt with the water that was the key to its prosperous farming economy. That same river plays a dramatic part in the biblical story of Israel.

The Dead Sea Scrolls

Modern scriptural studies can be greatly affected by discoveries such as the Dead Sea Scrolls.

Possibly before the Roman invasion of Palestine in the first century C.E., a community called Qumran hid its library of scrolls in caves near the Dead Sea. There they remained until 1947, when shepherds discovered them.

Before the discovery of the Dead Sea Scrolls, the earliest manuscripts in Hebrew came from the ninth century C.E. The scrolls from Qumran date back almost a thousand years before that and serve as a check on the accuracy of later manuscripts. These scrolls confirm that Jewish scribes copied their manuscripts with great care and precision.

with a name and an address was once kind to a man beaten by robbers is irrelevant to Jesus' point, which was to illustrate true love of neighbor.

Contradictions in the Biblical Stories

Imagine finding a book with passages in the styles of Louis L'Amour's westerns, Stephen King's horror stories, Judy Blume's teenage novels, and Mark Twain's *Huckleberry Finn.* It would be clear that the book was a weaving together of pieces written by four different American writers. Similarly, modern scholars have found that the Bible is a weaving together of writings from different people with different points of view about their ancestors' history and traditions. When scholars became aware of the various literary styles in the Bible, they also realized that it had been edited and re-edited.

Rather than choose one version and discard the others, the biblical editors wisely kept them all, often working them together so skillfully that only scholars can identify the different strands. Understandably, this led to contradictions in the Bible's stories—for example, two different stories of the Creation. But the existence of different versions of the same event merely confirms that it took place! The wonder is that out of many bits and pieces, the storytellers and writers fashioned tales with such craft that they often sound like eyewitness accounts.

The Fierce "God of the Old Testament"

Emerging from the worship of their tribal gods, the Israelites chose as a model of their God the most noble figure at hand: the patriarch, a powerful and respected elder. From this model came the image of God as an old man with a long, white beard, a hurler of thunderbolts and lightning. They imagined God as an outraged ruler who ordered that offenders be stoned or burned and as a triumphant warrior who had enemies slain and women and children enslaved. These last actions were the customs of war at the time—horrible customs, but no more so than our own. Marching under the banner of the LORD, the Israelites believed that every victory and every punishment had God's blessing.

God has not changed over the centuries, but human perceptions of God have. As the mystery of God's love became

> Write a brief statement explaining how you would respond to someone who insists that Adam and Eve actually existed.

more apparent, the people of Israel no longer saw God solely as a warrior-king. By the time the Hebrew Scriptures were in final form, the image of God was very different—loving, forgiving, and compassionate. Jesus' teachings about God as a loving parent were not foreign to the Jews of his time.

A related note: In order to move away from an exclusively masculine image of God, an attempt has been made to eliminate from this book masculine pronouns—*he, his,* or *him*—referring to God. They do appear, however, in direct quotations from the Bible, where their use is unavoidable.

The Sins of the Biblical Heroes

In the Hebrew Scriptures, sin is often exposed and rarely excused. For example, the prophet Hosea condemns the patriarch Jacob for tricking his brother Esau, and the story of David's sin and Nathan's condemnation of him are related in detail. The biblical writers and editors did not try to hide the sins and failures of Israel's heroes because the purpose of the Bible was not to glorify heroes. The Bible was meant to be a revelation of how God could take human beings, full of sin and weakness, and make them heralds of love and salvation.

The Inspiration in the Scriptures

To say that the Scriptures are inspired does not mean that God literally put words in the minds of the scriptural writers or spoke to them through a "heavenly address system." The term *inspiration* means that God alone communicated the truth and beauty found in the Scriptures. The writers' own choice of words, literary style, and oral tradition reveals not only the existence of the one God but also God's love, mercy, justice, and infinite wisdom. Ultimately such a message could only be the work of God—in other words, inspired.

Compare this idea to the way Catholics understand the Eucharist. They know that the bread and wine at Communion are made by human hands. Yet they also see this food and drink as transformed into the body and blood of Jesus. Similarly, believers see the Bible as both the work of human writers and the word of God.

With all this in mind, open the first book of the Hebrew Scriptures—the Book of Genesis, which tells the story of the Creation and of the first people on earth. As you proceed, keep in mind the words of the great Jewish thinker Martin

The biblical Jews' image of God as a male ruler and warrior was based on the patriarch, the most noble figure in their society.

Buber, referring to the Hebrew Scriptures and addressed to
Christian readers:

> To you, the book is a forecourt;
> to us, it is the sanctuary.
> But in this place,
> we can dwell together,
> and together listen to the voice
> that speaks here.

In your own words, explain the
meaning of Martin Buber's statement.

For Review

1. Of the six reasons given in this chapter, explain the two reasons for studying the Hebrew Scriptures that make the most sense to you.

2. Describe the two ingredients—other than the Bible and this book—that you need to make this course a success.

3. Explain what is meant by *oral traditions*.

4. Who are the patriarchs and the matriarchs of the Jewish faith?

5. What was the name of God that was revealed to Moses?

6. What were the names of the two kingdoms established after Solomon's death?

7. Who were the Jews of the Dispersion, and why were the Scriptures so important to them?

8. What does the word *Bible* mean?

9. What are the major sections of the Hebrew Scriptures?

10. Give the two names for the first five books of the Hebrew Scriptures. What do they mean?

11. List the wisdom books of the Bible.

12. The Pentateuch comes from what four sources?

13. Name the three groups of writing prophets.

14. Explain why contradictions are found in the Bible.

15. Why did the Israelites see God as a warrior-king?

16. Why did the biblical writers relate the sins of Israel's heroes?

17. What does the word *inspired* mean when used to describe the Bible?

2

Beginnings:
Stories About God's
Creation and Promises

THE first words of the Bible are the first words of the Book of Genesis: "In the beginning . . ." Yet Genesis tells us about much more than the beginning of the world. Genesis also describes the role of people in the world and the destiny of the world according to the plan of God.

In Genesis, we see God's nature as both *universal,* creating all things, and *eternal,* existing before time itself.

The Goodness of Creation

The first eleven chapters of Genesis are an introduction to the great drama that follows. The ancient stories, first told by storytellers and folksingers early in biblical history, are filled with fragments of Near Eastern myths that the Jews later transformed into beautiful and powerful religious tales.

Like the Greeks and the Romans, many people in the ancient Near East practiced **polytheism**—that is, they worshiped many gods. Self-serving, violent, and destructive, these gods made the earth for their own pleasure and humankind for their slaves. Theirs was a world of chaos. To those who believed in gods like these, the story of the Creation in Genesis would come as a complete surprise because it tells about the God who creates order, not chaos.

The First Story of the Creation

God creates lovingly, and the Creation is good. In this story, the sun and the moon and the stars are not gods but creations, as are the great sea monsters that the people of the Near East formerly perceived as evil demons. When God creates man and woman, they are godlike and are stewards of the earth, not slaves of the gods.

Read Genesis 1:1-31; 2:1-4a.

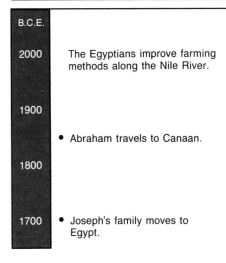

B.C.E.	
2000	The Egyptians improve farming methods along the Nile River.
1900	
	● Abraham travels to Canaan.
1800	
1700	● Joseph's family moves to Egypt.

The God of Genesis lovingly creates the world and proclaims it good.
Facing page: A poppy field in Israel reflects the beauty of God's Creation.

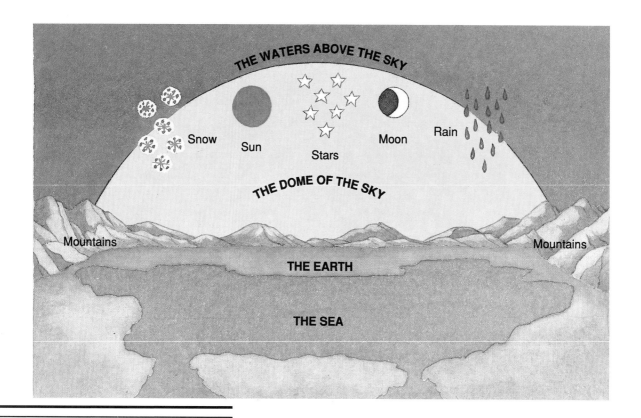

The following labels appear on the illustration:

THE WATERS ABOVE THE SKY

Snow Sun Stars Moon Rain

THE DOME OF THE SKY

Mountains   Mountains

THE EARTH

THE SEA

The earth according to Genesis, chapter 1: the Priestly Writer's image of the world was that of a flat disk topped by a bowl-shaped, transparent sky and bordered by water both beneath the earth and above the sky.

The Creation and the Sabbath

The author of this first story of the Creation is the Priestly Writer, who lived near the time of the Babylonian exile, in the sixth century B.C.E. During the Babylonian exile, when the final text of the Hebrew Scriptures began to be shaped, only two customs—the Sabbath and circumcision—remained to mark Israel as unique among the nations. So the Priestly Writer listed the Sabbath as another act of the Creation, a day to rest and to praise God. This story of the Creation is a tribute to the poetic genius of the Priestly Writer, who with very few words put everything in place.

Adam and Eve

In the second story of the Creation, Adam and Eve are caught up in disobedience and guilt. They have eaten the forbidden fruit, and feeling naked, they try to cover themselves. When they hear God approaching, they hide. God calls Adam, and his excuse for hiding is his nakedness. Yet earlier Adam was naked and unashamed. God asks if he has eaten the fruit of the tree of knowledge, and Adam, unwilling to take the blame, tries to shift it to Eve. Eve, just as unwilling, accuses the serpent of tricking her.

Thus sin has done its work and ruined Adam and Eve's relationships—with God, between themselves, and with Creation. Now God foretells the consequences of their sin: man's work will not give him perfect pleasure but will be difficult and weary him, and woman will be subject to her husband and bear children in pain.

Read Genesis 2:4b–25; 3:1–24.

The sin of presumption

Written at an earlier time (before the first story) by the Yahwist, this second story of the Creation tells of **the Fall**—that is, the first sin in human history. The "knowledge of good and evil" is the knowledge of all things, and this is God's alone. The divine command is that human beings should not try to be equal to God—the ultimate act of presumption.

Sin's Spread

Like ripples in a pond, sin will spread out over the ages and touch everyone. Genesis describes sin's spread first with a story about hatred between brothers that ends in murder, then with a story about depravity in society, and finally with one about arrogance among the nations.

Cain and Abel

The story of Cain and Abel tells of two brothers—the first a farmer, the second a shepherd—offering gifts to God in sacrifice. God blesses only Abel's sacrifice and encourages Cain to rise above his jealousy. Angry, Cain murders Abel and then insolently responds to God's inquiry, " 'Am I my brother's keeper?' " (4:9). So the first sin has begun to affect the human family.

Read Genesis 4:1–16.

A shepherd's story

Although Cain is a farmer and Abel is a shepherd, their story supposedly takes place centuries before the development of farming and shepherding. Scholars suggest that the story is taken from an early shepherd's tale about the change to a settled, farming way of life. We have similar stories about the change from a manual to an industrial lifestyle—for instance, the legend of John Henry, the miner who raced against a digging machine and died immediately after his victory.

Write a brief comment on these words spoken to Eve: " '. . . your husband . . . shall be your master' " (Genesis 3:16). Do you think this was a "revelation" or a choice of words influenced by the culture of the writer?

The story of Cain and Abel is a story about sin as well as a lament about change. Brainstorm and list at least five social changes that have disturbed people.

In writing, give an example of how a single act of sin can touch others until great evil results. Then describe an example of how goodness works in the same way.

Noah and the Flood

The account of the Flood almost begins with "Once upon a time," so accustomed are we to hearing it as a nursery tale. The story tells of such depravity on the earth that God regrets creating the human race. Here we see God, through the eyes of the biblical storytellers, as one who makes mistakes and regrets them.

Only one man, Noah, finds favor with God and is instructed to build an ark to protect himself, his family, and the animals from destruction. Noah does as God commands, the Flood comes, and the ark safely rides the waters until they recede. All other creatures are destroyed.

Read Genesis 6:1-22; 7:1-24; 8:1-19.

A corrupt society ignores God's word

The story of Noah is probably related to the accounts of a global flood found in ancient literature, which may or may not connect the Flood with the melting of the great glaciers. But the tale's authors (the Yahwist and the Priestly Writer) were not interested in the Flood's historical causes. Their story teaches the powerful truth that whoever hears and obeys God will be saved and whoever does not, will be lost.

Saved from what? is the question. We know that devout people are not necessarily saved from disaster. Even those whom Jesus says will live forever are not saved from calamity in this life.

The answer is that hearing and keeping God's word saves our heart from turning to stone, saves us from forgetting how to love and serve. When we *do* forget how to love, something happens inside us, where it is unseen. Unlike Pinocchio, our nose does not grow when we lie—or we would lie only once. Lying, like other sins, leads to the loss of integrity, to no longer knowing what is true and what is not or who we *really* are. It is like drowning in a sea of dishonesty. Perhaps the storytellers were saying this by using the image of the Flood with all its victims.

God's Covenant with Noah

Leaving the ark, Noah offers a sacrifice of thanksgiving. The story of Noah ends with God's first covenant—with Noah because he obeyed.

Read Genesis 8:20-22; 9:1-17.

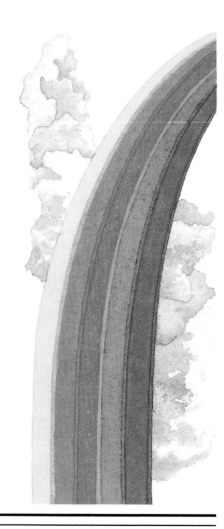

A rainbow marked the end of the Flood and the presence of God with the world.

The rainbow

The end of the Flood was marked with a rainbow as a sign of God's presence with the world. The colors in light are always present, yet we need a prism to reveal them. In the same way, we need the eyes of faith to see God in the world around us.

Babel

The last of the introductory stories in Genesis is the tale of Babel. Once again humankind tries to carve out a destiny of its own making. Here the presumption of Adam and Eve is projected on a grand scale when the nations try to build a tower with its summit in the heavens so they can "make a name for themselves." God comes down to see the tower and disperses the peoples; otherwise " 'nothing will later stop them from doing whatever they presume to do' " (11:6).

Read Genesis 11:1–9.

The presumption of the nations

The story of Babel is not about the origin of languages or the dispersal of peoples. Rather, it shows how sin has spread to affect even the behavior of the nations, who seek glory in power, might, wealth, superiority, and dominance—without a thought for God. Today the nightly newscasts are filled with stories of such attempts, as well as stories of the pain, corruption, and devastation they beget.

God as "We"?

In the first chapters of Genesis, you might have noticed bits of language suggesting that more than one God exists. For example, in Genesis 3:22, God says, " 'See! The man has become like one of us.' " Similarly, in Genesis 11:7, God says, " 'Let us then go down and there confuse their language.' " The fact that these remnants of polytheistic language remain in the final version of the Scriptures helps us appreciate the long, intense struggle toward the worship of the one God.

The Stories About Abraham

The first eleven chapters of Genesis explain why things went wrong in the world. The stories that follow are about how God chose a people to start setting things right again.

Read John 9. Write a paragraph explaining the connection between this funny, beautiful story and the idea that God is always present but not always clearly "present" to everyone.

The Near Eastern *ziggurat*, a stepped temple with a shrine at its top, may have provided the model for the Tower of Babel.

Like the stories about the Creation, the stories of the founders were remembered and told for centuries before they were written down. Unlike the stories of the Creation, the stories of the patriarchs and the matriarchs take place in historical times. Their setting is the period about four thousand years ago (2000 to 1700 B.C.E.).

The first of these stories is about Abraham, the father of biblical faith—who appears first with the name *Abram.*

Abram's Call and God's Promise

Among the Semitic nomads wandering along the highlands of the Near East is a man named Abram. He travels from the city of Ur to the city of Haran (see the map on page 45), and it is in Haran that he hears God's call. God bids Abram to take his family away from all that is familiar and go to a land " 'that I will show you' " (12:1). And God promises that out of Abram will come a blessing on the nations. Abram goes. This is the first mention of God's Promise.

Read Genesis 12:1-9.

A new God

The story of Abram's call, written as though God is speaking directly to him, is about Abram's struggle to understand the mystery of the gods—until it comes to him that one God is above all other gods. Abram's call probably came the way that God's call comes to anyone: silently, subtly, during the search for answers that we call prayer.

Interestingly, the biblical stories do not suggest that Abram worshiped God as the *only* God. Even though belief in the one God is the cornerstone of Judaism, it was not yet clear to the people of Abram's time. What is significant here is that Abram's God had no connection with any of the other gods of the Near East.

Letting God lead

Abram, a man whose wife is barren and beyond her child-bearing years, lets God lead him—and becomes the father of the faith of the Jews, the Christians, and the Muslims. His story is a stunning contrast to the story of Babel.

God's name

Abram might have known his God by the name *El Shaddai* (which means "the One of the Mountain") instead of *Yahweh.* That name came into use much later, about the time of Moses, and its significance will be discussed in the next chapter of this book.

A painting based on a mural from an Egyptian tomb, dating from the time of Abraham and depicting Semitic nomads in colorful attire

The Semites

The word *Semite* describes not only the Israelites but also other ancient peoples of the Near East—including Arabs, Aramaeans, Assyrians, Babylonians, Canaanites, and Phoenicians. The term *Semite* originated in *Shem*, the name of one of Noah's three sons.

Scholars continue to debate the origins of the Semitic peoples. Traditionally the Semites were viewed as nomadic peoples, but today they are understood to have included both shepherding and more settled, farming groups. The enduring contribution of the Semitic peoples is the first alphabet, dating from sometime before 1550 B.C.E.

Today the term *anti-Semitism* is often used to describe prejudice specifically against Jews.

Abram and Melchizedek

A famine comes to the land of Canaan, so Abram and his wife, Sarai, journey to Egypt. When they return from their stay, Abram rescues his nephew Lot from capture by four allied kings. After this mission, Abram is greeted by the priest-king of Salem, Melchizedek, who brings him bread and wine and blesses him in the name of God.

Read Genesis 14:13-24.

The city of Salem

The author's intention in mentioning the city of Salem was to place the patriarch Abram in the vicinity of the settlement that would one day be called Jerusalem. This is like our need to say that national heroes have been in our towns and cities, claiming such things as "George Washington slept here" or "Abe Lincoln studied here."

Offerings of thanksgiving

Ritual sacrifice was an ancient rite, evidence of which has been discovered where great cave paintings still exist in France, Spain, Austria, and elsewhere. Early humans probably enacted rites of petition or thanksgiving for good hunting in such places, and the sacrifices of Abel, Noah, and Abram were the same kinds of rites. Their burnt offerings, usually animals, were food—a symbol of the offering of their life. After the gift of life, the most precious gift we have is food, which sustains life in us. Once offered, such gifts became sacred, and if not destroyed by fire, they were eaten by those present. Thus the offering became a sacred meal.

Abram's Doubt

Abraham is the father of biblical faith, yet even he doubted. Write a brief description of a moment of doubt—religious or otherwise—that you have experienced.

Abram, having waited faithfully and grown older, begins to doubt that he will have a son. Imagine him sitting in his tent one night, gently complaining to God in prayer. He has no child, his wife is barren—is he to adopt a son?

In answer, God tells Abram to look up at the stars and count them if he can. God promises that Abram's descendants will outnumber the stars.

Read Genesis 15:1-6.

God's Promise repeated

By *descendants* God refers to all who believe or will believe because Abram believes. It is a beautiful story for a starry night or for a time when faith burns low and discouragement seems to press the spirit.

The Birth of Ishmael

Sarai continues to be childless and finally proposes that Abram take her Egyptian maid, Hagar, as a concubine and beget a child by her, which would legally belong to Sarai. Once pregnant, Hagar becomes scornful toward Sarai, who complains to Abram, who in turn tells Sarai to do as she pleases with the girl.

Resentful at the resulting ill-treatment by Sarai, Hagar runs away. In the wilderness, a messenger of God appears to her. At his command, she returns to submit to her mistress, fortified by the promise that her unborn son, Ishmael, will grow to manhood wild and free. (Tradition has made him a *Bedouin*—that is, a nomadic Arab—and the father of the Arab peoples.)

Two covenants between God and Abram are recorded, the most familiar being the sign of circumcision, which identifies Abram's people as God's people. To reflect this new status and identity, Abram's name is changed to *Abraham* and Sarai's to *Sarah*.

Read Genesis 16:1-16; 17:3-22.

Hagar, the concubine

Curiously, Hagar emerges from this episode more noble than Abraham and Sarah. The Jews did not try to whitewash their ancestral heroes, only to show that God had chosen a people far from perfect. Yet in spite of their faults, God was able to make them a light to the world.

Concubines and polygamy

We cannot judge the people of the Bible by our standards, but their customs of taking concubines and of practicing *polygamy*—that is, taking more than one wife—deserve an explanation: If a wife was barren, a female servant might become a surrogate childbearer, a *concubine* to the husband. Or the husband might take a second wife in order to give the family children. Both of these practices helped to assure the survival of the tribe. The story of Adam and Eve suggests, however, that *monogamy*—taking only one wife—was the biblical ideal.

Abraham's Visitation

Abraham is sitting at the entrance to his tent when he is approached by three strangers—who, we later learn, represent God. In a beautiful display of graciousness, Abraham offers them refreshment, water for bathing, and a place to rest.

Tradition has made Hagar's son Ishmael a Bedouin—that is, a nomadic Arab.
Above: A present-day Bedouin living in the Sinai region of Egypt

According to the custom of the time, Sarah, as a woman, is not present in this scene, but she is listening behind the flap of the tent. When she hears one of the visitors say that in a year she will bear a son, she laughs out loud; then, rebuked by the visitor, she denies having done so. The story, rich in color and detail, repeats God's promise to Abraham that one day he will be a father of nations.

Read Genesis 18:1-15.

Hospitality

The story of Abraham's visitation highlights a solemn obligation of biblical times: the giving of hospitality. For a traveler in the wilderness, hospitality was a matter of survival, and to be refused it was sometimes a death sentence.

"Laugh"

Both Abraham and Sarah laugh when told that they will have a son of their own (17:17, 18:12). These verses contain a bit of wordplay: *Isaac,* the name that God gives to their son-to-be, means "laugh" in Hebrew.

Abraham's Intercession for Lot

Now the storyteller shifts from the image of three strangers to "the man" and hence to "the LORD." As Abraham accompanies God on the road to Sodom, God reveals a plan to destroy that wicked city if the complaints against it are found true. Abraham pleads for the safety of his nephew Lot, who lives there. As Abraham again and again presses God not to destroy the just people with the wicked in this infamous city—even if they number only a few—God graciously agrees. This story is about a man praying for his family.

In Sodom, the wicked inhabitants propose the rape of some young men (or angels) to whom Lot has given shelter. Rape is evil at any time but doubly heinous considering the life-giving hospitality required by guests. Lot offers his own daughters in order to protect his guests—to no avail. So the city will be destroyed. The angels rescue Lot and his family. In the well-known ending to the story, the curiosity of Lot's wife turns her into a pillar of salt—a famous but unimportant biblical detail.

Read Genesis 18:16-33; 19:1-29.

The just God

None of the prophets in the Scriptures listed sodomy—that is, sexual intercourse between persons of the same sex—

When Lot and his family fled Sodom—which was near the Dead Sea—the curiosity of Lot's wife turned her into a pillar of salt.
Above: Salt pillars in the Dead Sea, which has a high saline content due to an extremely fast rate of evaporation

among the crimes of Sodom, whose name has given us the term. The prophet Jeremiah accused the residents of adultery, living in lies, and siding with the wicked (23:14). Later, the prophet Ezekiel condemned Sodom's citizens as vain, greedy, complacent in their prosperity, and uncharitable to the poor and the needy (16:49). Needless to say, all of these crimes are as evil as the one for which the city is reputed.

The Birth of Isaac and Abraham's Test

Isaac is born, and now Sarah's laughter is of a joyful kind. Hagar is expelled because Sarah fears that Ishmael might threaten Isaac's inheritance. Again, we must admire Hagar's behavior. Alone in the wilderness with no water left and thinking that her boy will die, she walks some distance away from him because she cannot bear to watch his suffering. Then, aided by an angel of the LORD, Hagar finds a spring and saves her son. The story is a tribute to her perseverance and faith.

The next story is often called "Abraham's Test." In it, God bids Abraham to take the son whom he loves with all his heart to a place on a mountain and sacrifice him as a **holocaust**—that is, a burnt offering. In anguish, "hoping against hope," as Saint Paul wrote (Romans 4:18), Abraham climbs the mountain with the boy. In answer to Isaac's question about what they will sacrifice, Abraham can only say, filled with faith, that God will provide a victim.

Read Genesis 22:1–19.

Abraham's test

The biblical writer displayed only admiration for Abraham's obedience. Clearly the writer had no problem with this story. But we do! How can we come to terms with a God who would ask such a thing, even if not intending to carry it out— to say nothing of a father who would acquiesce? The God whom Jesus calls Father in the Gospels would never play games with a man's love for his son, as we know from a passage in Luke.

Read Luke 11:11–13.

What if Abraham only thought that he knew what God wanted? He came from a culture that occasionally reverted to human sacrifice in times of national crisis, as a desperate attempt to secure divine help. We do not know for certain if this was the case with Abraham, but people have often thought that they knew what God wanted and have been

In this story, Abraham prays for his nephew Lot. Write a fifty-word "conversation" with God about something dear to your heart.

Abraham led his son Isaac to the sacrificial altar but was not allowed to kill him as an offering. This confirmed once and for all that God forbade human sacrifice.

Sometimes disasters happen and there is nothing we can do to make them go away. We try to avoid them, but finally we must face them. When they are over and we have survived them, we can have some strong feelings. Write about a tough moment that you have had to face. How did you feel when it was over?

Make a list of your "heroic ancestors," including family heroes as well as national ones. Write a brief reflection on the importance of these heroes to your identity and self-respect.

mistaken. Only when the angel stayed his hand did Abraham know what his God expected of him. This story confirms once and for all that God forbids human sacrifice.

Isaac and Rebekah

Abraham returns home and at Sarah's death buys a field in which to bury her, the first piece of ground that his people possess in a land that will one day be theirs.

Isaac grows up, and Abraham, facing his own death, instructs his steward to find a bride for Isaac from among their tribe in Haran. Now we have a *novella*—a little masterpiece of storytelling. Rich detail, exotic marriage customs, and Rebekah's loveliness and generosity are woven together in the most beautiful of all the biblical romances. We meet Rebekah's brother, Laban, for the first time. We glimpse Rebekah's adventurous spirit when she agrees to leave Haran immediately, over the protests of her kin. The story ends with the bride glimpsing Isaac as she approaches her new home and Isaac taking her to his tent, where he marries her. In Rebekah he finds comfort after the death of his mother.

Abraham marries again and has many children by another woman. When he dies—at the age of one hundred and seventy-five—Isaac and Ishmael bury him next to Sarah in the family's field.

Read Genesis 24:1–67.

Abraham's great age

Abraham's unbelievable age at his death is an exaggeration common in biblical stories. It is a way of saying that Abraham was wise and blessed.

The Stories About Jacob

The stories about Isaac and Rebekah's son Jacob continue the theme of God's Promise to the descendants of Abraham. Jacob is a much more complicated character than Abraham was, and his portrait is the most skillfully drawn in the Hebrew Scriptures. He is a man filled with life, faith, and intelligence as well as a calculating man who perhaps also harbors great doubt.

Rebekah Decides

As Jacob's story opens, Rebekah is pregnant and puzzled by the commotion in her womb. A visit to a holy place reveals that she is carrying twins and that the younger will supersede the elder. That is, he will take over the elder's role as principal heir. From this point on, Rebekah has only one thought: to maneuver her younger child into the role of heir. The twins are born, the shaggy, redheaded Esau first and Jacob second, grasping Esau's heel—as though trying to get ahead of him. Esau becomes a hunter and his father's favorite; Jacob, the stay-at-home, is his mother's favorite. Undoubtedly Jacob learns of his destiny from her.

In the first story of the twins' struggle, a ravenous Esau returns from the hunt, finds Jacob cooking bean soup, and asks for some. Jacob, apparently with tongue in cheek, agrees to give Esau soup in exchange for his birthright—which includes seniority in the line of inheritance and twice the goods that will be inherited by the other sons. The holder of the birthright will become the leader of the tribe. Esau replies that his birthright will do him little good if he starves, and he seems not to take seriously what Jacob is proposing. Jacob, his interest quickened, asks slyly, "Do you swear your birthright to me?" Still unaware, Esau swears, and the deed is done. To swear is final! The birthright is Jacob's. The writer sums up the deception by saying that obviously Esau cares little about his birthright—which is not true, as we will see.

In time, Isaac—aging, his eyesight failing—wishes to give Esau the patriarchal blessing to seal his right to head the clan. He asks Esau to hunt some game and prepare his favorite dish; after eating it, Isaac will bless him. Rebekah overhears this, bids Jacob to bring two young goats for her to prepare for Isaac, and orders him to put on Esau's best clothes, take Esau's place, and obtain the blessing. Jacob has enough sense to be afraid that he might be cursed instead and says so. Rebekah's reply, "Let any curse fall on me," reveals at least her good intentions. She gives Jacob pieces of goatskin to cover his neck and wrists, ensuring that he will feel hairy like Esau, and sends him to Isaac with the food.

When Isaac asks how Esau's task has been accomplished so quickly, Jacob blasphemes. He assures his father that God blessed his hunt. Still suspicious, Isaac has his son come closer; the voice is Jacob's, but touching his hands, Isaac finds him hairy. Ah yes, it feels like Esau. Isaac eats, and finally convinced when he smells Esau's clothes, he blesses Jacob. Scarcely has he done this when Jacob leaves and Esau returns with venison stew and asks for Isaac's blessing. Isaac is struck with a terrible trembling, and the truth dawns, too late. Esau, furious, vows to kill Jacob when Isaac dies.

Read Genesis 27:1-41.

Rebekah became convinced that she must maneuver her youngest child, Jacob, into the role of Isaac's heir.

Rebekah's plot

For all her presumption, Rebekah sincerely believes that the will of God in this affair is in her hands. She strives to obey it at great personal risk.

Esau cheated?

Given Esau's later identification with the tribe of Edom, Israel's enemy, it serves the storyteller's purpose to present Esau as an oaf. That is why Esau is described as redheaded. In ancient times, red hair was considered barbaric or even evil. Even later, in the Middle Ages, Judas was depicted as a redhead—which is eminently unfair to redheads.

Jacob Journeys to Haran

Two accounts of Jacob's flight to Haran are interwoven. In one, when Rebekah hears Esau promise to kill Jacob, she suggests to Isaac that they send Jacob to Haran, out of harm's way, to get a bride from their own tribe. She bids Jacob to go, "Lest I lose the two of you in one day," she says—knowing that she has lost Esau's love but not realizing that she will never see Jacob again.

In the other account, Rebekah's concern is merely that Jacob not marry a Canaanite woman. Isaac agrees, and Jacob—young, feisty, and self-satisfied—sets off. Camping the first night, he dreams of angels ascending and descending from heaven, hears the voice of God repeat the Promise made to Abraham, and names the place Bethel, meaning "the house or abode of God."

Read Genesis 27:42-46; 28:1-22.

In writing, describe a time when you bargained with God. Use an example from your childhood or from a recent experience.

A brash young man

In the final scene of this episode, Jacob seems to choose the terms of the relationship with God (28:20–21), but God, not people, initiates covenants. Jacob sounds like a brash young man who feels that it is his prerogative to bargain with God.

Jacob Marries Rachel—He Thinks

Jacob arrives in Haran, meets Rachel, falls madly in love, and discovers that her father is his uncle Laban. Jacob begins working for Laban, and after a month his uncle asks what wages he wants. Jacob answers, "Rachel!" Laban agrees that if Jacob works for him for seven years, he may have her.

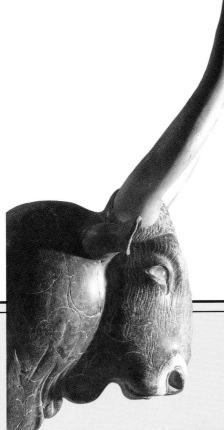

A Cretan drinking cup in the image of a bull, found in an excavated palace at Knossos

Historic Happenings
Between 2000 and 1700 B.C.E.

Africa
The Egyptian pharaohs no longer build pyramids as their tombs. Instead they are buried in tombs deeply tunneled into the walls of the hills on the western side of the Nile River.

America
The Eskimo culture begins on the Bering Strait. Pottery is made in Mexican villages.

China
The potter's wheel is introduced. Pigs, dogs, oxen, goats, and sheep are domesticated.

Europe
Early cultures begin using bronze to make tools and weapons. The Stonehenge circle in England is used for religious and astronomical ceremonies. Culture on the island of Crete is at its height; the bull-god is worshiped at the city of Knossos.

India
Chickens and elephants are domesticated. Sacrifice is offered in the worship of a mother-goddess.

The Near East
Around 2000 B.C.E., the destruction of Ur, the Near East's major city, results in the decline of the dominant culture.

When the seven years are up, the wedding is celebrated with great festivity. At nightfall, the bride, veiled from her head to her toes, is escorted to Jacob's tent. In the morning, he discovers not Rachel but her older sister Leah, and he is outraged. Laban's only reply is that the oldest daughter is always married first and that if Jacob will promise to work for another seven years, he may wed Rachel at the end of a week. So Jacob gets two wives and bondage for another seven years, and the cunning Laban gets two weddings for the price of one feast.

Read Genesis 29:14b–35; 30:1–43.

Jacob Returns

Fourteen years pass, and the second phase of Jacob's life finds him older and wiser, although no less conniving. He has two wives, two concubines, and many children, and is totally disenchanted with Laban. In a kind of mid-life crisis, he remembers the land of Canaan and God's Promise and wants to return home. Contriving to divide the huge flocks that his labors have acquired for Laban, and taking one-half at Laban's insistence, Jacob announces his intention to return to Canaan and waits until Laban is away before he leaves. Legally, Jacob's wives and children belong to Laban, but both Leah and Rachel are angry at their father for spending their dowry money and ignoring them, so they are pleased to go.

Midway to Canaan, Jacob remembers Esau. Fearful of his anger, Jacob sends herdsmen ahead with large flocks of animals to be given as gifts to placate him. In his fright,

Leah and Rachel willingly went to Canaan with their husband, Jacob, and his flocks.
Right: In the Sinai region of Egypt, Bedouin women herd flocks—much like Leah and Rachel did.

Jacob reminds God, to whom he was almost flippant many years before, of the promise of protection, which he now desperately needs.

Reaching the border of Canaan, Jacob shepherds his family and flocks across a river and, staying alone on the other side, has a strange encounter, the meaning of which continues to puzzle scriptural commentators.

The mysterious being who meets Jacob in this story has been called by translators a stranger, a man, an angel—some even suggest a demon. All of them admit the difficulty of interpreting this ancient tale. This "someone" wrestles with Jacob until the break of day, when Jacob, refusing to let go, asks for a blessing. In reply, the stranger asks his name, and when he says that it is Jacob, he is told that from now on he will be known as **Israel,** meaning "one who has contended with divine and human beings." Left alone as the sun rises, Jacob marvels that he has seen God face to face and has not died.

Read Genesis 32:23-32.

A struggle with God?

The interpretations of this episode are so numerous that we are almost free to interpret it for ourselves. Was it a night of prayer? Was it a struggle with God? with conscience? with the temptation to turn back? Was it a dream? Jacob—separated for fourteen years from his ancestral home and faced with Esau's possible rage—could well have been terrified and torn between going on and turning back. In the context of biblical history, it is a curtain-raising story. Jacob is returning to the destiny long ago promised, to the land of Canaan, and to his place among the people chosen to be a blessing to the nations.

The interpretations of Jacob's struggle with the mysterious being are numerous. Was it a struggle with God? with Jacob's temptation to turn back?

Jacob Initiates His Family into the Worship of God

Jacob continues on to meet and make peace with Esau. He then goes to Bethel and builds an altar on the spot where he heard God's Promise on his outward journey. He orders his family to rid themselves of the trappings of their pagan religion—not only the household gods but also their ornaments, earrings, even clothing—in a purification rite that initiates the family into the worship of the God of Israel. Again God transfers to Jacob the blessing given to Abraham and Isaac, the Promise of the land of Canaan and a royal line that is to be a blessing to the nations.

The name of the nation of Israel comes from the name given to Jacob. Think about your own names. Ask your parents about them. What do your first, middle, and last names mean? Write a paragraph about the appropriateness of your names.

In a short passage, we are told of the death of Rachel at the birth of her second son, Benjamin. Jacob returns home and finds Isaac still alive. At his death, Jacob and Esau bury their father in the field where Abraham and Sarah lie.

Read Genesis 35:1-29.

The Stories About Joseph

The stories about Joseph are also about his father because God is not finished with Jacob yet. These famous tales also repeat the major theme of the patriarchal history: Keeping God's word brings rewards far beyond anything imaginable.

Sold into Slavery

Joseph's brothers used his bloody coat to convince Jacob that Joseph had been killed by a wild animal.

Joseph, Rachel's first son, is seventeen years old and Jacob's favorite, but not his brothers'. Dan, Naphtali, Gad, and Asher dislike Joseph because after he tended flocks with them, he told his father tales about their behavior. The others resent him for being his father's favorite, the son of Jacob's beloved Rachel. Jacob has had a long, flowing tunic made for Joseph—the garb of tent dwellers, not shepherds, and unlike the short, coarse garments that his brothers wear. Worse, Joseph's dreams contain portents that one day he will lord it over his family. When he rashly recounts these dreams, even Jacob rebukes him. The scene is set for his undoing.

One day the brothers are tending the flocks some distance away from home, and Jacob sends Joseph to see if things are well with them. As the brothers watch him approach wearing his long, flowing coat—hardly the clothing for a hike in the country—they plot to kill him and throw his body down a well. But Reuben has no heart for such a deed and suggests that instead they put Joseph into a dry well, for Reuben plans to return later to rescue him. The brothers do this and then sit down to eat—the writer's comment on their callousness.

Seeing traders on the way to Egypt, Judah suggests that they sell Joseph instead and avoid having his blood on their hands. The deed is done, and the brothers hide it by showing Joseph's coat, which they have dipped in goat's blood, to Jacob. Seeing the bloody coat, Jacob believes that Joseph has been killed by a wild animal, tears his own garments, and mourns the loss of Joseph for many days.

Read Genesis 37:1-35.

A melodrama

Here are all the elements of a family saga. Consider the parts of this melodrama:

- Jacob's favoritism
- Joseph's talebearing and boastfulness
- the brothers' envy and betrayal
- the brothers' deception of their father (they seem to have inherited some of his traits)

The wonder is that sinful and guilty as they are, God will lead these men to self-knowledge and remorse, some even to heroism and holiness.

Joseph and Potiphar's Wife

Once in Egypt, Joseph is bought by Potiphar, the pharaoh's chief steward, who puts him in charge of his household and all his possessions. Now Joseph is strikingly handsome—which might be expected because his mother and grandmother were such beautiful women—and this fact does not go unnoticed by Potiphar's lustful wife. Attempting to seduce him, she is rebuffed when Joseph refuses to betray his master. This rejection, needless to say, does not sit well with the lady, and the next time she is alone in the house with Joseph, she approaches him again. He flees, but she snatches his cloak and, using it as evidence, accuses him of rape. So Joseph ends up in prison.

Read Genesis 39:1–20a.

A long way from home

In most versions of Genesis, this episode is called "Joseph's Temptation." Separated from his family, Joseph was probably lonely and in need of consolation. The biblical text says that God was with him, but Joseph could well have questioned that. Most of us interpret ill-fortune as a sign that God is not with us. Where, then, did Joseph find this reservoir of courage and honor? Perhaps hardship and loss uncovered a core of integrity.

Joseph as Governor of Egypt

Even in prison, Joseph is singled out. When the pharaoh's baker and wine steward have dreams, he interprets them—with the help of God. Later, when the pharaoh's counselors cannot interpret his dreams, Joseph is brought from prison to try. He acquits himself so successfully that he gains the pharaoh's favor.

Do you naturally identify with the feelings of any of the characters in this opening story about Joseph: the favorite son? the half brothers? the caring half brother? Write a paragraph describing how families can be harmed by jealousy or favoritism.

By the time Joseph is thirty years of age, he is the governor of Egypt, the most powerful man in the land other than the pharaoh. He marries a beautiful Egyptian woman and fathers two sons, Manasseh and Ephraim. Then famine strikes the Near East, and hungry people from all over go to Egypt for grain.

Read Genesis 39:20b–23; 40:1–23; 41:1–56.

Famine: Joseph's Brothers Go to Egypt

Among the people threatened by the famine are Jacob and his family, and we next see the old patriarch barking at his sons about standing around when there is grain in Egypt. He sends them off, all except Benjamin. As Rachel's only other son, Benjamin is now Jacob's favorite, and he will not let the boy out of his sight.

Arriving in Egypt, the brothers are ushered in to see the governor, and although Joseph knows them, they fail to recognize him. After all, they are sure that their brother is a slave, and this man is plainly an Egyptian noble. Joseph speaks to them only through an interpreter but, of course, understands their Hebrew and eavesdrops on all they say.

Pretending to believe that they are spies, Joseph questions his brothers in detail until they mention that they have a younger brother named Benjamin at home. Joseph locks them up, saying that one of them must return home and bring back the youngest brother.

Later, changing his mind, Joseph keeps only Simeon and gives the others grain and permission to go, on the condition that they return with Benjamin. When they comment among themselves that they are being punished by God for their long-ago crime against Joseph, he learns that Reuben had tried to save him. Before the brothers leave, Joseph has his servant return their money to the grain sacks, and at the night's encampment they are alarmed and puzzled to discover it.

At home, when the brothers tell Jacob about their visit and the strange request for Benjamin, he berates them, lamenting not only the loss of Joseph but that of Simeon as well. In a cry familiar to all of us, he wails, " 'Why must such things always happen to me!' " (42:36). Reuben offers his own sons as a pledge for Benjamin's safety, but Jacob is adamant. They may not take Benjamin!

Read Genesis 42:1–38.

The Founders' Journeys

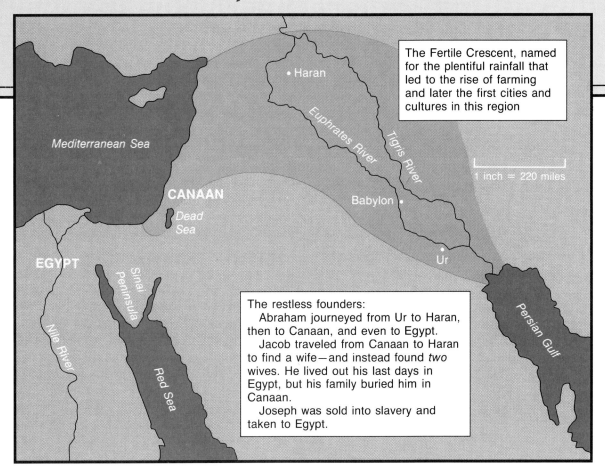

The Fertile Crescent, named for the plentiful rainfall that led to the rise of farming and later the first cities and cultures in this region

Mediterranean Sea

Haran

Euphrates River

Tigris River

1 inch = 220 miles

CANAAN

Dead Sea

Babylon

EGYPT

Sinai Peninsula

Ur

Nile River

Red Sea

Persian Gulf

The restless founders:
   Abraham journeyed from Ur to Haran, then to Canaan, and even to Egypt.
   Jacob traveled from Canaan to Haran to find a wife—and instead found *two* wives. He lived out his last days in Egypt, but his family buried him in Canaan.
   Joseph was sold into slavery and taken to Egypt.

Stories Jesus heard

The personalities in the story of Joseph are so alive and believable and the events drawn in such detail that they seem to be eyewitness accounts. This is oral history at its best, reworked by skillful writers, and these are the tales that Jesus heard—tales told to him by Mary and Joseph, by the rabbi at the synagogue school, or on feast days at worship. The blood of Joseph and his family flowed in Jesus' veins, and he must have loved them with all his heart.

The Second Journey

Once again Israel needs grain, and when Jacob orders his sons to go to Egypt, they remind him that without Benjamin, they cannot go. After bemoaning the price he must pay, Jacob finally consents to part with Benjamin because the people must live. The sacrifice will take him to his grave, he cries—surely plucking out his beard—but he will do it.

Read Genesis 43:1-14.

The great Jacob

We want to shout, "Hooray, Jacob!" Recall the story of Abraham going up the mountain to sacrifice his son and what he learned about God at the top. Compare this with Joseph's journey through betrayal, exile, prison—which has revealed gifts of perseverance and strength in him that he did not know he possessed. Consider Jacob's lifelong deceit, craft, and greed. Not until the moment when he sacrifices Benjamin does Jacob reach heroic heights and become one of the great saints of the Scriptures.

Return, Reunion, Reconciliation

Back the brothers go to Egypt, and on arriving they are invited to Joseph's house for a banquet. They are so guilt-ridden that they fear a trap and frantically explain that they have brought back the money they found in their sacks. When Joseph sees Benjamin, he leaves the room to weep. Later, when Joseph sits down to eat, he sends tidbits from his own plate to share with Benjamin as a gesture of royal favor.

When the brothers prepare at last to leave with their grain, the steward hides Joseph's own goblet in Benjamin's sack. Once they are on their way, Joseph sends servants after them. The cup is found, and Joseph orders Benjamin to stay behind as a slave. Now Judah steps forward and in a beautiful speech pleads with Joseph to consider the aged father who will die if Benjamin fails to return. Judah pledges his own life in Benjamin's place, and Joseph, close to tears, sends everyone but the brothers from the room.

Weeping so loudly that the others hear him in the hall, Joseph finally reveals his identity, forbidding his brothers to blame themselves for their past misdeeds. Everything was allowed to happen, he says, so that when they were in danger of starving, someone would be there to feed them. Joseph's story is a tale of reconciliation and redemption.

So all ends happily. The brothers return home, fetch Jacob and his family, journey back to Egypt, and settle there. Jacob is rewarded for his sacrifice of Benjamin by seeing all his sons reunited. In his old age, Jacob adopts Joseph's two sons, Manasseh and Ephraim—which is why they are listed as two of the twelve tribes of Israel. When Jacob dies, Joseph takes his body back to Canaan for burial. Joseph also lives to old age and makes his brothers swear that whenever their people return to the land of God's Promise, his bones will be taken there to be buried in the field where Abraham, Sarah, Isaac, and Jacob lie.

Read Genesis 43:15–34; 44:1–34; 45:1–28.

Happy endings

The stories of the patriarchs are all tales with happy endings—astonishingly so. Joseph's last request reveals, however, that the saga of ancient Israel is not over.

> Which of the stories in Genesis is your favorite? Write a one-page essay explaining your choice.

For Review

1. Who wrote the first passage of Genesis, and when did that author live?

2. What is the significance of the story of Cain and Abel?

3. What does obeying God save us from?

4. To whom does God offer the first covenant? Why is it offered, and what is the symbol of that event?

5. Who is called "the father of biblical faith"?

6. Who does God say will outnumber the stars?

7. Who is traditionally known as "the father of the Arab peoples"?

8. Explain why polygamy and the taking of concubines were practiced in biblical times.

9. Why is Sodom destroyed?

10. What is emphasized as a forbidden act in the story of Abraham's test?

11. What does Rebekah learn when she visits a holy place?

12. Describe Laban's character.

13. What new name is given to Jacob by the mysterious being? What does this new name mean?

14. What is the major theme of the patriarchal history?

15. Why do Joseph's brothers dislike him?

16. Summarize the story of Joseph's temptation.

17. Describe the moment when Jacob reaches the heights of heroism.

18. What is the significance of Joseph's last request?

3

Freedom:
The Exodus
and the Covenant of Sinai

THE Book of Exodus was close to the hearts of the biblical editors for many reasons:

- As the story of the Exodus begins, the Israelites are living in a foreign land. The postexilic Jews, who did the final writing and editing of this story, were fresh from a similar experience in Babylon.
- At the time of the Exodus, the people of Israel were slaves of the Egyptian Empire. The Priestly Writer recorded this story when the people of Israel were subjects of either the Babylonian or the Persian Empire.
- The people of the Exodus struggled in a frightening and hostile wilderness. Similarly, the exiles in Babylon had made a long, painful journey to the lands where they were taken.
- Most important to the biblical editors was God's revelation to their ancestors in the wilderness. Through Moses the people of Israel discovered the identity of their God, and through the Covenant they found their own identity. Similarly, in Babylon, after repenting of their sins, the exiles had rediscovered their true identity.

Enslaved in Egypt

The Book of Exodus begins about four hundred and fifty years after the death of Joseph. The reigning pharaoh of Egypt, unlike the Semitic pharaohs of Joseph's time, hates and fears the people of Israel and orders them enslaved and all Israelite males slain at birth.

The story of Moses begins when his mother, to save her infant son, puts him in a basket and floats it on the Nile near the villa of an Egyptian princess. As soon as the princess discovers the baby, a little girl darts out of the rushes with the information that a woman nearby could nurse the baby. Would the princess like her fetched? The princess hires the woman to care for the child until he is weaned, when he is

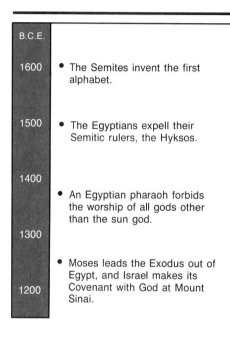

B.C.E.

1600 • The Semites invent the first alphabet.

1500 • The Egyptians expell their Semitic rulers, the Hyksos.

1400

• An Egyptian pharaoh forbids the worship of all gods other than the sun god.

1300

• Moses leads the Exodus out of Egypt, and Israel makes its Covenant with God at Mount Sinai.

1200

At the time of Moses, Egypt enjoyed an era of prosperity and conquest. *Facing page:* The Nile River has served Egypt as a highway since ancient times.

In protecting the Israelite slave, Moses is thrown into adulthood. The passage from childhood to adulthood is marked by many losses. Just as Moses loses the security of his princely position, we too lose things as we grow. Make a list of five losses or difficult changes you have endured in your passage to adulthood.

returned to the princess' household. Because the little girl and the woman are Moses' sister and mother, he grows up knowing that he is really an Israelite—although he is raised as an Egyptian prince.

Reaching manhood, Moses sees an Egyptian slave driver beating an Israelite one day. Angrily, he attacks the slave driver, kills him, and buries his body in the sand. Told the next day that the murder is known, Moses fears the pharaoh's anger and flees Egypt eastward to the land of the nomadic Midians. There he meets a priest, marries one of his daughters, and becomes a shepherd.

Read Exodus 1:6-22.

The Burning Bush

When the Israelite slaves, who no longer know God, cry out in agony, God is mindful of their suffering. One day, while tending sheep, Moses sees a strange sight—a bush aflame but not consumed. Drawing near, he hears God command him to return to Egypt to order Pharaoh to let the Israelites go. Moses, alarmed, protests that he is unsuited for such a task, but God insists. Again Moses protests: he does not know God's name. Who will he tell the people that their God is? God reveals the sacred name to be *Yahweh,* meaning "I am who am." Once again Moses excuses himself: the people will not believe him. God gives him a sign by which to convince the people—or at least himself! Still Moses argues: he is slow of speech and tongue (perhaps having a speech impediment). Finally, God becomes angry and says that Moses' brother, Aaron, will accompany him and do the talking—but Moses is to go!

Read Exodus 3:1-22; 4:1-17.

The name *Yahweh*

The name *Yahweh,* translated in the scriptural text as "I am who am," is better translated, "I am the One who is always present." For centuries people had believed that they were the slaves of the gods. A God who was not only supreme but also a constant and caring presence was a revolutionary idea.

Scholars suggest that the worship of the God named Yahweh was, in fact, unknown before the time of Moses. Although the early Israelites began to worship Yahweh within their own group, they did not necessarily see Yahweh as the one and only God or as the God of all the nations. This belief came later on. The concerns of Moses' people probably did not extend much beyond their own families and tribes.

Moses' call to lead his people to freedom came at Mount Sinai, sometimes referred to as Mount Horeb. His attention was drawn to a bush aflame but not consumed.

For Jews, the name *Yahweh* stresses the unutterable mystery of God, and out of reverence they have preferred not to pronounce it. Instead they substitute titles such as *Adonai,* meaning "the LORD"—a practice continued in many Christian versions of the Bible. This course will follow the same practice, with one exception: to underline the historical significance of the name *Yahweh,* this chapter will adopt the scholarly practice of using it where appropriate.

Moses' Return to Egypt

In Egypt, Moses and Aaron give Yahweh's message to the Israelites, who exult because God has seen their affliction. Yet Pharaoh is unmoved: Why should he heed a God of slaves? Isn't he, Pharaoh, a god also—son of the great god Ra? Besides, freeing his work force would upset the system! Accusing Moses of luring the Israelites from their work, Pharaoh doubles their burden. The people cry out that Moses' promise of Yahweh's protection has not freed them but only increased their sufferings. They want no more to do with Yahweh! Now God promises to take action.
Read Exodus 4:27–31; 5:1–23; 6:1.

The forgotten God
Notice that the Israelites have to be convinced of God's presence by miracles. They have been in Egypt for over four hundred years, and they no longer know their God. Yet God knows them.

The Ten Plagues

Moses and Aaron return to Pharaoh and repeat their demand, Pharaoh ignores them, and then the plagues begin. Water turns to blood, frogs overrun the land, and gnats and flies torment the Egyptians. Sickness afflicts their cattle, boils plague the people, hail destroys the crops, and locusts eat what is left. Darkness covers the land, and then Moses proclaims the final plague—death for the firstborn of Egypt. Pharaoh will beg them to leave, Moses says—but still Pharaoh is adamant.
Read Exodus 6:28–30; 7:1–29; 8:1–11; 11:1–10.

Miracles or natural disasters?
The usual question is, Were the plagues miracles or natural phenomena? As natural disasters, they were not unknown to Egypt. But the point is that God freed Israel from Egypt—whether through miracles or the powers of nature.

Jesus called God *Abba,* meaning "Papa" or "Daddy." Saint Paul said that using this name in a profound spiritual sense is a sure sign of conversion. Yet most Christians prefer the more formal title *Father* or the generic term *God,* which means "breath" or "spirit." Write a brief essay on what Jesus' name for God suggests and why you think it is not regularly used.

In a way, we are often like Moses —longing for freedom for ourselves and for those who are shackled in many ways. But sometimes we are like Pharaoh—arrogant, ignoring counsel, unwilling to face what is true. Write a brief reflection on three of the qualities of Pharaoh that you sometimes see in yourself. Or write a brief essay about a character from a TV show, film, or novel who exhibits traits like Pharaoh's.

Egypt of the Pharaohs

The classical period of Egyptian history dates from 3200 to 200 B.C.E., an era of relative peace and prosperity in the lower Nile region. Egypt possessed a warm climate, fertile soil, and a safe position between two deserts—all of which assured its inhabitants a stable, orderly, and secure existence.

Egyptian religion reflected this stability. Its myths grew up around gods who, in a serene and orderly hierarchy, presided over every city, temple, and home. The dominant concerns of creation and death were reflected in the chief deities, Ra and Osiris. *Ra* was the sun god, whose tears brought forth humanity and in whose divinity the pharaohs shared. *Osiris* was the god of the underworld, of eternal life, and of the renewal of life. From the size of the temples, their hieroglyphic inscriptions, and other records, we know that the rituals to Ra and Osiris—and to the many other gods of Egypt—were lengthy, serene, and solemn. These rituals were presided over by a powerful priestly class that flourished during a long period of ancient Egypt's history.

The pyramids and sphinxes stand in mute testimony to the ancient Egyptians' belief in the afterlife. They believed that life continued after death and that this survival depended upon the preservation of the body. For this reason, enormous efforts were made to save the body through mummification

Facing page: A superb statue of the pharaoh Khafre, who ruled Egypt in the twenty-sixth century B.C.E., when Abraham's ancestors were nomads in the Near East
Left: Khafre built one of the great pyramids—the second-largest one shown.
Below: The mummy of the pharaoh Ramses II, who may have reigned at the time of the Exodus

and to protect it in a pyramid or hide it in a cave. Such customs were reserved for nobles and especially for the divine pharaohs.

Semitic pharaohs?

Some scholars connect the migration of Joseph's family with the movement of other Semites to Egypt and with the Semitic group called the *Hyksos,* which actually ruled Egypt starting about 1667 B.C.E. The royal favor extended to the Israelites was much more likely to occur at this time than during any other period.

Sometime in the following century, the Hyksos were expelled by the native Egyptians. Little evidence of the Hyksos reign remains. No doubt it was a humiliating chapter of history for the Egyptians.

Who was Moses' Pharaoh?

Because historical evidence for the Exodus itself is slight, identifying the pharaoh of Moses' time proves to be almost impossible. The date often given for the Exodus, 1250 B.C.E., places the event in the reign of Ramses II (1304 to 1237 B.C.E.). During his exceptionally long reign, Ramses undertook an ambitious construction program, forcing foreigners to do all sorts of work for his empire: manning the army, tilling fields, erecting a new palace, and constructing two new cities almost from the ground up.

Pharaoh's stubbornness

Pharaoh's performance reads like that of a character in one of the nighttime TV soaps. Note the following:

- Pharaoh's arrogance in 7:22b-23
- how he bargains in 8:4-11
- how he ignores his counselors in 8:15
- how he wavers in 8:21-28
- how he resists advice in 9:11-12
- how he feigns repentance in 9:27-28
- his craftiness in 9:33-35
- his ransom plan in 10:10-11
- his hypocrisy in 10:16
- his offer of terms in 10:24-27

Did God harden Pharaoh's heart, or was he naturally stubborn? The Scriptures say both things, ten times each, and both may be true. The human heart is hardened by flinging itself against the will of the loving God, and proud, powerful rulers do not give in easily, especially to slaves. The God of the lowly Israelites was in Pharaoh's way.

Preparation for the Passover

Yahweh gives Moses instructions in preparation for the journey out of Egypt. Each family is to slay and roast a yearling lamb or kid, eat it with unleavened bread—a yeast dough would take too long to rise—and be ready to leave. Then they are to smear the top and posts of their doorway with the blood of the lamb so that the angel of God will *pass over* their home when striking down the firstborn of Egypt. The Israelites are to celebrate this meal every year as a perpetual reminder of the **Pesach,** or Passover.

Read Exodus 12:1-14.

Jesus' Last Supper

The memorial meal of the Israelites became the Passover *Seder,* or ritual meal, of the Jewish people. Although we do not know for sure, the Last Supper might have been a Seder. We do know that Jesus used the language, food, and ritual of the Passover to help his disciples understand the meaning of his own death in the context of their history. The Jewish Seder celebrates freedom from slavery in Egypt and the longing for freedom everywhere in the world. The Last Supper has become the Christian Eucharist, which celebrates freedom from the power of sin and death through Jesus' teaching, death, and Resurrection.

The Israelites were instructed to smear their doorways with the blood of a lamb so that the angel of God would pass over their homes when striking down the firstborn of Egypt.

Unleavened bread is a traditional food at the Passover Seder.
Left: A Seder meal set by Israeli Jews and including unleavened bread

Unleavened bread

At subsequent Passovers, the Israelites rid their households of all *leaven*—that is, fermented dough kept from one baking to another, a form of yeast—and all leavened bread. Starting afresh with new dough symbolized a new life of freedom. Jewish families today do this during the Passover season and serve only unleavened bread, called *matzo*. From this custom came the Christians' use of unleavened bread in Communion.

Departure

At midnight, a loud cry rises up over Egypt as the firstborn of every household is discovered dead. As Moses has foretold, Pharaoh summons him and cries out that Moses and his people must go: " 'You will be doing me a favor' " (12:32).

At last the people of Israel leave—a ragtag crowd of slaves, foreigners, men, women, and children, unarmed and on foot, leading their milking animals, and carrying all their belongings—including the bones of Joseph.

Read Exodus 12:29–39.

Again, the point of the story is *that* Yahweh freed the Israelites, not *how* Yahweh freed them. The slaying of the Egyptians' firstborn is not described.

Crossing the Sea of Reeds

God, in a pillar of cloud by day and a pillar of fire by night, leads the Israelites. Hardly have they left when Pharaoh, in

a rage, starts after them. The Israelites see his chariots in pursuit, are terrified, and cry out to Moses accusingly: "Were there not enough graves in Egypt? Is that why you brought us out to the desert to die?" Moses bids them to wait to see what Yahweh will do. The cloud moves to the rear of their camp and hides them from the Egyptians. Then the wind blows all night, parting the Sea of Reeds, and in the morning the Israelites cross safely—just ahead of the Egyptians. The water returns, and Pharaoh's troops drown. Moses and his sister Miriam, together with their people, sing a *canticle,* or song, praising God for the victory.
Read Exodus 13:17-22; 14:1-31; 15:1-21.

A modern story of a crossing

Did the crossing really happen the way the ancient story describes it? A modern story of a similar crossing offers an answer: During the struggle of the black people for civil rights in the United States—on the Easter Sunday following the jailing of Dr. Martin Luther King, Jr.—a crowd of two thousand people marched to the Birmingham, Alabama, jail to pray and sing outside under the windows. Police officers with dogs and fire fighters with hoses awaited them. Blocked, the crowd dropped to its knees to pray, and after five minutes someone jumped up and cried: "The LORD is with this movement! We're goin' on to the jail!" Everyone rose and started walking. To their astonishment, the police officers, fire fighters, and dogs simply stood still and let them go past. Bull O'Connor, the sheriff of Birmingham, yelled, "Turn on the hoses!" But no one moved as the people slowly marched to the jail, singing. The point of both this story and the ancient one of the crossing is that however they happened, the events were the work of the saving God.

Moses and Miriam's canticle

Scholars believe that the oldest parts of the Hebrew Scriptures might be found in Moses and Miriam's canticle (Exodus 15:1b,21b). Notice that in these verses, God is the Liberator of the Israelites, not the Creator of the world. The image of God as Creator of all peoples and the universe came much later in Jewish history, and the events of the future referred to in the canticle are also later additions.

The Murmuring Stories

The people of Israel have hardly finished celebrating their new freedom when they begin to complain about the hard-

The Birmingham march of 1963 offers us a modern story of a miraculous crossing.
Above: Photographed through the window of a police wagon, some of the estimated two thousand demonstrators sing and pray during their march on the Birmingham jail.

Have you had something happen to you that you hoped for but that had seemed impossible? Describe the event in writing and explain your feelings about it. Did you feel that God saved or liberated you at that moment?

ships of the journey. When the water is bitter, Yahweh sweetens it. When they lack food, Yahweh sends manna and quail. When again they need water, Moses strikes a rock and water gushes out.

Read Exodus 15:22-27; 16:1-36; 17:1-6.

Manna

Scholars are not sure what the food was that the Israelites called manna. One possibility is the sweet sap that forms on one variety of desert tree. Most of the story is by the Priestly Writer and might be a late elaboration on an early legend.

What has God done for us lately?

Have you ever been filled with joy over some turn of events in your life and then found that the feeling did not last? Events that seem perfect can become disappointing when the novelty drains off. The Israelites had this human experience as they wandered through the wilderness of the Sinai peninsula.

Arrival at Mount Sinai

When the Israelites arrive at Mount Sinai, Moses goes up the mountain. There God bids him to tell the people that Yahweh has brought them safely to this place and that if they keep the Covenant, they will be Yahweh's holy nation, dearer than all other peoples. Moses returns to the people and repeats this message, and the people say that they will do everything Yahweh asks of them.

On the third day, as the people prepare themselves for Yahweh's coming, a great storm breaks on the mountain. Lightning flashes, thunder peals, and dense clouds cover the peaks. Filled with fear, the people withdraw and beg Moses to be their spokesman with Yahweh lest they die. Then Yahweh gives Moses the Ten Commandments.

Read Exodus 19:1-11,16-19.

A theophany

The Priestly Writer embellished this account of divine visitation, referred to as a *theophany,* with details from Israel's later liturgical celebrations. The trumpet blasts and clouds of smoke, or incense, that were used to symbolize Yahweh's arrival were probably part of its celebration of the great event in the years that followed.

Make a quick list of symbols and symbolic actions used by the church to celebrate special times in our life. Explain their meaning.

The Ten Commandments

The Ten Commandments, or **the Decalogue,** date from Moses' time (1250 B.C.E.). Many other laws were added to them over the years and are included in Exodus—as well as in the Books of Leviticus, Numbers, and Deuteronomy. These later laws will be treated in the next chapter. Here we will look at the Ten Commandments in their historical context.
Read Exodus 20:1–26.

No other gods

The first commandment did not say that no other gods existed, but it did declare that there was only one God of the Israelites and that they should worship no other. This commandment also prohibited idolatry. In the Near East at the time, people commonly worshiped idols that represented gods—for example, a statue of a bull or a sun symbol. The first commandment stated that human efforts to depict God were bound to fail and should not be attempted.

Do you see idol worship today? How? Where? Write a one-page response to these questions, giving examples.

These inscribed pillars, reminiscent of the traditional tablets of the Ten Commandments, were discovered in the Sinai region on the site of an Egyptian temple.

God's name

The second commandment forbade the use of God's name in irreverent, sacrilegious ways. As mentioned earlier, devout persons rarely spoke God's name, but those less devout sometimes abused it in the belief that using the name *Yahweh* in prayer or when swearing an oath would magically force God to do their will.

The Sabbath

The third commandment called upon the Israelites to keep Saturday, their seventh day, as the Sabbath—free for worship in honor of God's rest on the seventh day in the story of the Creation. Later, by contrast, Christians chose Sunday as their holy day in honor of the Resurrection, which they believed signaled the first day of the New Creation.

Parents

Today we associate the fourth commandment, "Honor your father and your mother," with children and obedience. Originally, the law addressed adults and sought to protect aging parents. A wise politician once said that any society must be judged by how it treats its youngest and oldest citizens.

Murder

The fifth commandment, "You shall not kill," is more accurately translated as "You shall not murder." In nomadic groups, a person's life and dignity were protected only by the assurance that kinsfolk would revenge any injury or insult. Acts of revenge often escalated to bloody feuds and sometimes resulted in the extinction of entire family groups. At the time of the Exodus, the purpose of the fifth commandment was to lessen the violence arising from hatred, malice, and the taking of the law into one's hands. Much later, speaking of this commandment, Jesus denounced other forms of destructiveness—for example, anger, slaying with words, contempt, and vicious gossip.

Read Matthew 5:21-26.

A bishop once said that capital punishment is a sin against hope. Write a brief statement explaining what he meant and why you do or do not agree with him.

Adultery

The sixth commandment, "You shall not commit adultery," had as its end the protection of marriage and the family. In ancient times, the well-being of the family took precedence over the individual's desires because the stability and even survival of the community depended upon it. Adultery, which often led to vengeance and feuds, was held

The top of the seven-foot-tall *stele,* or pillar, containing King Hammurabi's code of laws

The Code of Hammurabi

Numerous codes of law predate the Ten Commandments. Probably the earliest is the code of Ur-Nammu, dated about 2100 B.C.E.—over eight hundred years before the Exodus. The code is named after the king of the city of Ur, a major city of an early Near Eastern civilization.

The best-known early code of laws is the code of Hammurabi, named after the king who ruled Babylon from 1792 to 1750 B.C.E. At the beginning of our century, a black stone pillar engraved with the code was unearthed. A portrait at the top of the pillar shows Hammurabi standing before Shamash, a god of justice. Inscribed below are laws that discuss trade and commerce and impose fees and wages—including the fees for doctors and severe penalties if medical treatment were to fail. For example:

If a doctor has mended a citizen's broken bone, or has healed an injured muscle, the patient shall pay the doctor five shekels of silver. . . .

If a doctor has made a major incision on a citizen with a bronze lancet, and has caused that man's death, or if he has cut open a citizen's brow and has blinded the man's eye, they shall cut off his hand.

in great horror among the Israelites, and its punishment was death. Although the hurt and harm of adultery is just as real today, some of these destructive consequences have been limited by the courts. Later laws of ancient times addressed other wrongful sexual relationships.

Stealing

"You shall not steal," says the seventh commandment. Stealing is a sin that accuses God of caring for us inadequately as well as a sin against the neighbor whose goods are stolen. Consider this idea too: stealing can also be defined as persons with abundance not sharing with others, who go without necessary food, shelter, or employment.

False witness

The eighth commandment forbids giving false testimony, especially in cases being judged by elders or in courts. At the time the Commandments were given, when a liar intended to bring about a sentence of death, the penalty for false witness could also be death.

Coveting a married woman

The ninth commandment given was later divided, and the second half was made into the tenth—which is how we will treat them here. Both commandments have to do with covetousness, or greediness, and both reveal a profound understanding of the path of sin. Sin begins in the mind and the heart. Entertaining the idea of a sin leads to the act. For example, coveting a neighbor's wife can be the first step toward adultery.

Greed for a neighbor's property

The tenth commandment relates to coveting a neighbor's goods, an envious craving that is the first step to injuring one's neighbor. Such greed leads not only to "keeping up with the Joneses" but also to trying to surpass them, and life can become a nightmare in which people are possessed by their possessions.

Write a brief reaction to the following statement:
- People can become addicted to buying things and to credit card spending.

Other Laws of Israel

"The Book of the Covenant," which follows the Ten Commandments in Exodus, treats laws of worship, civil laws, and laws controlling morality. Many of these laws were radical steps forward for the time. Other laws in "The Book of the Covenant" strike us today as clearly unjust, such as the law that was quoted at one time to justify owning slaves. This law said that if the owner of a slave struck the slave but did not kill him or her, that person would go unpunished because the slave was property.

Read Exodus 21:20-21.

Slavery

The other laws of Israel were not solely divine ordinances; they were the customs of many cultures of the time. In the ancient world, few undertakings could be completed without human power, and the use of slaves, bought or captured in war, was a universal practice. However, slavery has always been a violation of human rights; and when, in time, people saw this, they either freed their slaves or refused to own them. Much later, Western society began to see that slavery was a hideous custom, and with the arrival of the Industrial Revolution, machines and hired workers could do the work of slaves.

Sealing the Covenant of Sinai

In preparation for ratifying the Covenant of Sinai, Moses builds an altar with twelve pillars representing the twelve tribes of Israel. He has young bulls sacrificed for offerings, dividing their blood into two bowls. Half of the blood he splashes on the altar as a symbol of Yahweh's presence, and the other half he sprinkles on the people as a sign of the binding of God and the people in a kind of marriage. Doing so, Moses proclaims the Covenant of Sinai. Then Yahweh bids Moses to ascend the mountain again to receive the stone tablets on which the Law has been written.

Read Exodus 24:3-8.

The symbol of blood

In the Hebrew Scriptures, blood is the sign of life itself. In fact, laws of the time prohibited the consumption of animal blood because life was God's dominion, not humans'.

The Covenant of covenants

The sealing of the Covenant of Sinai is the high point of Israel's story. You have read about other blessings, promises, and covenants that God made with Adam, Noah, Abraham, and Jacob. Other covenants, made between human

Jesus said that he founded a New Covenant in his blood (Luke 22:20). Write a one-paragraph reflection on the meaning of his statement.

parties, are also mentioned in the Hebrew Scriptures. The Covenant of Sinai, however, surpassed all others in the minds of the biblical editors. At Sinai, Yahweh proclaimed for all time that the people of Israel were the people of God. In Judaism, the Covenant of Sinai is a never-to-be-repeated event—the testament that gave its name to what has been called "the Old Testament." This event is also of profound importance to Christians, who as believers in God are also children of Abraham and the people of Israel.

Something else is worth remembering: By the time the finishing touches were put to the Hebrew Scriptures, the Jews better understood what it meant to be the people of God. Theirs was a privileged role but not an easy one. To be called as witnesses to the one God for all the world was an extraordinarily difficult mission.

The Golden Calf

The story of Exodus continues with an account of immediate and shocking infidelity. When Moses returns to the mountaintop and remains for forty days and nights with God, the people think that he has left them. They grow bored and hunger for diversion, and astonishingly, they ask Aaron to make them an idol. More astonishingly, he does. Gathering the gold ornaments of the women and children, Aaron melts them, fashions a golden calf, and proclaims that it is Yahweh, the God who brought them out of Egypt (or, some scholars surmise, the animal on whose back God's throne rests). The people offer sacrifices to the golden calf.

Read Exodus 32:1-6.

Miles of commentaries have been written on this ageless tale—about the human heart, its inconstancy, and the need for redemption. When God seems to be absent, we quickly make gods of things that seem more real to us—or at least are more visible.

The Tablets Destroyed

Yahweh, knowing what the people have done, vows to destroy them, but Moses intercedes. He descends the mountain, discovers their revelry, and breaks the tablets of the Law, which has already been broken by the people. Angrily, Moses confronts Aaron, orders the idolators slain, and returns to beg Yahweh's forgiveness for the rest of the people.

Refusing to accompany the Israelites, Yahweh orders them to continue on their way to the land flowing with milk

The story of the golden calf tells how easily people can make things into idols.

and honey. However, upon further pleading by Moses, Yahweh agrees to be present in a pillar of cloud before the tent of the meeting, but only when they halt.

Read Exodus 32:7–20; 33:1–11.

The Love Between Moses and Yahweh

One of the most moving passages in the Scriptures is a conversation between Yahweh and Moses that is like two lovers talking. Moses begs Yahweh to go with the Israelites so that all the world will know that they are God's people. Yahweh agrees. Then, in a burst of longing, Moses begs, "Let me see your glory!" Yahweh replies that no one can look upon the face of God and live, but Yahweh will pass by and shield Moses so that he can safely see God from the back.

Read Exodus 33:12–23.

The Covenant Renewed, the Tablets Rewritten

Yahweh tells Moses to bring new tablets, and before engraving the Commandments on them, Yahweh reveals what God is like. (The Jewish teachers called this scriptural passage "The Thirteen Attributes of God.") Yahweh then renews the Covenant, promising to work marvels for Israel that the world has never seen before—if Israel keeps God's word.

Descending from the mountain, Moses is radiant with the glory of God. Because the people are afraid to approach him, Moses covers his face with a cloth, removing it only when he goes to speak with Yahweh.

Following God's instructions, a dwelling place for the ark of the Covenant is completed and Aaron and his sons are ordained as priests. The cloud indicating the presence of Yahweh settles down over the ark's dwelling place and fills it. When Yahweh moves, as a cloud by day and as fire by night, the people of Israel follow. Where Yahweh stays, the people stay. Thus the Israelites resume their journey.

Read Exodus 34:1–35; 40:1–38.

"The God of the Old Testament"

The thirteen attributes of God are briefly explored in the following list:

1, 2. *The LORD, the LORD:* This repetition indicates that Yahweh is the God of all things and all creatures and is the beginning and end of all time.

The Ark of the Covenant, the Tent of the Meeting

According to the Priestly Writer, the ark of the Covenant was a small wooden box, about the size of an orange crate, kept within a tent sanctuary while the people of Israel were in the wilderness. On the top of the ark was a plate of gold called the *mercy seat,* the throne where God met the people of Israel. Thus the sanctuary itself was called the *tent of the meeting.* The ark was carried at the head of the column when the people traveled through the desert and before the army in battle.

Later, Solomon established the sanctuary in the Temple in Jerusalem. In English versions of the Bible, the sanctuary is called the *tabernacle,* which simply means "tent."

Jews still celebrate the *Feast of Tabernacles,* known as *Sukkoth,* commemorating God's providence during the time in the wilderness. During this week-long, autumnal feast, many Jewish families put up simple booths, decorate them with harvest fruits, eat their meals there, and sleep under the stars.

The Israelites carried the ark of the Covenant with them through the wilderness and before the army in battle. At campsites, it was kept within a tent sanctuary.

3. *A God*

4. *Merciful:* The Hebrew word for *merciful* is the same as that for *womb,* which suggests that God possesses a mother's tender understanding of a child's weakness.

5. *Gracious:* The Hebrew word for *gracious* is the same as the word expressing the kindness of the good Samaritan —suggesting kindness for its own sake.

6. *Slow to anger*

7. *Rich in kindness:* This phrase refers to Yahweh's fidelity to the Covenant even when Israel has disobeyed.

8. *Fidelity:* The Hebrew word for *fidelity* means "steadfast love," suggesting that Yahweh is not only present but is always offering love to us. In the Christian Scriptures, the term that comes closest in meaning is probably *grace.*

9. *Continuing for a thousand generations:* The word *thousand* implies endless. Think of the faith that for thousands of years contributed to Christian faith today, starting with Abraham and Israel, reshaped by Jesus and the Apostles, carried on by missionaries, reaching the recent history of your grandparents and parents.

10, 11, 12. *Forgiving wickedness, crime, and sin:* The literal translation of these attributes is "bearing crookedness, and rebellion, and failure." The implication is that God's love and goodness are stronger than evil.

13. *Yet not declaring the guilty guiltless, but punishing the children and grandchildren to the third and fourth generation:* Yahweh forgives those who want forgiveness. As for those who do not, the sin against the Holy Spirit—which Jesus says is not forgiven in this world or the next—is believing that we have no need to be forgiven.

This attribute sounds extremely harsh, but the intention is to suggest that Yahweh does not let wrongs go unpunished. Remember that belief in personal punishment in an afterlife developed later in Jewish history. So if an individual died without being punished for injustices, it was believed that the punishment must then have fallen on his or her children.

People who see "the God of the Old Testament" as angry and vengeful should ponder Exodus 34:6–7 in order to see in it the God whose attributes are made present to us in Jesus. God's self-revelation to Moses in this portrait well matches the gospel portrait of the father in the story of the prodigal son.

Choose one of the thirteen attributes of God that strikes you as significant and write a brief reflection on it.

A Final Note on Exodus

You have completed the Book of Exodus, but the people of Israel have only half completed their journey to the Promised Land. The rest of the journey is more than simply a matter of miles. The Israelites cannot enter the land of Canaan until they comprehend more fully the Law and the Covenant. So the people have more to learn in the wilderness.

For Review

1. Give four reasons that the Book of Exodus was close to the hearts of the biblical editors.

2. Give two translations for the Hebrew name *Yahweh*.

3. What is the final plague proclaimed by Moses?

4. What does the Passover Seder celebrate?

5. What image of God is given in Moses and Miriam's canticle?

6. Define the term *theophany*.

7. Why did the first commandment prohibit idolatry?

8. Why was adultery held in great horror among the Israelites?

9. Explain the understanding of sin revealed in the ninth and tenth commandments.

10. What does blood symbolize in the Hebrew Scriptures?

11. Why did the Covenant of Sinai surpass all other covenants in the minds of the biblical editors?

12. Explain the reason behind the last attribute of God: "punishing the children and grandchildren to the third and fourth generation."

4

The Law:
Living Out the Covenant

THE keystone to the Book of Exodus is the Commandments, which establish the terms of the Covenant of Sinai. The next three books—Leviticus, Numbers, and Deuteronomy—expand the Commandments and further define relationships within the community of Israel.

In some ways, the Commandments are like the U.S. Constitution, which establishes a community built on justice and rights. But even before the Constitution was ratified by the states, amendments were needed to specify more clearly the laws of the land. Similarly, many laws were added to the Ten Commandments over the centuries.

These additions treated matters that Israel had not yet experienced at the time of Moses and the Decalogue. They included laws about land ownership, houses, vineyards, and situations that were nonexistent in the lives of the wandering Israelites. These added laws became permanent biblical Jewish Law because, like the amendments are to the Constitution, they were in the spirit of the Commandments. Some of these laws appear in Exodus, but Leviticus, Numbers, and Deuteronomy contain many more. In its entirety, this collection of laws is called the *Law of Moses,* the *Mosaic Law,* or simply **the Law.**

Leviticus: Holiness and Ritual

The Book of Leviticus is named after the Levites, members of the tribe of Levi, who were set apart to serve as priests. The book is attributed to the Priestly Writer. The purpose of much of the Priestly writing is to answer the question, How can Israel survive as a people believing in one God while living in a foreign culture whose people worship other gods?

The Mosaic Law helped the Israelites survive their years in the wilderness, and it helped their descendants survive in the wilderness of pagan cultures in which they were forced to live.
Facing page: A shepherd tends his flock near Bethlehem in Israel. Although the Israelites later took up farming, crafts, and commerce, shepherding was never abandoned entirely.

Write a brief reflection on this question:
- If someone goes to church each Sunday and keeps the rules but shows little or no concern for justice and peace, can that person be considered a good Christian?

In response, Leviticus, which is a handbook for worshipers, offers precise instructions for Israel's rituals. In Leviticus, formal worship is considered central to the moral and spiritual lives of the Israelites. Some of the instructions might have their origin in ancient teachings. Most of the material, however, probably stems from rituals in the Temple in Jerusalem, which the Jews rebuilt after their return from exile in Babylon. Leviticus presents these regulations in the form of direct statements from God to Moses or the Israelites, in the style of the Covenant of Sinai.

Above all, the Priestly Writer wanted the Jews to see their worship in the Temple as related to their life in the community. The Covenant with God was meant to frame the whole of life, so the idea of holiness in Leviticus includes not only worship but also the conscientious avoidance of sin. In short, true worship leads to a concern for human rights.

Leviticus is rarely a favorite book of the Bible, yet to think that it contains nothing of interest for us would be a mistake. The Book of Leviticus encourages its readers to

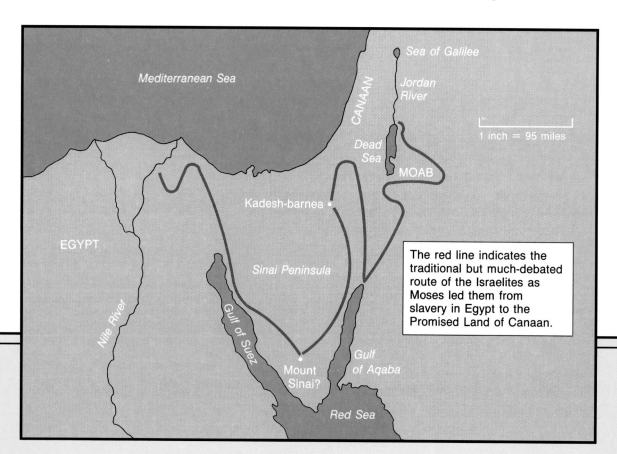

The red line indicates the traditional but much-debated route of the Israelites as Moses led them from slavery in Egypt to the Promised Land of Canaan.

Out of Egypt into the Wilderness

honesty, reverence, respect, tolerance, compassion, and generosity—virtues that are as needed now as they were at the time of its writing.

Sacrifices of Atonement

Leviticus treats the rituals of the Temple, which included different kinds of prayer and sacrifice. Since its beginning, humankind had felt that sin broke its relationship with the gods and created a debt payable only by sacrifice. As the story of Abraham's test suggests, this was sometimes human sacrifice. Early in their history, the nomadic peoples of the Near East substituted animal sacrifice in atonement for sin. The blood of the animal, poured out on the altar, signified the offerer's sorrow; the altar signified the presence of God.

The rituals described in the first half of Leviticus are sacrifices of atonement. In addition, once a year, on the *Day of Atonement* (called *Yom Kippur* by the Jews), the high priest entered the sanctuary called the holy of holies, where God was believed to dwell. There the priest first offered incense, then the blood of a bull representing himself and his tribe, and finally the blood of a goat representing all Israelite people. After the Dispersion began, Jews continued to celebrate Yom Kippur as the holiest day of the year, although the day no longer included sacrifice.

The atonement of Jesus?

The unknown author of the Epistle to the Hebrews, writing to Jewish Christians, used the familiar rituals of atonement to give meaning to the death and Resurrection of Jesus. He called Christ the true High Priest—who offers the victim, who is also the victim, whose blood is spilled for the people, and who reconciles humankind to God with his perfect sacrifice.

Unfortunately, over the centuries popular theology had distorted the image of perfect atonement into a portrait of an unforgiving God, whose anger at sin would not be satisfied until a bloody price was paid. This image does not fit either the loving and forgiving God described in Exodus 34:6–7 and elsewhere in the Hebrew Scriptures or the loving parent whom Jesus reveals in the story of the prodigal son. Explaining the mystery of redemption is extraordinarily difficult, but it is enlightening to see that much of the vocabulary with which Christians have struggled to describe redemption comes from the Book of Leviticus.

Read Hebrews 8:1–12; 9:11–14.

In writing, describe a time when you felt the need to be forgiven by someone.
- Were you conscious of a feeling of sorrow for your wrongdoing?
- Of the need to admit your fault?
- Of a desire to make up for the offense?
- Of a determination not to repeat it?

These are the traditional four elements of a good confession. Can you recall how they were worded in religion class?

The Holiness Code

The holiness code in Leviticus, chapters 17 to 26, contains many teachings that predate even the Hebrew Scriptures. These address matters such as the purification of people and dwellings, death sentences for certain crimes, and threats of disaster for disobedience.

Most remarkable are the code's advanced moral teachings. For example, Israel is told the following:

- Leave some of the harvest for gleaning by the poor.
- Do not withhold the wages of a laborer until the next day.
- Do not curse the deaf or put a stumbling block in the way of the blind.
- Do not stand by idly while a neighbor's life is at stake.
- Do not persecute foreigners.
- Do not fashion dishonest weights and measures, used for determining prices.

In addition, every fifty years, debts are to be canceled, and those who have lost their property are to have the opportunity to redeem it.

Read Leviticus 19:9-18,33-35; 25:1-23.

Aaron and His Sons

The one story in Leviticus is a lesson in how the compassion and understanding of God supersede even the important ritual instructions.

During the week of their ordination, two of Aaron's sons break the rules by bringing fire to the sanctuary in their incense burners instead of using the fire that burns perpetually on the altar. The biblical text says that God, in anger, strikes them down with fire. Warned by Moses not to leave his priestly post to mourn his sons' death nor to touch their bodies and become unclean, Aaron grieves in silence while the bodies are carried outside the camp.

Moses instructs Aaron to sacrifice a goat in atonement. When he discovers that Aaron and his remaining sons have not eaten the flesh of this sin offering, he angrily rebukes them, asking why they have once again disobeyed the rules. Aaron, bereaved, answers that when such a terrible misfortune has befallen him this day—would God expect he could eat? And Moses understands.

Read Leviticus 10:1-7,16-20.

Moses' principles and compassion

This story of Aaron and his sons stresses the importance of ritual to the survival of the community. The many regula-

In ancient times, prices and taxes were calculated according to the weight, area, or volume of an item—based on royal standards.

The great Indian chieftain Tecumseh said that he could not sell land to the white people anymore than he could sell them the air because both were given by the great Spirit for the good of all. **Reread Leviticus 25:23.** In writing, compare the chief's concept of owning property with that of the Priestly Writer.

tions surrounding Israel's worship were necessary to protect Israel from the idolatrous customs of its neighbors, who worshiped many gods. The outcome of the story recalls Jesus' statement that " 'the sabbath was made for man, not man for the sabbath' " (Mark 2:27). In other words, the authentic needs of the person cannot be ignored for the sake of legalism. This story, written centuries after the Exodus, reveals the forceful, zealous, yet also compassionate character of Moses—and the writer's understanding of the compassion of God.

Numbers: Priestly Regulations and Inspiring Stories

The Book of Numbers is a complex work by many authors and editors. Its present title comes from the census mentioned in the first part of the book, which reports exaggerated numbers of Israelites as well as lists of priestly regulations. The original Hebrew title, "In the Wilderness," describes the latter part of the book, telling of Israel's wandering in the

The Israelites' journey through the wilderness was both a spiritual and a physical feat.
Left: A satellite photo shows the fertile Nile Delta and the barren lands of the Sinai Peninsula.

wilderness on the way to Canaan. This second section contains a number of inspiring stories about jealousy, rebellion, and greed.

The First Part of Numbers

Notes on two brief, unrelated excerpts from the first part of Numbers will be useful in discussion later on.
Read Numbers 1:20–21,45–46.
Read Exodus 13:1–2,11–12; Numbers 3:5–13.

The numbers of men

The Hebrew word for *one thousand* might be more accurately translated as "battalion." So Numbers 1:21, describing the tribe of Reuben, should read "forty-six battalions totaling five hundred" rather than "forty-six thousand five hundred." This reading brings the sum of all men in the camp to between twenty-five thousand and thirty thousand—a much more reasonable size than the over six hundred thousand mentioned in verses 45 to 46. One scholar has said that if the Israelites had been as numerous as reported, perhaps they would have stayed in Egypt and taken over.

The Levites

After the Babylonian exile, the ritual offering of sacrifice was reserved for Aaron's line—a clan of the tribe of Levi. The other Levites were restricted to less important sanctuary duties.

The priestly role of the Levites is reflected in the story of Zechariah and Elizabeth in the first chapter of Luke. In Luke 1:5–17, Zechariah, of the tribe of Levi, is told by an angel that he and his wife, Elizabeth, of the line of Aaron, will have a son and name him John. Thus, John the Baptist came from the tribe dedicated to serving God.

More Murmuring

The second part of Numbers begins with another version of the murmuring tales from Exodus, using contributions by the Yahwist and the Elohist. Here the people complain about the food, lamenting loudly for cucumbers, melons, onions, and garlic rather than "nothing but this manna." When Moses, distraught, asks God to let him die, God promises that the people will eat the meat they want—until it comes out of their noses! A strong wind drives flocks of quail in

According to the Book of Numbers, when the Israelites tired of the manna sent by God, they gorged themselves on flocks of quail driven in from the sea.

from the sea, and the people gorge themselves so greedily that some of them die.

Read Numbers 11:1-23,31-34.

The Jealousy of Miriam and Aaron

The next story, about Miriam and Aaron, has a familiar ring. Moses' sister and brother claim authority equal to his. Does Moses think that he is the only prophet around? Angrily, God rebukes them, saying that other prophets have visions and dreams of God but only Moses sees the LORD "face to face," that is, intimately. At the end of God's denunciation, Miriam's skin is white with a disease referred to as leprosy. A week spent outside the camp for purification is required for her healing. The people cannot start out again until she is brought back.

Read Numbers 12:9-15.

The sinning, healing community

Some people say that going to church is not necessary—that faith, prayer, and good deeds are all that is needed. These *are* truly needed, yet the work of Christians is to heal the world, and we cannot do this as individuals. Healing the world takes the efforts of a believing, serving community.

The story of Israel is about the beginnings of the community that Christians call the Church. That community was made up of people who were, like people today, weak and sinful, and sin took its toll. In the story of Aaron and Miriam, the people cannot continue their journey until Miriam has been healed and restored to them. In the same way today, sin hinders the journey of the Church, yet repentance and God's healing forgiveness get it back on its way.

Exploring the Land of Canaan

In the next story, God has Moses send a man from each tribe to cross the border and explore Canaan. They return with tales of a land flowing with milk and honey but, they fearfully add, occupied by giants, next to whom the Israelites would seem like grasshoppers. Two of the scouts, Caleb and Joshua, want to enter the land nevertheless, but the people begin to mutter. Forgetting that God has broken the might of Egypt for them, the people complain that it would be better to have died in Egypt or to die now in the desert than to go into Canaan and be slaughtered.

The mission of Christians is to work in community to heal the world. ***Above:*** A Salvadoran refugee prays for a member of his family who died in a tent camp in Honduras.

On the Nile River lies the marvelous temple of the queen Hatshepsut, who ruled Egypt from 1503 to 1482 B.C.E. She was the only woman to rule Egypt as a pharaoh. In Hatshepsut's time, the temple symbolized her divinity as well as the power of imperial Egypt.

Historic Happenings Between 1700 and 1250 B.C.E.

Africa
The Egyptians extend their empire eastward into Asia and southward into the Sudan. By 1600 B.C.E., the cat has taken up residence in Egyptian homes.

America
Agricultural villages, which grow corn and other crops, become numerous in Central America.

China
A system of writing, in which each word is a picture, is used to communicate with the spirit world. Armies use chariots and wooden bows, reinforced by horn and sinew.

Europe
The Greeks lay siege to the city of Troy in what is now modern Turkey, giving rise to the legend of the Trojan War.

India
Hindu priests collect the religious hymns of the *Rig Veda*. One of these hymns praises "the unknown god," who is lord of all that exists.

The Near East
After 1500 B.C.E., the warlike Assyrians from northern Iraq become a leading power in the region. Their kings trade gifts with the pharaohs of Egypt.

God takes the people at their word and declares that for each of the forty days spent scouting Canaan, they will spend a year in the wilderness, until every member of the generation brought from Egypt has perished. Only Caleb and Joshua will live to see the land, along with the offspring of the first generation. Immediately the people change their tune. They will enter Canaan! Moses warns them not to disobey God; but the people go anyway, are defeated, and return disheartened.

Read Numbers 13:1-3,17-33; 14:1-44.

Faith without risk?

The story above is about faith and risk taking. Here a frightened Israel again forgets the generosity and mercy of God. The people choose instead the fragile security of the desert—and they get to stay there.

Giants?

The people of Canaan were not larger than the Israelites, but the huge stone walls around their fortified cities evidently frightened the tent-dwelling Israelites. They thought that a race of giants had built them.

The Rebellion Stories

Two rebellions repeat the theme of jealousy that is found earlier in the story of Miriam and Aaron. First a Levite challenges the religious authority of Aaron. Then two men of the tribe of Reuben incite a political rebellion, accusing Moses of leading Israel out of Egypt on a wild-goose chase. In a grim turn of events, the text says, they are all destroyed with their families.

Read Numbers 16:1-35.

Punishing the innocent?

The punishment of whole families, which horrifies us, might have been the result of some natural disaster, although an early, primitive custom did include the practice. In the Israelite culture, such events were commonly interpreted as punishment from God. A later verse in Numbers suggests that in fact, the children of Korah were not destroyed (26:11).

In a way, circumstances exact the same penalty in the modern world. The entire family of a person who commits some great wrong will suffer its consequences—through heartache, humiliation, or sometimes loss of reputation or livelihood.

Write a one-page essay describing the greatest crisis you have ever faced. How did faith get you through that crisis?

Write a brief description of a news story, film, or novel that tells about innocent people being injured because of others' misdeeds.

Aaron's flowering staff symbolized his tribe's special role as the priesthood.

Aaron's Status Confirmed

In a charming story, God has each tribal leader, including Aaron, leave his staff before the ark of the Covenant. In the morning, almond blossoms and a few almonds are found growing on Aaron's staff. Thus God gives a sign once and for all that Aaron's tribe has been chosen for the priesthood and is not to be challenged.

Read Numbers 17:16-26.

The Punishment of Moses and Aaron

In the next story, the people settle at a place called Kadesh, more often called Kadesh-barnea. Again they complain about the hardship of the wilderness compared to the lush life in Egypt. God bids Moses to strike a rock with a staff. He does so, but only after he and Aaron have angrily berated the people as rebels. Water gushes forth from the rock, but the LORD is angry about the brothers' outburst and punishes them, saying that they will die without entering Canaan.

Read Numbers 20:1-13.

Faith, not fear

Why do Moses and Aaron deserve such a harsh penalty? The explanation seems to be that each time the people's faith has weakened, God has shown unfailing care and inspired them through a mastery of nature. This time, Moses and Aaron resorted to angry sarcasm, changing the people's experience from one of renewed faith to one of fear.

The Bronze Serpent

Once again the people of Israel cry out for Egypt. And God, becoming angry, sends serpents to poison them. The terrified people confess their sin and beg Moses to intercede for them. God tells Moses to make a bronze serpent, mount it on a pole, and tell the people that anyone who repents and looks at it will recover—which they do.

Read Numbers 21:4-9.

This brief story underlines once again that God forgives and forgets people's sins, if they repent.

Balaam and His Donkey

Now comes one of the best stories in Numbers. As the Israelites journey through lands occupied by other peoples, they are forced to detour, bypass, or sometimes do battle—at which they are very successful. Balak, the king of Moab, hears of these successes and decides that Moab must not be overcome. He sends members of his court to summon a soothsayer named Balaam.

The princes of Moab offer gifts to Balaam and deliver the request, and Balaam tells them to stay the night while he consults God. God tells Balaam that the Israelites are blessed, that he must not curse them, and Balaam refuses the commission. The Moabites report this to Balak, who, believing that flattery and bribery will induce anyone to do anything, sends more distinguished emissaries to Balaam with promises of more glorious gifts. Balaam says that he must again ask God, and this time God tells him that he may go to Moab but he must do as God says. Things are looking up, thinks Balaam.

Starting out on his donkey, Balaam rides until the donkey halts before an angel with a fiery sword standing in the road—whom Balaam cannot see. The donkey turns off into a field until the angry Balaam beats her and gets her back on the road. In a while, as they travel on a narrow lane, the angel appears again. The donkey shrinks against a stone wall, grazing Balaam's knee, and again he beats her. On they go until a third encounter takes place and the donkey falls to the ground. Balaam, beating the creature mercilessly, is astonished to hear the donkey speak. By what right, she asks, does he beat an animal who has so faithfully served him over the years? Balaam, terrified, suddenly sees the angel, who says that but for his donkey, Balaam would have been killed. Balaam's lust for gold and silver had blinded him to the presence of God.

Read Numbers 22:2–35.

Straight from the donkey's mouth

The story of Balaam and his donkey is a parable about obsession with material things. Balaam's mind, filled with visions of riches, is blinded to God's will, represented by the angel. Opening one's eyes to this kind of obsession can be as difficult as getting a donkey to speak!

Balaam's Oracles

Balaam, arriving at Moab, instructs Balak three times to build seven stone altars, on which Balak is to offer young bulls and rams. Each time the sacrifices are made, Balaam steps aside to seek oracles, and God puts blessings for Israel,

The story of Balaam and his donkey carries a clever message about greed and God's will.

not curses, in Balaam's mouth. A fourth blessing lists the nations that Israel will overcome and includes a passage referring to a star that will come from Jacob.
Read Numbers 24:14–17.

The figure of Balaam

Historical reference to Balaam has been found outside the Bible. At a shrine to Balaam, dating about 700 B.C.E., he is described as a soothsayer who received messages from the gods. Scholars suggest that Balaam might have been a famous folk figure known for centuries among many groups in the Near East.

Jacob's star

The star mentioned in Balaam's fourth blessing is probably an editorial reference to David, although some scholars think that it refers to the "stars of Jacob"—meaning his destiny. In either case, the early leaders of the Church often quoted it as a prophecy of Christ.

Some scholars propose that in Matthew's Gospel, the mention of the magi who follow a star to Bethlehem builds upon Balaam's story. In both tales, wise men meet a king with evil designs on Israel, and in both the wise men bless Israel. No doubt, Matthew's reference to the star and the wise men helped the first Jewish Christians understand that Jesus was the Promised One.

Matthew's reference to a star and the wise men helped the first Christians understand Jesus' identity.
Below: A star over Bethlehem

A Summary of Numbers

Saint Paul provided a fitting summary to the Book of Numbers in his First Letter to the Corinthians. Once again, we see how much is missing for Christians if, in reading the Gospels and the Epistles, they do not have an acquaintance with the writings in the Hebrew Scriptures.

Read 1 Corinthians 10:1-13.

Deuteronomy: The Law and Love

Deuteronomy is written almost entirely in the first person and in the style of three sermons given by Moses prior to his death—interrupted by random selections from the Law. The title of the book, meaning in Greek "the repetition of the Law," is not altogether accurate for this retelling of Israel's wilderness journey. Rather, Deuteronomy is an admonishment to love the Law and keep it.

Put together after the Babylonian exile, the book is compiled from a number of earlier writings, none of them from Moses' time. These writings of the Deuteronomists date back to the northern kingdom of Israel and to the first Temple in Jerusalem. Much of the book is beautifully written with language that is not only deeply touching but sometimes quite folksy.

On the other hand, the accounts of battles and of the destruction of cities and their inhabitants are scandalous. Israel obviously did these things in accordance with the customs of war in those times and attributed them to the command of God. The God whom we know from the Gospels would neither desire nor command such brutality.

The First Sermon

Moses' first sermon reviews the journey from Sinai (here called Horeb) to Moab, the land on the east side of the Jordan River. From Moab the Israelites will cross over into Canaan.

Moses has implored God to let him accompany the people into Canaan, but his request has been refused. In his sermon, he blames the people's disobedience for his punishment rather than admitting his own fault.

Joshua will succeed Moses and lead Israel into the land.

Read Deuteronomy 3:23-29.

Taking into consideration all the events of Moses' life, write brief essay answers to each of these questions:
- What was Moses like at the beginning of his story?
- In what ways did he change?
- If you were casting an actor to play the part of Moses in a film about his life, who would you choose? Why?

No to Moses

Moses' blaming the people for God's refusal of his request shows the Deuteronomists' reluctance to find fault in the great prophet. An earlier example of this prejudice in favor of Israel's great men appears in Numbers when Miriam, the woman, is punished for jealousy but Aaron—the man and ancestor of the Priestly Writer—is not.

But the story of Moses reveals a powerful lesson: heroes are still human. Allowing Moses to enter the Promised Land seems only right, but the biblical writers remind us that human plans always give way to God's, even when we do not understand them. Christians are reminded that only Jesus served God perfectly—and even his plans took a painful and unexpected turn.

The Second Sermon

In Moses' second sermon, the Commandments are repeated with some variations:

- The Sabbath rule allows slaves to rest.
- Honoring one's parents is the condition on which long life and prosperity depend.
- The tenth commandment does not define a wife as a man's property—as was suggested in Exodus 20:17.

Read Deuteronomy 6:4–9.

> Write a brief reflection on the idea that Deuteronomy 6:5 is the commandment that contains all the other commandments.

The greatest commandment

Deuteronomy 6:4–9 is part of a Jewish confession of faith called the **Shema**. The Shema was repeated daily by all Israelites and would later be recited by Jesus, Mary, and Joseph.

Jesus quoted Deuteronomy 6:5 to the Pharisees who tried to trip him up with their question about which commandment of the Law was the greatest.

Read Matthew 22:34–37.

The temptation of Jesus

In the gospel story of Jesus' temptation in the desert, his responses to the tempter come from the Book of Deuteronomy.

- In response to the invitation to make stone into bread, Jesus quotes Deuteronomy 8:3: " '. . . Not by bread alone does man live, but by every word that comes forth from the mouth of the LORD.' "
- In response to the suggestion that he show his power by throwing himself off the Temple's wall, Jesus quotes Deuteronomy 6:16: " 'You shall not put the LORD, your God, to the test. . . .' "

The Mezuzah and Phylacteries

Some Jewish families write the verses of the Shema (Deuteronomy 6:4–9; 11:13–21 and Numbers 15:37–41) on parchment and fasten this scroll to the doorpost of their house. This scroll is called the *mezuzah.* Other Jews keep the verses in two small square leather boxes called *phylacteries,* which are worn on the forehead and the left arm when the verses are recited.

Left: In Jerusalem, two young men prepare for prayer by putting on their phylacteries.
Above: A mezuzah

- In response to the promise of riches and power, Jesus quotes Deuteronomy 6:13: " 'The LORD, your God, shall you fear; him shall you serve, and by his name shall you swear.' "
  Read Matthew 4:1–11.

Loving the lowly

In Deuteronomy 7:7–8, Moses reminds Israel that it has been chosen by God not because it is the largest of the nations but because it is the smallest, because of God's love for the people, and because of God's promises to the patriarchs.

The reforms of Josiah

The Deuteronomists inserted a code of laws into the second sermon of Moses. The code includes the following:

- Every seven years, debts must be forgiven, although the approach of the "release year" must not deter one from lending money to a poor neighbor.
- Slaves who have served six years must be released in the seventh.
- Interest on a loan may be demanded of a foreigner but not of an Israelite.
- Selling an Israelite into slavery is punishable by death.
- Millstones owned by the poor may not be taken in pledge, for without them they cannot grind flour.
- Parents and children may not be punished for one another's crime.
- Under the **levirate law**, a widow has the right to marry her husband's brother in order to bear a child who can carry on the name of the late husband and inherit his goods.
- Feasts, judges, and judgments are described, along with the procedure to be followed should Israel desire a king.

Scholars think that these laws were taken from a book found in the first Temple during the reign of King Josiah (about 640 to 609 B.C.E.). Following the book's discovery, Josiah, horrified at Israel's infidelity to the code as well as to the Covenant it represented, instituted extensive reform.

The Third Sermon

Moses' third sermon teaches that the Covenant extends to more people than the adult males of Israel. Women, children, all who live in the camp, those who hew wood and draw water—usually slaves or foreigners—and later generations are all included as God's people. Moses sets forth the penalties for disobedience, idolatry, and infidelity; promises mercy; reads the Law; and commissions Joshua as his successor. In what is called the Song of Moses, the entire story of the Covenant is retold. This canticle was probably inserted in the book long after its writing, because it is filled with allusions to later events.

Moses climbs a mountain to take a final look at Canaan, into which he is not allowed to cross, and he blesses the tribes of Israel. He dies and is buried; and Joshua, filled with wisdom because of his great love for God and his long apprenticeship under Moses—who laid his hands on Joshua—becomes Israel's leader.

Read Deuteronomy 34:1–12.

From a mountaintop Moses could see Canaan, but he was not allowed to enter it.
Above: An aerial view of Canaan and the hills near Jerusalem

A Final Note on the Pentateuch

We have completed our study of the Pentateuch, the five books that Jews consider the most essential of all the Hebrew Scriptures. At the heart of the Pentateuch is Sinai, where the people's relationship to God is spelled out in their obligations to God and to others. The biblical writers evoked the stories of the Torah time and again to remind Israel of its roots—and not just Israel but the Christian world as well.

Compose an essay, cartoon, poem, or song that retells one of the stories about ancient Israel's journey through the wilderness. Use a modern setting and modern characters.

For Review

1. What is the keystone to the Book of Exodus?

2. Leviticus is a handbook for whom?

3. Explain the original concept of a sacrifice of atonement. How did this concept become distorted over time?

4. Name three of the advanced moral teachings found in the holiness code in the Book of Leviticus.

5. Describe the two parts of the Book of Numbers.

6. Explain what the story of Miriam and Aaron tells us about sin and the community of God's people.

7. What does the story of Caleb and Joshua tell us about faith?

8. What does the story of the punishment of Moses and Aaron tell us about faith?

9. The story of Balaam and his donkey is a parable about material possessions. Explain.

10. In what style is the Book of Deuteronomy written?

11. Define *Shema*.

12. Explain the levirate law.

13. The Pentateuch is the religious masterpiece of the Hebrew Scriptures. What is at the heart of the Pentateuch?

5

Enemies and Friends:
Saving Israel from Itself

THE Books of Joshua, Judges, and Ruth are all stories about the period between Moses' death and the beginning of the monarchy, usually dated from about 1250 to 1030 B.C.E. The books come from early oral and written sources. In the case of Joshua and Judges, these sources include the Yahwist and the Elohist, whose materials the Deuteronomists rewrote and edited.

The Books of Joshua and Judges deal with the problems the Israelites face in taking the Promised Land from the people residing there. The question is how to treat the Canaanites—as friends or as enemies? The stories in Joshua and in Judges answer the question bluntly: Other people, as unbelievers, are enemies to be treated harshly. By the time the postexilic editors added the story of Ruth, however, Israel had discovered that foreigners could be neighbors and that Israel's worst enemy could be its own greed and weakness.

B.C.E.	
1300	• The Egyptians control Canaan and Syria.
1200	• The Israelites cross the Jordan River into eastern Canaan, and the Egyptians allow the Philistines to occupy southwestern Canaan.
1100	

Joshua:
Bringing the People
into the Promised Land

The Book of Joshua tells about one of Israel's great heroes. Joshua's military genius has been respected down through the centuries—so much so that a statue of Joshua stands in the hall of fame at the United States Military Academy at West Point. The book tells how Israel, after centuries away from the land promised to Abraham, returns to it, takes it, and settles there. Here is an account of Israel's faith at its most primitive. God, it is believed, calls for the sacking of

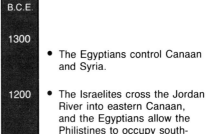

The crossing of the Jordan River marked the Israelites' entrance into Canaan.
Facing page: A section of the Jordan River valley

cities and the slaughter of their inhabitants, with never a hint of the love and mercy praised by the biblical prophets or revealed in Jesus.

Was God different in those days? Or did Israel, still new to the Covenant of Sinai, perceive God as a stern taskmaster and assume that its customs of war and vengeance had God's blessing? The Book of Joshua reminds us that the human race progresses slowly on its journey to know God.

Joshua's Commission

The book opens with God's sending Joshua to take the land of Canaan, urging him to be brave and steadfast, and reminding him to keep the Law and that God will be with him.
Read Joshua 1:1–9.

Walking away from God

Although Joshua's story is set around 1250 B.C.E., it was put together hundreds of years later, when the Babylonian exile was looming or had already happened. For the Jewish exiles, hope was all but gone and the future bleak. The story of Joshua reminded them of their need to turn to God again. As these verses remind the reader, Israel's exile was the result of ignoring the Law of Moses and rejecting the love of God.

Joshua's plan

Moses has brought the people east of the Jordan River, a position ideal for launching an invasion of Canaan. Now Joshua, a new and much younger leader, promises that in three days they will cross over into the Promised Land.
Read Joshua 1:10–18.

Rahab and the Spies

Joshua sends two spies to scout Jericho, the first city across the Jordan. Entering it without trouble, they go to a lodging house run by a prostitute named Rahab, who recognizes that they are Israelites. When the king's men come to question her about the visitors, she sends the spies to hide under the flax drying on her roof and misdirects the search party to the countryside. After dark, Rahab bargains with the spies. She will help them escape if they will promise safety for her family when Jericho is invaded. The men give her a red cord to hang in the window of her house, which is built into the city wall, and they promise not to harm anyone in

Reminders to keep God's Law can sound like "how to keep God happy." But morality, far from being something we must do to please God, is meant to protect us. Write a brief essay about some law that irks you; argue both the pros and the cons in separate paragraphs.

Joshua was a born leader—and Hitler was also. Write a paragraph about how to choose leaders who are worth following and how to avoid those who are not.

The Canaanites

Along with other Semitic peoples, the Canaanites held the Promised Land long before the Israelites arrived. Canaanite kings ruled rural towns in the area of Palestine and evidently quarreled endlessly among themselves. Although this disunity made matters simpler for the invading Israelites, once they were settled, they became involved in these disputes.

Israel hated the Canaanites' religion, with its worship of many gods and the Canaanite practice of male and female prostitution. But when from time to time the Israelites were unfaithful to their God, the Canaanites' storm god, Baal, seemed more attractive to them and became a rival to their LORD. Israel also adopted the Canaanites' language, their alphabet, and probably their festivals.

The Phoenicians, wealthy seafarers who dominated the Mediterranean, were descended from the Canaanites. The name *Canaanite* was also used for other groups in the region, including the Amorites, who inhabited the forested mountain areas.

A glazed tile, from the twelfth century B.C.E., depicts a richly robed Canaanite noble.

the house marked by the cord. The spies return to Joshua with news of the city's terror as it awaits invasion.
Read Joshua 2:1-24.

The spies and the prostitute

We might criticize Rahab for her betrayal of the city. Is she a traitor in choosing the survival of herself and her family? The biblical writers seem undivided in their opinion that she is doing the will of God. Rahab reappears in a surprising passage in the Christian writings.
Read Matthew 1:1-6a; James 2:24-25.

Crossing the Jordan River

Now comes another story of a miraculous crossing. Joshua orders the march; and as soon as the feet of the priests touch the riverbed of the Jordan, the waters cease to flow—piling up to the north and disappearing to the south. The people cross over, and one man from each of the twelve tribes carries a stone from the riverbed to build a memorial at the new camp, called Gilgal, the name meaning "circle" and referring to a circle of stones.
Read Joshua 3:1-17; 4:1-24.

Explanation of the crossing

The season in this story is spring, the time of heavy mountain runoff that forms powerful torrents and flash floods, annually overflowing the Jordan's banks. Did the Israelites actually walk into the river in full flood, with the waters standing back miraculously? Or was the crossing timed to escape the first onslaught of the floods and made while the river was still shallow and fordable?

Another possibility is that an earthquake took place, collapsing the banks of the Jordan north of the crossing and holding the flow of water for about a day. Still another proposal is that Joshua stationed scouts on hillocks at the numerous bends of the river to signal the approach of a flood.

All of these explanations make good sense, but none are satisfying because they imply that a miracle did not happen. To the Israelites, arriving in Canaan was nothing less than a miracle. This ancient story has passed through generations of storytellers. No one knows what really happened except that—and this is the point—God got the people of Israel across the Jordan and into Canaan. Like the crossing of the Sea of Reeds, the crossing of the Jordan River was a key moment in the history of ancient Israel.

Write a brief comment on the presence of a prostitute in Jesus' ancestry. Who was she?

Read Psalm 114. This psalm was written about three hundred years after the events described in Joshua. Write your reaction to the language used by the writer.

Evidence of some editing

Several older accounts of this crossing were combined by the Deuteronomists, and the story contains several contradictions. For example, in 3:17 the priests stand in the riverbed "on dry ground," but in 4:18 they must climb out of the bed to regain dry ground.

Israel in the Promised Land

Once in Canaan, the people eat for the first time the produce of the Promised Land, and the manna disappears. It is their first celebration of the Passover in the land of the Promise. In a mysterious encounter, Joshua meets the captain of the army of the LORD, and like Moses in Exodus 3:5, Joshua is told to remove his sandals because he stands on holy ground —possibly an ancient place of worship.

Read Joshua 5:1–15.

The disappearance of the manna

After the Israelites arrive in the Promised Land, the marvelous food provided for them in the wilderness disappears. In the past, commentaries have pointed to the manna as a *type*, or a foreshadowing, of the eucharistic food provided for the believers in this life. When their earthly journey is complete and they reach heaven, the presence of Christ makes the sacrament no longer necessary.

The captain of the army of the LORD

Verses 13 through 15 suggest that the coming war at Jericho will have the blessing of God and the help of angelic hosts.

The Siege of Jericho

Joshua's soldiers lay siege to Jericho, surround the city, and cut off its supplies. Then early each morning for six days, seven priests carrying rams' horns lead the Israelites out of camp. Behind these priests come other priests carrying the ark of the Covenant. Troops march before and behind the priests. The entire company, silent except for the blaring of the rams' horns, marches once around the city. At dawn on the seventh day, the Israelites circle the city seven times, and at a signal they begin to shout and storm the walls. Jericho falls, and only Rahab and those in her house are saved from the slaughter of all the people and animals in the city.

Read Joshua 6:1–19.

The ancient Israelites blew the *shofar,* a trumpet made of a ram's horn, in battle.
Above: In the modern Yom Kippur celebration, the shofar is sounded at the end of the synagogue services.

Jericho

Jericho may be the oldest walled city in the world, dating back to about 7000 B.C.E., which makes the pyramids comparatively modern buildings. With a nearby ford across the Jordan River, Jericho became a major trade center, and by the time of Joshua's arrival, the city covered about five acres and contained several thousand inhabitants.

A tower that has been excavated at the site of the ancient city of Jericho

The ban

The practice called **the ban** required the total destruction of an enemy city, including its inhabitants, their possessions, and their animals. Like some other laws of ancient Israel, the ban was a barbarous custom that was abandoned with the growth of a more enlightened morality. The practice disappeared before the reign of King David, in about 1000 B.C.E.

The walls of Jericho

Jericho's untended gates and its citizens' fear of invasion hint at walls already vulnerable, perhaps in disrepair. At the modern site of Jericho, nothing remains of this period—indicating that these walls were made of unbaked clay brick, which was easily demolished.

No one knows if the walls of Jericho fell down or if the expression is a figure of speech; history books often say that a captured city "falls." On the other hand, the Israelites might have *sapped* the walls. That is, soldiers might have tunneled under the walls in order to weaken their foundation and collapse them. Whatever happened, the biblical writers believed that God had helped Israel take Jericho.

Defeat at Ai

After Jericho's destruction, Joshua's men scout the town of Ai and predict an easy conquest. Yet Israel is defeated. Demoralized, Joshua prays to God, who tells him that someone has broken the ban by taking loot from Jericho. Assembling the tribes, Joshua discovers that a man named Achan is the culprit. Achan is executed by stoning, and his loot is burned and buried.

Read Joshua 7:1–26.

A tale of conceit and greed

Archaeologists who have dug at the site of Ai cannot reconstruct any of the above events. To understand why this story came to be part of the sacred Scriptures, we need to remember what biblical inspiration is all about: What God inspired in the writers of the Scriptures was their telling the story of ancient Israel's journey in faith. If the incident at Ai was part of the story as the Deuteronomists knew it, then the event teaches inspired lessons:

- God, not humankind, brings human work to fruition. The first attack on Ai was reckless, without consultation of the LORD.

- Greed and self-serving will always be the enemy of our attempts to serve God.

By the time the Deuteronomists wrote down the story of Ai, it had been accepted for centuries and its lessons taken seriously. If today's biblical scholars find that this is a folktale, the loss is negligible because the lessons remain inspired.

The Gibeonites' Deception

Afraid of the Israelites, the local kings form a confederacy for self-defense. The Gibeonites, who live in a cluster of four towns about twenty miles away, have a different idea. They disguise some of their citizens in torn clothes and ragged sandals. Carrying dried bread crusts and mended wineskins, the men arrive at Joshua's camp claiming that they have traveled from a distant land. They ask for a protective alliance—which they know the Israelites would not grant to a local tribe.

The author of Joshua wrote that the walls of Jericho "collapsed," but that may have been a figure of speech. List ten figures of speech used today that readers a thousand years from now might find nonsensical if interpreted literally. An example: "It rained cats and dogs."

Joshua smells the deception. Cleverly he lets the Israelite elders—called "princes" in some versions of the Bible—make the decision. An alliance with Gibeon is sworn on their recommendation. Three days later, the people discover the Gibeonites' identity and grumble against their elders. Yet the elders dare not break the contract, sworn in God's name. In retaliation, however, they humiliate the Gibeonites by making them drawers of water and hewers of wood—which is traditionally slaves' work.

The Sun Standing Still

When the five local kings learn that the Gibeonites are allied with Israel, they put Gibeon under siege. Its citizens cry to Joshua for help. Joshua's army marches under cover of darkness, takes the besiegers by surprise, and routs them. Joshua asks God to stop the sun in the sky the next day, and the storyteller marvels at God's obeying a human. The attacking kings—lumped together as "the Amorites" in some versions of the Bible—are found by Joshua and executed.
Read Joshua 10:12–13.

A miracle or a rooster tale?

Joshua's request that the sun stop in the sky is a fragment of an ancient song of victory from the lost Book of Jashar—apparently a book of poems celebrating Israel's heroes.

Did the sun really stand still? Undoubtedly the sun did not set until Joshua had overcome the local kings—which is to say that God helped him to victory before sundown. To explain this miracle, the author used poetic license, much as we do ourselves. For example, we might wish, Please don't let it rain until the game has ended . . . the wedding is over . . . the parade is finished. If rain does not ruin the event, we might report gleefully, "I told it not to rain, and it didn't." We feel that in some sense nature responded to our request. In fact, we are acting a bit like the little rooster who thought that his crowing made the sun rise every morning.

Next to the story about the fall of Jericho, this is probably the best-known and most-disputed tale in the Bible—and one of the least important. The story has been told for centuries, and as is so often the case, the seemingly miraculous detail has overshadowed the point of the story—that God helped Joshua to victory and his people to recovering their land.

At the trial of the astronomer Galileo, who was accused of teaching error—that the earth revolves around the sun—the story of Joshua's stopping the sun in the sky was used as evidence against him. Could a similar misfortune happen today? Explain your answer in writing.

Conquests, Tribal Divisions, and Cities of Refuge

The remainder of the Book of Joshua gives a simplified account of the conquest of Canaan, claiming that Joshua captures all the land and subdues all Israel's enemies. The division of the land among the tribes of Israel is reported—along with the setting aside of the cities of refuge, or asylum.

Read Joshua 20:1–6; Deuteronomy 19:1–13.

The twelve tribes of Israel

The twelve tribes of Israel are, strangely, listed as thirteen in Genesis 46:8–27 and Numbers 1:20–42 and referred to as eleven in 1 Kings 11:31–32. The varying figures are accounted for either by substituting for Joseph the tribes of his sons Ephraim and Manasseh or by leaving out the Levites, who were set aside to serve as priests. This brings the number to twelve, which became a symbolic number for Israel—and later for Christians. In Acts 1:15–26, for example, we read that the Apostles choose Matthias to replace Judas in order to complete "the Twelve," whom Jesus said would sit on twelve thrones to judge the twelve tribes of Israel.

Joshua's military successes

The writer's claim of a quick conquest of Canaan cannot be true because in the next book, Judges, we will see Israel living side by side with Canaanite tribes—sometimes dominating them, sometimes as their *vassals,* or subjects, even intermarrying with them.

The cities of refuge

Places of refuge probably came later than the time of Joshua, perhaps during the time of King David. The idea behind them was to protect people guilty of accidental or unintentional killing from blood vengeance of the victims' families. Down through the centuries, Egyptians, Jews, Greeks, Romans, and Christians all have followed similar practices of *sanctuary*—so called because the refuge was often at a religious shrine. Sanctuary remains a universal custom, offering aid to the persecuted and the homeless.

The Death of Joshua

In a solemn farewell, Joshua begs his people never to forget the one God who has done so much for them, and he warns

The practice of offering sanctuary to those in need is an ancient and universal custom.
Above: Refugees near the border between Democratic Kampuchea (Cambodia) and Thailand.

Sanctuary was originally given to accidental murderers to protect them from the vengeance of the victim's survivors. Ironically, today sanctuary is often denied to innocent people from war-torn countries who are trying to escape being murdered. Write a brief opinion in answer to this question:
- Do we have a moral obligation to offer sanctuary?

them of the consequences if they do forget. The Israelites renew the Covenant at a place called Shechem, and Joshua's work is done. He dies and is buried in his tribal land.
Read Joshua 24:1–33.

The renewal of the Covenant

Some scholars believe that the assembly before Joshua's death was an important event in Israel's history. At Shechem, various groups that had not been part of the Exodus were formally initiated into the covenantal community. Shechem thus became the earliest religious center for the Israelite tribes.

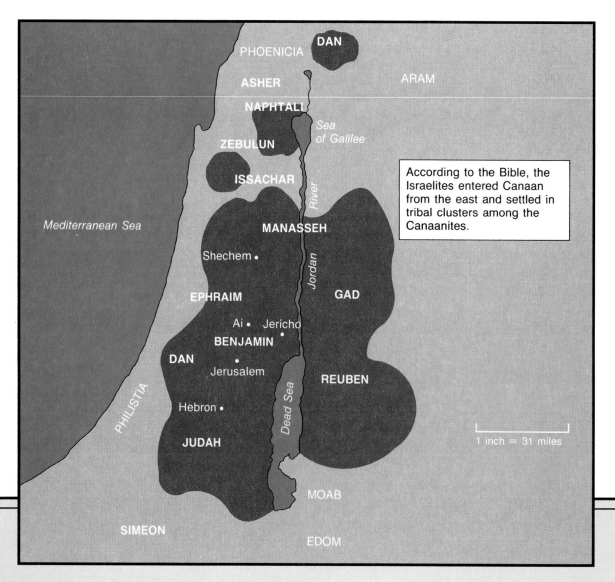

According to the Bible, the Israelites entered Canaan from the east and settled in tribal clusters among the Canaanites.

The Israelites Enter Canaan

The personality of Joshua

Joshua was one of Israel's greatest leaders—strong, courageous, careful, honest, unshaken by failure, a keeper of treaties, and an upholder of the Law. An inspiration to his people, Joshua's heart was on fire with love for God, and by obeying God, he brought Israel into the Promised Land.

Judges: Saving Israel from Itself

The Book of Judges, which has nothing to do with legal matters, might be better called the Book of Deliverers because its stories tell how God raises up deliverers to save Israel when, after settling in Canaan, it is unfaithful and overwhelmed by enemies.

These stories also make the point that such infidelities could have been avoided. With Joshua gone, the tribes fall into self-indulgence and idol worship, which eventually lead to their downfall. The Deuteronomists seem to be saying that a king would have prevented these disasters.

Twelve judges are mentioned in the book itself: six minor judges, barely mentioned, and six major judges—Othniel, Ehud, Deborah, Gideon, Jephthah, and Samson—to whom Eli and Samuel from the First Book of Samuel are added. The Book of Judges spans the years between the death of Joshua and the beginning of the First Book of Samuel (about 1200 to 1025 B.C.E.) but was put together long afterward.

The stories of the judges are derived from very early songs and poems—much like the tales of King Arthur and Queen Guinevere. These heroes, however, are not nobles but peasants. Nor is their behavior particularly noble. Rather, they are people called by God to deliver Israel—regardless of their personal weaknesses.

Once again Israel is a mirror for us. Our calamities, like those of the Israelites, can be the result of forgetting our call to serve God and do what is right. When Israel forgets its call to reveal the one God to the nations, it falls into selfishness, timidity, blindness, and ends up dominated by idol-worshiping neighbors.

Israel's Infidelities

Judges opens with a description of Israel in Canaan that is very different from the picture given in the Book of Joshua.

There we read that all Canaan was captured and its people overpowered. Here Israel has not only settled down among the Canaanites but even intermarried and worshiped with them.
    Read Joshua 21:43-45; Judges 1:21-36; 3:1-6.

Othniel and Ehud

The first judge, Othniel, rescues Israel from a neighboring tribe, and aside from this, nothing is known of him.

The story of Ehud, next, is a grisly slapstick. The tribe of Benjamin has been oppressed for eighteen years by Eglon, the king of Moab. Then God raises up Ehud, whose task is to conduct the annual tribute to Eglon. Ehud, who is left-handed, makes a two-edged dagger and conceals it under his clothing on his right thigh—not on his left, as was the custom. The knife apparently goes undetected when the guards frisk him as they would right-handed people. Ehud delivers the tribute to Eglon, gaining the king's confidence, and then leaves.

Later Ehud returns to Eglon as though with a message from God for the king. Curious, Eglon dismisses his servants and ushers Ehud into his private apartment on the roof of the house. Ehud stabs his knife into the king's stomach, which is so fat that the knife disappears. Then he slips the bolt on the door and escapes through the window.

Ehud and his followers lie in wait to slay the terrified Moabites as they try to flee across the Jordan, and the tribe of Benjamin lives in peace for eighty years.
    Read Judges 3:12-30.

A bit of gloating

The purpose of the story of Ehud is not to document God's approval of stabbing people in the stomach but to recount the many ways that God helped Israel free itself from its enemies. The Jewish exiles who later listened to this story certainly needed a victory to gloat over—needed to believe that someday, somehow, they too would be freed.

Deborah the Prophet and Barak the Soldier

Deborah, referred to as both a judge and a prophet, is a magistrate of the tribe of Naphtali, deciding local disputes for her people. The tribe has fallen under the domination of the Canaanite king Jabin, whose army, with its nine hundred iron chariots, has kept the people subject for twenty years. Deborah reveals to Barak, the commander of the Israelite militia, that God wants him to lead an army against Jabin's general Sisera. Barak fearfully agrees to go if Deborah will accompany him, and she consents but says that he will lose the credit for the victory.

When Sisera assembles his army in the valley, torrential rains render his chariots useless, and he and his troops are routed. Sisera deserts his troops and flees to the tent of a friend, whose wife Jael welcomes him, serves him refreshment, and bids him to rest while she stands guard. Outraged at Sisera's desertion, Jael hammers a tent peg through his skull when he sleeps, and ever after she is glorified in the savagely triumphant Canticle of Deborah. Defeat at the hands of a woman, even in this case—a woman who breaks her word and betrays the sacred law of hospitality—is the ultimate disgrace for a warrior. A final sarcastic touch to the story is the glimpse of Sisera's mother and wives waiting in the harem to divide the spoils that he will never bring.

Read Judges 4:1-24; 5:1-31.

More glee

Imagine the hilarity with which the Jews of the exile greeted this story, which, for all its violence, nurtured hope in their hearts. Deborah's canticle is one of the oldest writings in the Bible, dating back almost to the time of the events it describes.

Gideon the Lowly

Gideon's tribe, Manasseh, together with all Israel, is oppressed by Midianite desert dwellers, who raid the tribe's land and ruin its crops. We first glimpse Gideon secretly threshing wheat in his family's winepress when an angel calls him to save his people. Gideon protests that as the youngest of the lowliest family in Manasseh, he is hardly a candidate for such a heroic task. Yet God assures Gideon of victory and consumes Gideon's sacrificial offering with fire as a sign of favor.

Read Judges 6:1-24.

The ugly duckling

In fairy tales, a repeated theme has the youngest child first scorned as good for nothing and then vindicated as a savior. Help comes disguised as a fairy godmother or a friendly genie, timidity gives way to confidence, and marvelous things happen. The stories of the judges have this same quality.

In the Book of Judges, the judge Deborah orders an attack on the Canaanite troops, and another woman, Jael, slays their general.

How do the stories in Joshua and Judges compare with today's films containing violence? Do they serve the same purpose? Write a one-paragraph opinion.

Gideon and the Altar of Baal

In a dream, Gideon is told to destroy the altar of the Canaanite god Baal, built by unfaithful Israelites. When he does, the outraged townspeople order Gideon's father, Joash, to slay him. Joash cunningly suggests that if Baal is a god, he should kill Gideon himself. No doubt to mock the god, Gideon is given the nickname Jerubbaal, meaning "Let Baal take action."

Gideon asks for another sign that God has chosen him to save Israel: placing a sheepskin outdoors on the threshing floor, he asks God that dew fall on it and not on the ground—which it does. When Gideon reverses the request, the wool remains dry.

Read Judges 6:25-40.

Fearful heroes?

The worship of Baal has to be wiped out among Gideon's people before he can expect a victory over the Midianites. But even after that has been accomplished, Gideon still is not confident. The sign with the sheepskin assures him. Insecurity and fear were frequent companions of the judges, and later the prophets, when answering God's call.

Gideon's Victory

After gathering a large army, Gideon is rebuked by God; victory will be credited to the size of his forces, not to divine help. He must send some men home. Keeping only those who drink water cupped in their hands—with their eyes alert as they drink—Gideon ends up with three hundred men. He divides these into companies, and each man is given a horn and an empty water jar in which is hidden a lighted torch. On a moonless night, they surround the Midianite camp, break their water jars, reveal the torches, and blow their horns. The Midianites believe the attack force to be much larger than it is because only Midianite officers (each officer commanding ten men) carry torches. In the dark, the Midianites begin fighting each other, and the survivors flee in terror. Gideon's men seize the Jordan ford and slay all of the enemy who attempt to cross.

The grateful Israelites beg Gideon to be their king, but he insists that God alone is their king. However, he will erect a cultic object to celebrate the victory. Collecting the Israelites' golden ornaments, he creates an *ephod*—a receptacle for use in seeking oracles. Unfortunately, the people begin

List three episodes from the Pentateuch in which the people fear and doubt that God can save them. Write a brief essay on fear and faith in your own life.

to worship the object as an idol, and in the end it spells the ruin of Gideon's family. Following Gideon's death, his son Abimelech murders all but one of his own brothers.

Read Judges 7:1-8,16-22; 8:22-35; 9:1-6.

The best-laid plans

God inspired Gideon to execute the brilliant bit of psychological warfare that brought him victory, but Gideon's own scheme to erect the ephod—without consulting God—was his undoing.

Although Gideon's son Abimelech was proclaimed king, the biblical writers did not recognize him as such. His savage behavior excludes him from most lists of the judges as well.

Jephthah's Victory and Vow

The son of a prostitute, Jephthah has been expelled from his Gileadite family and is a chieftain of a band of mercenaries. When war with Ammon threatens the Gileadites, they swallow their pride and ask Jephthah to bring his troops to defend them. Should he be victorious, they will make him their leader. Jephthah agrees, assembles the Israelites for battle, and foolishly vows that if he wins he will sacrifice by fire whoever comes first to meet him on his return.

On his triumphant return, Jephthah is greeted by his only child, a beloved daughter, who runs out of the house to embrace him. Both believe that Jephthah cannot default from his vow, but the daughter asks for two months in which to grieve over her lost future, including marriage and maternity. When she returns from the mountains, her father sacrifices her. Every year thereafter, young women of her tribe mourn her death for four days.

Read Judges 11:1-15,27-40.

A horrifying vow

Jephthah's vow indicates an exceedingly primitive notion of God, and his horrifying promise turns victory into tragedy. The story once again reminds the reader that human sacrifice is forbidden.

Samson

The stories about Samson are variously accounted as folktales by some scholars and as history by others. They were told around campfires in the days when the Philistines dominated the tribes of Dan. Later, when Israel had lost even

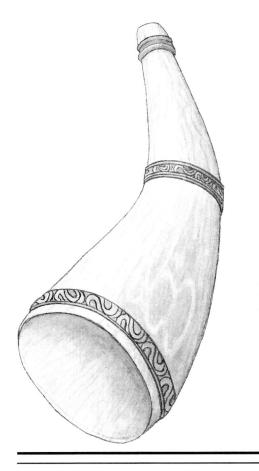

Gideon ordered his troops to blow horns and carry torches, tricking the Midianites into thinking that his force was much bigger than three hundred men.

more territory to Philistia, the people found comfort in these tales of a village hero who, in both life and death, proved to be too much for the hated enemies of his people. Present-day scholars who hold the stories to be history feel that the amount of detail in them indicates that they were based on a historical person.

When the story of Samson opens, the Philistines have dominated Israel for forty years. Samson's birth is foretold by an angel, who says that Samson is to be a **Nazirite**—a person consecrated to God from birth, never to touch strong drink or cut his hair or his beard.

Read Judges 13:1-25.

Some good advice

Notice that the angel advises Samson's mother not to consume wine or strong drink during her pregnancy—a recommendation that we think of as quite modern.

Samson's Exploits Against the Philistines

Samson falls in love with a Philistine woman, and there follow the famous tales of his great strength. He kills a lion barehanded, slaughters thirty Philistines, discovers that his wife has been given to another, and in a rage sets three hundred foxes afire in the Philistines' fields. Captured, Samson breaks his bonds and kills a thousand Philistines with the jawbone of an ass.

Eventually Samson becomes infatuated with Delilah, who is probably an Israelite woman bribed by the Philistines to find out the secret of his strength. Ever unable to resist the enticements of women, Samson finally tells her of his consecration to God and that the secret of his strength is the length of his hair. He falls asleep, she cuts his hair, and he is captured.

Samson's eyes are gouged out, and he is put to grinding grain like a beast at the mill wheel. But his hair grows again, and his strength returns. When the Philistines make sport of him in the temple of their chief god, Dagon, Samson stands between two pillars and pushes them over. The temple collapses, killing Samson and all the Philistines.

Read Judges 14:1-20; 15:1-20; 16:1-31.

Strong back, weak character

Samson has little to recommend him. He is a violent man with an uncontrolled passion for women—like a host of un-

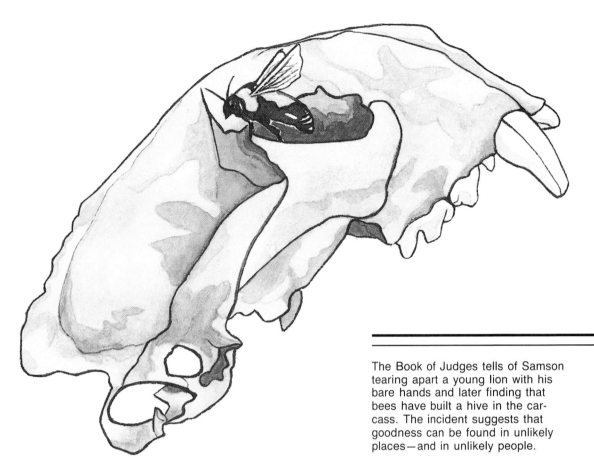

The Book of Judges tells of Samson tearing apart a young lion with his bare hands and later finding that bees have built a hive in the carcass. The incident suggests that goodness can be found in unlikely places—and in unlikely people.

disciplined, self-destructive characters in both fiction and history. His story is the tragedy of a morally weak man who might have been great if he had used his gifts for good.

The details of Samson's birth—including the angel and the Nazirite calling—are probably late additions to justify how such an unsavory character could be a judge.

Given Samson's character, why did the Deuteronomists list him among the judges? Perhaps their purpose was to marvel at the kind of people God can make use of.

Even if Samson the judge were not a historical person, his rages and lusts often appear in real life. When finally he is the cause of his own downfall, the story becomes a classic yet familiar human tragedy. No wonder Samson has inspired so many operas, writings, movies, and paintings.

The Remaining Stories

The remaining two stories in Judges are horror tales unrelated to the judges, each revealing extremely primitive and repugnant attitudes toward women.

An Egyptian stone carving, from the twelfth century B.C.E., depicts Philistine warriors wearing crested helmets. The carving celebrates an Egyptian victory over these seafaring people, but actually the Philistines may have forced the Egyptians to give them land in Canaan.

The Philistines

The Philistines were one of the *sea peoples* who invaded the eastern coastlands of the Mediterranean, beginning around the twelfth century B.C.E. The Philistines' expansion into the interior of Canaan coincided with the Israelites' invasion from the east. Thus, in the days of the judges—and later of Samuel, Saul, and David—the Philistines were a constant rival to the Israelites.

The Philistines were not Semitic people by origin. Like the other sea peoples, they probably came from the Greek Islands. But the gods of the Philistines had Semitic names, suggesting that these people quickly took up the religion of the Canaanites.

Metalworking was a special skill among the Philistines. Their use of iron weaponry was a severe threat to the Israelites, who had only softer, more expensive bronze weapons.

Ruth:
A Different Israelite

The Book of Ruth had its beginning in Israel's oral tradition and was probably told by storytellers who appeared in villages and towns at the popular festivals. Their audiences sat around the town spring or gathered in the plaza by the city gates. This story might have come out of a small town. After all, most of Israel's prophets came from small towns.

First heard in the period of the early kings (about 800 B.C.E.), the Book of Ruth was finished in the postexilic period. Its purpose was twofold:
* to teach how God could create a blessed ending out of a difficult situation
* to tell how it came about that Israel's noble King David had a Gentile as his great-grandmother

In Ruth's concern for the survival of her mother-in-law, her strength of character far exceeds that of some of the judges.

A Family Faces Calamity

The Book of Ruth almost starts with "Once upon a time," the time being the days of the judges. When famine strikes Israel, a man from Bethlehem named Elimelech journeys with his wife, Naomi, and their two sons to start life again on the plain of Moab. Soon after their arrival, Elimelech dies and leaves Naomi to raise their sons alone. When the sons are grown, each of them marries a Moabite woman—one named Orpah and the other Ruth. After ten years, the young men die, and Naomi, grief-stricken, plans to return to her homeland because she has heard that the famine is over.

Naomi starts out, and the two young widows accompany her for a distance. Then she stops, bids them good-bye, and asking God's blessing on each one, urges them to return home to find new husbands. But Ruth and Orpah want to stay with her. Naomi, trying to lighten the moment, says that she is too old to marry and have more sons, and that even if she could, the daughters-in-law would have to wait for them to grow up. Furthermore, she adds, they must not throw their lot with hers because God has a bitter fate in store for her. All three women weep, and after affectionate farewells, Orpah returns to Moab but Ruth remains with Naomi.

Read Ruth 1:1–18.

Three widows

Naomi is probably between forty and forty-five years of age. The life expectancy of women at the time was not much longer—thus Naomi's protest that she is too old to marry again. Naomi's love for the young women is evident in her insistence that they return to Moab, marry, and bear children. She resigns herself to seeing the end of her husband's family line—although she might have urged Ruth and Orpah to marry members of his clan. The levirate law, as noted in the last chapter, guaranteed that childless widows had a right to have male children by their husband's next of kin, in order to carry on his name and to inherit his property.

Ruth's famous speech

The Book of Ruth is most famous for its portrait of the beautiful relationship between Ruth and Naomi. Ruth's magnificent speech (1:16–17) binds her not only to Naomi but to God. In her selfless commitment to Naomi, her God, and her people, Ruth makes a covenant with the God of Israel.

Naomi and Ruth Reach Bethlehem

Naomi and Ruth reach Bethlehem during the barley harvest in early April, and their arrival causes a stir throughout the town. When Naomi is greeted by old friends, she expresses her bitterness toward God, calling herself not Naomi but Mara (meaning "bitterness") and saying that she left Bethlehem with abundance but God has brought her back destitute.

Read Ruth 1:19-22.

The name *Mara*

Naomi's exchange of her given name for the name *Mara*—meaning "bitterness"—recalls the story in Exodus where Moses makes the bitter waters of Mara sweet.

Ruth Meets Boaz

During the barley harvest, Ruth informs Naomi that she wants to glean the barley fields; apparently the two women need food. Naomi agrees, and Ruth goes by chance to the field of a farmer named Boaz, who is a kinsman of Naomi's late husband and a man of wealth and influence.

When Boaz arrives from Bethlehem, he notices Ruth. Asking his workers, he discovers that she is the Moabite girl

Harvesting in Ancient Israel

The story of Ruth uses harvesting terms that might be unfamiliar to you.

Gleaning means gathering the grain left by those who *reap*, or cut down the stalks of, the field.

Once cut, the grain must be loosened from the stalks. These are spread on the *threshing floor* outside and are beaten, walked on, or loosened with a studded board pulled by an animal. Next, the *husk*, or thin outer covering of the grain, is broken by a heavy wooden sledge pulled over the grain by an ox or an ass. The threshed grain is then *winnowed*—tossed into the air with winnowing shovels on a windy day. The breeze carries away the paper-thin husks, or *chaff*, while the heavy grain drops to the ground, ready to be stored in the barn.

Left: In Israel, a woman harvests wheat with a reaping knife.
Above: Also in Israel, a man winnows grain.

Boaz, a character of faith and generosity, ordered his harvesters to allow Ruth a peaceful and plentiful gleaning.

who returned with Naomi. Boaz realizes that through marriage to Naomi's son, Ruth is now one of his kin. He invites Ruth to glean in his field, instructs the young men not to bother her, and bids her to follow close to the women as they harvest. Ruth, astonished, throws herself on the ground and asks why a foreigner should be treated so generously. Boaz reveals that he knows of her and praises her loyalty to Naomi. When he asks the blessing of the God of Israel upon her, he reveals his knowledge of her conversion.

At lunchtime, Boaz offers Ruth bread, invites her to dip it in his bowl of wine, and gives her a portion of roasted barley to eat. When she goes to glean again, he orders his harvesters to drop grain on the ground for her to pick up.

At the end of the day, when Ruth beats the barley to remove the grain from the stalks, she finds that she has nearly one *ephah,* or a little more than a bushel. Ruth takes the barley home, and Naomi asks where she has gleaned. Hearing that it was in Boaz's field, Naomi excitedly reveals that he is a kinsman. She welcomes Ruth's good fortune as a sign that God has not abandoned them after all. A marriage between Ruth and Boaz would not only provide Ruth with a splendid husband but could also produce a longed-for son. Ruth gleans daily in Boaz's fields until the end of the barley harvest and, later in the spring, during the wheat harvest.

Read Ruth 2:1-23.

The Law, not theft

Ruth and Naomi are examples of "the poor and the alien," of whom the Law, and later the prophetic and wisdom books, speak. Gleaning is not theft, nor is it begging. Ruth has a right to glean because the Law requires that gleanings be left for the poor.

Read Leviticus 23:22.

Respect, not lust

That Boaz and Naomi are the same age by no means makes him an old man, but he is older than Ruth. Family loyalty seems to be his initial concern, not romance. When he instructs his women harvesters to let Ruth glean behind them, Boaz is warning them not to make her wait at the end of the row until they finish—a common behavior toward gleaners. He has told the young men to treat Ruth respectfully, neither being rough with her nor approaching her with immodest remarks.

Naomi Makes a Match

While Ruth has been gleaning in the fields of Boaz, Naomi, like Rebekah before her, has been hatching a plan. At winnowing time, she reveals it.

Naomi bids Ruth to bathe, perfume, and dress herself in her best attire. Then she is to go to the threshing floor, where Boaz and his men are working late into the evening, and stay out of sight. When the men have eaten and drunk and lain down to sleep, Ruth is to go where Boaz lies, uncover a place beside his feet, and lie there. " 'He will tell you what to do,' " wise Naomi says (3:4).

Ruth does as Naomi bids, and when Boaz awakens and finds her, she asks him to cover her with his cloak. Boaz understands that Ruth is invoking the levirate claim and blesses her. He will do all he can to arrange the marriage, although first a kinsman with closer ties to Ruth must be consulted. If this man does not want her, Boaz does! He tells her to sleep but to rise before the men awaken so that there is no suspicion of scandal. In the morning, when Ruth returns and tells Naomi what happened, Naomi assures her that Boaz will not rest until he has settled the matter.

Read Ruth 3:1–18.

Ruth's request

Ruth's request that Boaz cover her with his cloak is not a sexual advance but, rather, a proposal of marriage. Covering a woman with a garment was a traditional way of claiming her in marriage.

Boaz's honor

Up to now, Boaz has viewed Ruth as exemplary but not as a potential wife. Naomi's plan is for Boaz to see Ruth as a wife. Naomi must be sure of his character; someone less honorable might take advantage of Ruth. But Boaz takes precautions to protect Ruth's reputation and, aware of the meaning of her actions, plans to marry Ruth in a way that is proper and legal.

Boaz Marries Ruth

The following morning Boaz takes a seat at the city gate. When he sees the man who is next of kin, Boaz says that Naomi is selling Elimelech's land and asks the man if he wants it. He adds that whoever buys the land must take Ruth to wife in order to raise a new heir to the property. The man has no interest in either the land or a wife and relinquishes his rights to Boaz, encouraging him to claim the property.

The contract is agreed to according to an ancient Israelite custom: the man releasing the claim to the land gives his sandal to the one who claims it. Boaz accepts the sandal, asking the gathered elders to witness the contract. They do so and offer Boaz their congratulations.

And so Ruth and Boaz marry. In time Ruth bears a son, whom they name Obed, who becomes the father of Jesse, who in turn becomes the father of David.

Read Ruth 4:1–22; Deuteronomy 23:4–7.

David's Moabite forebear

The significance of David's Moabite great-grandmother derives from the above passage from Deuteronomy. The author evidently wrote to answer the question about whether it was right or good that a Gentile be welcomed by marriage into the community of Israel. The question was long debated among the Jews, but this story of the famous and much-loved Moabite Ruth reveals the LORD's choice of a Gentile as forebear to their great king David—and a far nobler person she was than some of the others!

What characters in films or on television remind you of Naomi, Ruth, and Boaz? Write a brief answer, including character sketches of how the three biblical figures are reflected in the three film or TV figures.

By the time of Ruth, the Israelites had become farmers like their Canaanite neighbors. They cultivated grains, vegetables, and fruits such as the pomegranate, *right.*

A Final Note

The Books of Joshua and Judges begin with barbarity, killing, and land grabbing—by a people who see God as merciless
to outsiders. But in hearing the story of Ruth, postexilic
Israel realized that its God was compassionate and caring.
Slowly the people were learning that tolerance, justice, and
peace were God's way. The story of Ruth says that the God
of Israel is the God of all the nations, the God to whom "there
is neither Jew nor Greek . . . for you are all one in Christ
Jesus" (Galatians 3:28).

For Review

1. Describe the primitive image of God found in the Book of Joshua.

2. Who is Rahab, and what help does she give the Israelites?

3. Describe the practice called *the ban*.

4. What two lessons does the story of Ai teach?

5. The story of the sun standing still is an example of what?

6. What was the original reason for the practice called *sanctuary?*

7. What happens to the Israelite tribes after the death of Joshua?

8. How are the judges different from he-roes of other stories—for instance, King Arthur and Queen Guinevere?

9. In the story of Deborah, why does Jael kill the general Sisera? How is her deed dishonorable?

10. Why does God tell Gideon to reduce the size of his forces?

11. What is Jephthah's vow? What custom is confirmed as forbidden in this story?

12. Explain the cause of Samson's down-fall.

13. What were the two purposes of the Book of Ruth?

14. Does Ruth have a right to glean Boaz's fields? Why?

15. Compare the Book of Judges with the Book of Ruth. How are they different? What does this reveal?

6

The Nation:
Anointing David,
Capturing Jerusalem,
Building the Temple

THE two Books of Samuel tell how Israel became a nation in about 1000 B.C.E. They include the stories of great biblical characters—including Eli, Samuel, Saul, Jonathan, and David. Originally called the Books of Reigns or the Court History of David, their authors are unknown—although some scholars see in them traces of the Yahwist and the Elohist. The Deuteronomists put together the final versions of Samuel around the time of the Babylonian exile.

Earlier, in Genesis, we saw the shift from the nonhistorical material in the stories about the Creation to the beginnings of history in the stories about Abraham and Sarah. In Exodus, Joshua, and Judges, the material had a stronger historical basis. In Samuel, the historical references are even clearer. These books are possibly the oldest written history there is—predating by five hundred years even the Greek historian Herodotus, who is known as "the father of Western history."

The purposes of the Books of Samuel were these:
- to show that God was present with the Israelites during their exile in Babylon
- to help the exiles reflect on God's saving works in the past
- to give the exiles hope that things would be right again in the future

The story of David introduced God's promise of the continuation of David's line as leaders of Israel. This eventually gave form to the expectation of a future leader whom the Jews called the Messiah, who would save Israel and initiate a reign of peace and justice. Christians believe that this promise is fulfilled in Christ.

B.C.E.

1050

1000

900

- Samuel anoints Saul.
- David takes Jerusalem and unites Israel.
- Solomon builds the Temple in Jerusalem.

Before becoming king, David spent years hiding in the region of Judaea. *Facing page:* A hillside settlement in the Judaean desert—the type of place that David would have sought out for refuge.

The Rise and Fall of Saul

Samuel's Birth

The First Book of Samuel opens with Samuel's mother, Hannah, as yet childless, grieving at the shrine at Shiloh. She is observed by the judge-priest Eli, who rebukes her for drunkenness. When Hannah explains her grief, Eli blesses her, and within a year she bears a son, Samuel. When the child is weaned, Hannah offers him to God as a Nazirite and leaves him in the care of Eli. She sings an exultant song praising God for helping those in need.

Read 1 Samuel 1:1-28; 2:1-11.

> **Read 1 Samuel 2:1b-10 and
> Luke 1:46-55.** Mary's Magnificat
> is said to have been modeled
> after Hannah's hymn. List the
> similarities. Then write a brief
> essay on the meaning of these
> songs for our times.

Samuel's Call

Samuel grows up serving God faithfully. Eli's two sons, however, are a different story. As priests, they behave sacrilegiously—in spite of Eli's warnings. God announces through a holy man that the family line will end.

One night, while sleeping in the sanctuary where the ark of the Covenant is kept, Samuel hears his name called. He goes to Eli, who merely sends him back to bed. A second and third time this happens. Finally Eli realizes that God is calling Samuel and tells him to respond, " 'Speak, for your servant is listening' " (3:10). God tells Samuel of the coming fall of Eli's family. Samuel reluctantly tells Eli God's message, and Eli accepts God's will.

Eventually this and other prophecies reveal to the people of Israel that Samuel is a prophet to whom God speaks, a man who will one day be their leader.

Read 1 Samuel 2:12-36; 3:1-21.

> Eli is described as both a judge
> and a priest, implying that in
> Israel, politics and religion were
> inseparable. Why was that?
> Do you see issues of poverty,
> injustice, and corruption primarily
> as political or as religious? Write
> a paragraph explaining your
> stance.

The Loss
of the Ark of the Covenant

Attacked once again by the Philistines, Israel is defeated, even though Eli's sons bring the ark of the Covenant to the battlefield. Eli's sons are killed, and Eli dies of grief. The Philistines capture the ark, but after being afflicted with misfortunes, they blame the ark and return it to the Israelites.

Samuel rebukes the Israelites for their lack of faith and promises victory if they will obey God. Finally the Philistines are defeated. As long as Samuel is its leader, Israel enjoys peace.

Read 1 Samuel 4:1-22; 5:1-12; 6:1-16; 7:1-17.

The ark as good luck charm?

Israel's use of the ark in battle is more an act of superstition than of faith. The people see the ark as a sort of rabbit's foot or mascot. The danger of superstition always surrounds the use of sacred objects.

A plague of mice

The Philistines' affliction was tumors, often translated as "hemorrhoids," which were probably caused by the deadly bubonic plague—spread by infected rodents. Evidently mice were on ships arriving at the shores of Philistia.

A King for Israel

Samuel has grown old, and his sons are unfit to take his place as judge, so the people cry out for a king. Samuel angrily complains to God, who replies, " 'It is not you they reject, they are rejecting me as their king' " (8:7). God bids Samuel to give the people a king but to warn them of the consequences: A king will draft their sons to make arms, build chariots, and reap harvests; their daughters to make perfumes, cook, and bake. A king will also take their fields, vineyards, olive groves, and a *tithe* of their grain—that is, one-tenth of it. He will then take their menservants, maidservants, donkeys, and sheep. Finally, the king will make the Israelites into slaves. When at last they cry out to God, it will be to no avail. But even with Samuel's warning, the people insist that they want to be " 'like other nations' " (8:20).

Read 1 Samuel 8:1-22.

Samuel the prophet

The Deuteronomists have Samuel speak here not as a judge but as the first of the prophets to stand up against the kings. For the prophets, only God is the king of Israel.

A nation apart

" 'Like other nations' " is precisely what Israel is *not* supposed to be. Yet questions about Israel's identity have continued through the centuries. In modern times, the eminent Jewish thinker Martin Buber has spoken against "that Jewish nationalism which regards Israel as a nation like unto other nations, and recognizes no task for Israel save that of preserving and asserting itself."

The term *Israel*

The term *Israel* has already been used in several ways. Let us take a moment to clarify the meanings.

Respond briefly in writing:
- Do lucky charms or mascots actually bring good luck? If so, how? If not, why do we often use them?
- What is their effect on the user?

Write a brief response to these questions:
- What was wrong with Israel's having a king?
- As spiritual descendants of the Israelites, are Christians also called to be "*un*like other nations"? How?

- After his nightlong struggle with the stranger, **Jacob** is given the name *Israel*.
- Later, **the people who claim descent from Jacob and the other founders** call themselves the people of Israel.
- In the Second Book of Samuel, **the ten tribes in the north** are called Israel. The two tribes in the south are called Judah.
- When David unites the tribes, **the nation** is called Israel.
- When the kingdom is divided after Solomon's death, *Israel* is the formal name given to **the northern kingdom**. This kingdom is the first one to be conquered, and it is conquered by the Assyrians.
- When the exiles return from Babylon to the province of Judah, they are called Jews; **the nation** is called Israel.
- From that time on, *Israel* means **the land and the people as a nation.**
- To some Jews, **the modern state** called Israel is a religious continuation of the ancient nation. To others, the state is primarily a political entity.

Saul Anointed King

Samuel, guided by God, meets Saul, an unassuming farm worker searching for his father's livestock. Samuel anoints Saul king and presents him to the tribes—even though Saul, a shy man for all his tall stature and good looks, tries to hide at the last minute.

Read 1 Samuel 9:1-27; 10:1-27.

Our gift to God

The theme of this story about Saul is familiar: God chooses the lowliest and least. A modern story about God's gifts comes from the film *Amadeus*. In that movie, the composer Mozart is the least likely person to possess the world's most brilliant musical gift. Mozart's enemy, the court composer Salieri, is outraged that God would give such a gift to a vulgar, silly, and poor young man. Salieri thwarts Mozart's career and connives to bring him to an early death. Yet the world soon acknowledges Mozart as a genius whose music is an incomparable gift to everyone.

Saul's Downfall

Saul wins a stunning victory for Israel over the Ammonites. Afterward, Samuel warns both the king and the people that

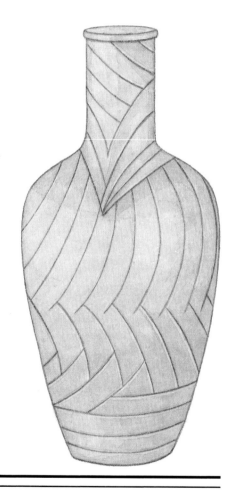

A drawing of a gold jug, the kind that might have held oil for anointing in ancient Israel

the key to their success will be fidelity to God—yet Saul soon breaks faith.

As the Philistines prepare to attack the Israelites, Saul and his men wait impatiently for Samuel to arrive and offer a prebattle sacrifice. But when some of the men begin to desert him, Saul illicitly offers the sacrifice himself. Later, when Samuel tells Saul to attack and destroy another of Israel's enemies—putting them under the ban—Saul fails to obey. Although he has been told to take neither survivors nor spoils, Saul saves the enemy king and the choicest live-stock. Samuel declares that Saul will now be rejected by God as king of Israel. The crown will be given to a more faithful man.

Read 1 Samuel 11:11-15; 12:13-18; 13:5-14; 15:1-35.

Unsuited for kingship

In the situation with the Philistines, Saul has apparent-ly panicked. Forgetting God's past rescues of Israel, he heeds his frightened soldiers rather than Samuel. To offer sacrifice, a practice reserved to priests only (the king may not do it), is totally unacceptable.

To break the ban—as horrible as that ban seems to us, but no more horrible than dropping an atomic bomb—is out-right disobedience. Israel needs a king more faithful and con-stant than Saul.

The Anointing of David

The theme of God's choice of the weakest and lowest is re-peated in the story of David. God sends Samuel to Bethle-hem, where he meets Jesse's sons, chooses David from among them, and secretly anoints him king. David will not be pub-licly declared king until later.

Two biblical traditions tell of Saul's meeting David. In one, David is brought to play the harp for Saul to lighten his dark moods. The other is the story of David and Goliath. In both stories, Saul likes David, finds him gifted, and asks Jesse's permission to keep him at court.

Read 1 Samuel 16:1-23.

Soldier or shepherd?

Verses 18 and 19 present two contrasting views of Da-vid. The first says that he is a trained soldier; the second, that he is a shepherd. Scholars suggest that David was more likely a soldier. The shepherd image probably came from early, popular stories that grew around David's memory. Similar stories of rags to riches are found throughout history—for instance, stories about Abraham Lincoln.

Another journey to Bethlehem

The story of David adds a historical dimension to the events that surround the later journey of Mary and Joseph to David's city, Bethlehem, and to the story of Jesus' birth.
Read Luke 1:26–33; 2:1–5.

David and Goliath

Next follows the famous story of David's victory over the giant Philistine warrior Goliath. Most everyone has heard it, but have you ever read it in full?
Read 1 Samuel 17:1–58.

A storyteller of genius

The biblical text contains many details that are rarely mentioned in shortened versions of the story of David and Goliath:

- a description of Goliath's height, his armor, and his weapons
- the Israelites' reaction to Goliath's challenge
- Jesse's gifts to his sons and to the field commander
- David's leaving his bundles with the baggage keeper
- Saul's promised reward
- the brother's anger
- David's telling of encounters with a lion and a bear
- David weighed down by Saul's armor
- the five smooth stones
- Goliath's taunt
- David's defense of " 'the God of the armies of Israel' " (17:45)
- David's quick action
- Saul's curiosity about David

Here, beyond a doubt, is the work of a storyteller of genius.

Story or history?

Scholars debate whether the story of David and Goliath is a historical account or a parable about little Israel overcoming giant Philistia—with opinions slightly in favor of an actual battle.

Historic Happenings
Between 1250 and 900 B.C.E.

Africa
Poverty and decadence plague the declining Egyptian Empire.

America
By 1000 B.C.E., the Olmecs in Mexico and the Chavín in Peru establish states with populations in the tens of thousands, along with priesthoods, civil services, and classes of traders and artisans.

China
The first Chinese dictionary is written, including over forty thousand written characters.

Europe
Classical paganism blooms in Greece. A temple to Hera—worshiped as queen of heaven, goddess of women and marriage, and wife of Zeus (king of the gods)—is built in the tenth century B.C.E. at Olympia.

India
Basic elements of Hinduism develop, including a belief in a cosmic order and also a class system of priests, nobles, merchants, and workers.

The Near East
The *Creation Epic* confirms the position of the Babylonian god Marduk as the maker of the universe. The city of Babylon becomes the spiritual capital of the region.

This Chinese vessel, used for ritual offerings, is from about the twelfth century B.C.E. It is shaped like a tiger protecting a man.

David tried unsuccessfully to soothe Saul's madness with harp music. *Right:* A harp of the kind used in ancient Israel

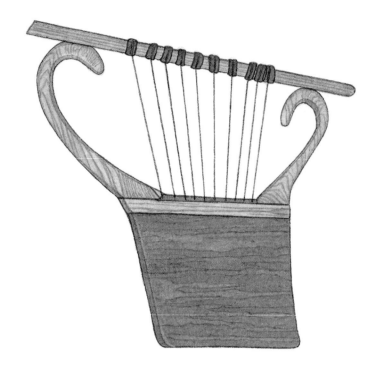

Saul's Jealousy of David

David's popularity, attractiveness, and skill begin to arouse jealousy in Saul until at last he tries to kill David. Both Saul's son Jonathan and his daughter Michal—who is also David's wife—help David escape Saul's murderous traps. Convinced of the king's irrational hatred, David finally bids farewell to Jonathan and Michal, leaves the court, and becomes a fugitive.

Read 1 Samuel 18:1-16; 19:1-18; 20:24b-35,41-42.

Saul's hatred

As Samuel prophesied, God is no longer with Saul, and from now on everything he does goes wrong. Twice when he tries to kill David, his spear misses. When Saul sends David to the battlefront, David's prowess wins the love of the people. Even Saul's children give their loyalty to David. Saul realizes that nothing he can do will stop David from becoming king.

Jonathan's love

The story of David and Jonathan is one of the world's greatest tales of friendship. Notice how Jonathan's love for David is described, his loyalty and the risks he takes for David.

Reflect on an example of true friendship from history, films, novels, or your own life. Then answer these questions in writing:
- Do loyalty and risk play a part in friendship?
- Do males and females share true friendship?

David as Outlaw

David flees to the shrine at Nob, which is near Jerusalem. There he contrives to get food from the priest Ahimelech by saying that Saul has sent him on an errand. Ahimelech gives David not only bread from the altar but the sword of Goliath as well. When Saul finds out, he orders the entire city of Nob destroyed, and only Abiathar, one of Ahimelech's sons, survives. David, contrite, admits his guilt to Abiathar and offers him protection.

Still loyal to his people, David next rescues an Israelite town from the Philistines. Then he and his troops flee to the desert and take refuge in a cave. Pursuing him, Saul stops in the cave to relieve himself and apparently falls asleep. David leaves Saul alive but cuts off a piece of his cloak. When Saul emerges, David calls from a distance and waves the cloth to show how close Saul has come to death.

Read 1 Samuel 21:1-10; 22:18-23; 23:1-5; 24:1-23.

David judged

The destruction of the city of Nob is a black moment in David's rise to kingship. After all, David had a part in the murderous deed—having deceived the priest within the hearing of one of Saul's men. Here is another example of how the biblical writers refused to whitewash their heroes.

David's loyalty and compassion

As David spares Saul, we see that his affection for Saul remains in spite of Saul's jealousy. David's touching and beautiful speech to Saul reveals the hand of a gifted writer.

Another Outlaw Story

David and his band survive by offering protection to the local inhabitants in return for provisions. But Nabal, a rich herdsman whose shepherds have enjoyed David's protection, refuses to pay. When David angrily moves to confront him, Nabal's wife Abigail intercepts David with supplies of food and wine. David is appeased, and later, when Nabal dies, he marries Abigail. Saul has already given David's wife Michal to another man.

Read 1 Samuel 25:18-43.

Abigail's plea

When Nabal's wife goes out to meet David, she pleads for her family and her people. She hopes that David will

After Saul tried to kill him, David fled the court and became a hunted exile in the desert of Judah.
Right: A pool in the Judaean desert, near the Dead Sea

become king—a merciful king, not like Saul, who sheds innocent blood.

David's and Michal's marriages

David's marriage to Abigail is prompted by his gratitude and admiration for her character. By contrast, Michal's remarriage was a political move by Saul, pure and simple. By marrying Michal to another man, Saul hoped to weaken David's claim to the throne. Later on, David will demand Michal back for much the same reason.

David with the Philistines

David decides to seek refuge with the Philistines and, to ingratiate himself with their king, pretends to attack Israelite towns. In reality, he is raiding Canaanite villages.

Threatened by the Philistines, a desperate Saul seeks out a witch to conjure up the spirit of the dead Samuel. When she does, the ghost reveals only that Saul and his sons will perish in battle the next day.

Meanwhile, at the Philistine camp, David is trying to outwit these enemies of Israel. His men, about to march into battle at the rear of the Philistine army, are apparently planning to attack them from behind during the battle.

But the Philistine chiefs distrust David and instead send his troops back to the village where they have been staying. Finding it sacked by marauders, with all the women and children kidnapped, David rescues the captives and slays their captors.

Read 1 Samuel 27:1-12; 28:4-20; 29:1-11.

Saul and Shakespeare

Saul's appeal to witchcraft reveals the depth of his madness and despair. Earlier, he outlawed fortune-tellers throughout the land. Shakespeare might have recalled this story when he wrote the plays *Hamlet* and *Macbeth*. In both, tragedy is preceded by ghostly apparitions. Like Saul, Macbeth is a false king striving to keep a throne that does not belong to him.

Saul's Death

Israel's battle goes as prophesied by the ghost of Samuel, and in a tragic end to a career that was once bright with promise, Saul kills himself rather than be captured. The Philistines fasten his body and those of his sons—including Jonathan—to the walls of their city Bethshan. But the Jabeshites, who were once rescued by Saul, march all night, rescue the corpses, and take them to Jabesh.

Read 1 Samuel 31:1-13.

In a page or less, write a character sketch of Saul: describe his personality and give your opinion of him.

Saul's demise, David's rise

The First Book of Samuel completes the first of the major themes in Samuel—namely, the reign of Saul. The other theme, the rise of David to his kingship, follows in the second book.

King David

The Second Book of Samuel opens with a different version of Saul's death. A young soldier from the front of Israel's battle reports to David that Saul is dead. The wounded Saul persuaded the soldier to strike a deathblow, lest Saul be captured. David is outraged that the young man would violate " 'the Lord's anointed' " (1:14) and has him killed. David mourns the death of Saul and Jonathan in beautiful and

touching words, once recorded in the ancient Book of Jashar.
Read 2 Samuel 1:17-27.

David's lament

The Book of Jashar, now lost, also contained the poem about Joshua's stopping the sun in the sky (Joshua 10:12-13). Notice the use of poetic license in David's lament: he curses the mountain ridge upon which Saul's shield lies rusting, commanding that no water reach it from above or below. But rain continued to fall on the mountains of Gilboa, in spite of David's curse—as indeed the sun did not stop for Joshua. Both David's curse and Joshua's order are literary devices to express the passion and intensity of the speaker.

David Anointed King in Judah

Israel is now without a king, but there are two rival leaders: Saul's general Abner in the north and David in the south. Abner makes Saul's eldest son, Ishbaal, king over the northern tribes, although Abner himself really wants to rule. David goes to Hebron, in the south, where he is anointed king of the southern kingdom of Judah.

Read 2 Samuel 2:8-11.

Actually, David is now *publicly* anointed king, since Samuel has already secretly anointed him (1 Samuel 16:13).

David, the King of All Israel

Abner proposes a duel between picked warriors on each side—with "winner take all," in the manner of Goliath's challenge—but the duel is a draw..

Aware that David's star is rising, Abner betrays Ishbaal, returns Michal to David, and persuades the northern tribes to choose David for their king. The people remember David's loyal service to Saul, assemble together with Judah, and anoint David king over all Israel. He is thirty years old.

Sandwiched between these events is a series of murders and betrayals that would do justice to a nighttime TV series. The plot would go like this:

- Abner, the powerful and ruthless vice-president of Israel, Inc., promotes to president the weak son (Ishbaal) of the deceased president (Saul). Abner also takes over the deceased president's mistress and tries to eliminate the lawfully designated president (David) by violence, but fails.

David mourned the death of Saul—and even more so the death of Jonathan. Both Saul and Jonathan died in battle.
Above: Military ceremonies mark the death of a sailor killed in a missile attack on his ship.

Insulted by Ishbaal, Abner next abandons his candidate for president of the company (Ishbaal) and persuades the stockholders whom he controls (the northern tribes) to vote for the lawfully designated president (David).

Returning from a business trip, Abner is waylaid and murdered by the new vice-president (one of David's generals), whose brother was slain by Abner. The new president (David) is horrified and mourns Abner's death.

In the meantime, two hit men from the north, certain that the president (David) will be pleased if his rival (Ishbaal) is removed, murder him. When the appalled president discovers the crime, the hit men are executed.

In short, David's reign begins with a bloodbath. Only his sincerity, his diplomacy, and the grace of God keep him out of the violence.

Read 2 Samuel 2:12-16; 3:6-13; 5:1-5.

David's soap opera?

Unfortunately, the human heart has not changed since ancient times. Scheming, jealousy, and violence are not only the stuff of TV programs; they are also the ingredients of many so-called success stories. The story of David's election by God, his long wait to take power, and his refusal to stoop to betrayal says something profound: God's plan can be trusted. We must wait to discover God's will. We need not sin to make it happen. We can work, pray, and learn—knowing that there is something unique that we have been born to do and that God will help us achieve that purpose.

The Tribes Unified at Jerusalem

Alarmed at Israel's unity, the Philistines force David into battle, and his victories drive them down to the coastal plain. The Philistines are never again a serious threat.

David's next move is inspired. He captures Jerusalem, a Canaanite city that has boasted that even the lame and the blind could defend it, and makes the city his capital.

Read 2 Samuel 5:17-25; 5:6-16, in that order.

Two great achievements

David's two great feats were ending the Philistine threat and unifying the Israelite tribes. Making Jerusalem his capital was a stroke of genius. Because Jerusalem had never belonged to any one of the twelve tribes, David could not be accused of playing favorites by bringing his court there.

Jerusalem was ideally located in territory between the northern and the southern tribes.

History has proven that David's decision was of much greater import than he would ever know. In Jerusalem, David established what would become a holy city for Jews, Christians, and Muslims—more than half of all religious believers in the world today.

Return of the Ark

Aware that the ark of the Covenant is a powerful symbol of God's presence to the people, David brings it to Jerusalem. On the journey, a man named Uzzah, one of the escorts, steadies the ark with his hand as it tips on the wagon. He dies on the spot. Upset, David waits three months before bringing the ark into the city.

When David joyfully enters the city, dancing before the ark, his wife Michal berates him for acting like a fool. He replies that if to give God praise he must look a fool, he will. The story ends with the note that Michal never bears a child.

Read 2 Samuel 6:1-23.

Uzzah's death

Sacred objects were held in great awe by the Israelites, and touching them was reserved for priests. Uzzah probably had a heart attack when he suddenly realized that he had committed a sacrilege. Such occurrences were always attributed to God.

David brought the ark of the Covenant to Jerusalem, carrying it on a wagon.
Right: A carving that may depict the ark on a wagon, from a third-century C.E. synagogue in Israel

Michal's fate

As for Michal's show of contempt toward David, clearly no bond of love remains between them. Their remarriage was purely political. The text implies that David never makes love to Michal again—a sad ending to a young love for which they had risked so much.

The Messianic Promise

When David reflects that while he is living in a house of cedar, God has only a tent as a dwelling place, he plans to build a house for the LORD. But the prophet Nathan says no to David's plan. It is revealed to Nathan that God will instead build a "house" for David—meaning a royal dynasty.

Read 2 Samuel 7:1-17.

Nathan's first prophecy

The prophet Nathan, one of the nonwriting prophets, played an important role in the lives of David and Solomon. In his first prophecy, Nathan revealed God's wish that the temple David had planned be postponed until his son could build it.

The Messiah

God promised that David's line would endure forever. In fact, David's line endured unbroken for four hundred years; then it dropped into obscurity. Afterward, devout Jews remembered this promise and waited for the reappearance of a leader from this royal line to be Israel's Messiah. The Hebrew word *messiah* means "anointed," referring to the anointing of a king. By the time of Jesus, the belief in the coming Messiah was widespread among Jews in Palestine. The early Christians believed the Messiah to be Jesus, who was from the line of David. The gospel writers referred to Jesus using the Greek word for *messiah—christos,* meaning "the anointed," from which the name *Christ* comes.

Read Mark 15:2,26.

David and Meribbaal

Now powerful, wealthy, and undefeated, David inquires about surviving heirs of Saul to whom he might show kindness for the sake of Jonathan. He is told of Meribbaal—Jonathan's son and Saul's grandson, a man lame in both feet. David has him brought to court, restores his inheritance, and offers royal protection. From that day on, Meribbaal lives in the king's house, sits at the king's table, and eats with the king's sons.

Read 1 Samuel 20:12–16; 2 Samuel 9:1–13.

Keeping a promise

In ancient times, a survivor of the enemy king was ordinarily executed, to protect the new king from pretenders to the throne. Keeping his promise to Jonathan, David instead restored Meribbaal's inheritance and his place at court. It was an astounding gesture of forgiveness and generosity.

David and Bathsheba

After years of war, David is tired, and one spring he stays home from battle. As he strolls on the roof of his palace, he sees a beautiful woman bathing nearby. She is Bathsheba, whose husband is Uriah, a warrior at the battlefront. David sends for her and makes love to her.

Later, when Bathsheba informs David that she is pregnant, he is alarmed. He brings Uriah back from the front, assuming that he will spend the night with his wife, but the plan fails. Out of deference to his comrades at the front and in obedience to one of David's regulations for his soldiers, Uriah spends the night in the barracks. The following night, David gets Uriah drunk and sends him home again, but again he returns to the barracks. Why does he not go to his wife? David asks. Uriah says that he cannot in conscience enjoy

David spotted Bathsheba from the roof of his palace.
Right: The rooftops of Jerusalem today

his home and his wife when even the ark of the Covenant is encamped on the battlefield.

Desperate, David sends Uriah back to the front with a sealed letter to his general directing him to place Uriah where he will be killed in battle—and this happens. When at last Bathsheba's mourning period is over, David marries her and she bears him a son.

Read 2 Samuel 11:1-27.

Two sins

This story tells about what wealth and power and boredom can do even to a man as great as David. He is guilty of both adultery and murder.

Nathan's Parable and Prophecy

Nathan the prophet now asks David to judge a case: A poor man had one ewe lamb, and a rich man had a flock of sheep. When a guest visited the rich man, the host stole the poor man's ewe instead of slaughtering one of his own for dinner. What should happen to such a man? asks Nathan. The fellow should die, cries David angrily, and Nathan says, " 'You are the man!' " (12:7).

Through the parable, David recognizes his sin and is appalled. When David pours out his sorrow, Nathan assures him that God forgives him and will not ask his life—but he will pay for his acts with grief. Soon after, Bathsheba bears a son, who is sickly and dies. Later, she conceives and bears another son, whom Nathan names Jedidiah, but he will grow up to be called Solomon.

Read 2 Samuel 12:1-25.

David's bad example

This famous parable of the Hebrew Scriptures is told to force David to examine his conscience. Surely his relationship with Bathsheba is known at court, and as king he must be responsible for the impact of his example. David will live to see the effect of his sin on both his family and his people.

Amnon's Crime

The fulfillment of Nathan's prophecy of evil for David's family further takes shape in Amnon's rape of his half sister Tamar and the violent events that follow. Amnon, David's firstborn and heir to the throne, desires Tamar and rapes her. When he then turns on Tamar and drives her away, her full

Read 1 Corinthians 13:4-7. Write a brief essay explaining the difference between love and lust and between love and infatuation.

As a young man, David had boundless hopes, but his later years were tortured with grief.
Above: The artist Michelangelo's statue of the youthful David

brother Absalom is enraged. David is angry, but he does not punish Amnon—because he is the heir to the throne.

Read 2 Samuel 3:2-5; 13:1-22.

Royal children and wives

David had a number of sons, but in those times the firstborn son always held the privileged position at court. Obviously, at that time girls were not thought of as important at all!

We might ask where all David's children came from. Polygamy was an accepted practice in Israel for those who could afford it. As noted in an earlier chapter, the primary reason for this custom was the fear of childlessness—or more accurately, sonlessness.

Royal wives, who were often acquired with the signing of treaties, also helped to ensure peace between the signers. David's principal reason for demanding the return of Michal, whom he had loved passionately in his youth, was to cement relations with the family of Saul in the north. A son from both David's and Saul's family lines would have been an ideal candidate for the throne, ensuring the unity of the northern and the southern tribes. But by the time she was returned to him, Michal no longer shared David's love for God—as we have seen—and she was like a stranger. Thus, Michal did not bear such a child.

Absalom's Plot

Two years later, Absalom, Tamar's full brother, invites the royal family to attend a feast at his estate at sheepshearing time. David excuses himself but sends his other sons, including Amnon. The vengeful Absalom has Amnon slain by his servants and escapes to his grandfather's home at Geshur, where he stays for three years.

Angry as David is, he loves Absalom and longs for his return. David's general Joab persuades him to call Absalom back, but it is a decision David will soon regret.

Read 2 Samuel 13:23-39; 14:1-24.

David, a permissive parent?

David, like Shakespeare's King Lear, is a fool where his children are concerned. Instead of consulting Nathan about Absalom and Amnon, he turns to Joab, a man whose mindset is war and violence. Neither of these sons is suitable to rule. Absalom is as deceitful and violent as Amnon, neither brother shows any awareness of God, and in the end their violent deaths are a boon to the nation.

Absalom's Rebellion

Now comes a long, involved story filled with striking portraits, passionate feelings, intricate details—and it is marvelously told. Absalom has made his peace with David but subtly begins to undermine the people's respect for the king. He successfully courts popularity for himself and, after four years, goes to Hebron, in Judah, with a large following. There Absalom declares himself king in David's stead.

David hears this and, wanting to spare the city bloodshed, flees Jerusalem across the Kidron Valley to the Mount of Olives. He sends two priests back to spy for him along with a trusted servant, Hushai, who is to gain Absalom's confidence and tell the priests of Absalom's plans.

As if one revolt is not enough, a servant of Meribbaal appears with a tale of his master's disloyalty. Meribbaal hopes to recover the throne as Saul's survivor. Another member of Saul's family curses David and attacks him with stones. Through it all, David weeps for Absalom, refuses to return evil for evil, and puts his confidence in God.

Read 2 Samuel 15:1–18a; 16:1–14.

The Death of Absalom

When Absalom enters Jerusalem, one of David's traitorous friends counsels Absalom to pursue the king immediately because David and his troops will be weary and easy to catch. Absalom asks Hushai's opinion, and he advises that because David is such a great warrior, an army should be formed first. Absalom agrees and waits to attack. Messengers from Hushai warn David, who withdraws his troops across the Jordan to safety.

When David's men, who refuse to let the king risk his life, go out to battle, he exhorts them to protect young Absalom. However, when the now-defeated Absalom tries to escape, his head of luxuriant hair becomes entangled in the branches of a tree, and his mule runs out from under him. Joab, finding Absalom hanging but still alive, kills him.

David, told of Absalom's death, mourns him piteously until Joab berates the king for weeping over a traitorous son yet treating his loyal soldiers as though they were the traitors. David then moves to reconcile the disgruntled tribes

In a paragraph, describe a character on television or in a movie who reminds you of Amnon or Absalom.

The Empire That David Built

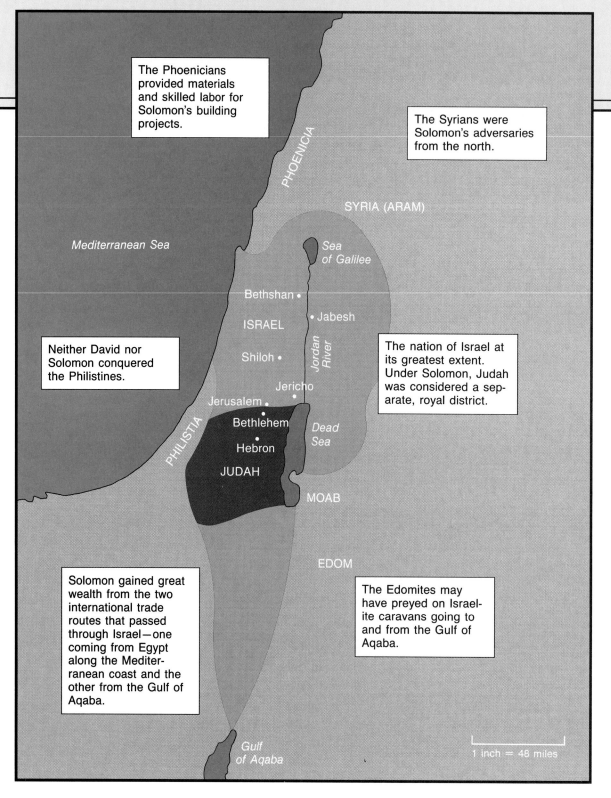

The Phoenicians provided materials and skilled labor for Solomon's building projects.

The Syrians were Solomon's adversaries from the north.

Neither David nor Solomon conquered the Philistines.

The nation of Israel at its greatest extent. Under Solomon, Judah was considered a separate, royal district.

Solomon gained great wealth from the two international trade routes that passed through Israel—one coming from Egypt along the Mediterranean coast and the other from the Gulf of Aqaba.

The Edomites may have preyed on Israelite caravans going to and from the Gulf of Aqaba.

PHOENICIA

SYRIA (ARAM)

Mediterranean Sea

Sea of Galilee

Bethshan

Jabesh

ISRAEL

Shiloh

Jordan River

Jericho

Jerusalem

Bethlehem

Dead Sea

Hebron

JUDAH

MOAB

PHILISTIA

EDOM

Gulf of Aqaba

1 inch = 48 miles

in both north and south and refuses to punish Saul's family—even Meribbaal.

David is enthroned once more in Jerusalem, and the kingdom is restored to a semblance of order. Yet the popularity of the aging king is not what it was. Animosity among the tribes is beginning to surface, and David—worn out, his judgment not always fair—is almost blind in his prejudice toward his favorites.

Read 2 Samuel 17:1-17; 18:1-17; 19:1-9a,42-44.

King and capital

By the end of David's reign, Israel is indeed a nation like other nations, with a king and a capital. The anointing of David and the capturing of Jerusalem are never-to-be-forgotten events in Jewish history.

Are you familiar with the story of King Arthur of Britain? Look up the legend of the Round Table. In a brief essay, compare Arthur's story with David's.

Solomon's Temple

For the rest of the story of the monarchy, we turn to the two Books of Kings. They tell of David's son Solomon (the topic of the remainder of this chapter), the breakup of the nation into the kingdoms of Israel and Judah, the infidelity of their kings, the prophets Elijah and Elisha, and finally the Babylonian exile. The literary sources for Kings were court and temple records and popular tales of the prophets—put together sometime after 561 B.C.E. by the Deuteronomists. The Books of Kings were written to remind the disheartened exiles in Babylon that it was they who broke the Covenant, not God. Yet their restoration in the future would be possible if they would repent and turn to God again.

The Last Days of David

The First Book of Kings opens with the last days of David. Adonijah, David's eldest son, seeing his father senile and close to death, gives a feast to celebrate his own imminent ascent to the throne. When Nathan hears of this, he sends Bathsheba to remind David that he has promised the throne to her son Solomon. Nathan manages to have Solomon anointed king before Adonijah is publicly acclaimed. Then deserted by his followers, Adonijah flees to a sanctuary until Solomon assures him of safety.

Read 1 Kings 1:1-22,28-40,49-53.

Nathan's invented promise?

David's promise to anoint Solomon king is not mentioned earlier. Nathan, whom we have come to know and admire, seems to be conniving with Bathsheba. The biblical text is not clear on this point, however.

David's Death

On his deathbed, David assures Solomon that if he and his line will remain faithful to God, they will always sit on the throne. In what seems a bloody reversal of his attitudes toward his own enemies, David counsels Solomon to settle the old scores. Upon David's death, Solomon does so.
Read 1 Kings 2:1-11.

Whose idea?

Were these murders Solomon's doing, with the court historians attributing them to David? Solomon would understandably want to rid his reign of David's strongmen in order to start with a court altogether on his side. The historical record might have been tampered with to serve the purposes of the monarchy.

Solomon's Dream

Solomon worships at one of the "high places," meaning an outdoor sanctuary. In a dream Solomon asks God for an understanding heart to distinguish right from wrong. Pleased, God promises Solomon not only the wisdom to judge rightly but riches, glory, and a long life as well—if he is faithful.
Read 1 Kings 3:1-14.

The high places

The Deuteronomists frowned on outdoor sanctuaries because the Canaanites used them in fertility rites and in the worship of Baal. Although Solomon's worship seems genuine, the story is hinting of evil things to come in its references to the high places—and to Solomon's Egyptian wife.

Solomon's Judgment

Solomon's understanding heart is immediately put to the test. Two prostitutes come before the king—one with a child, one without. The childless woman tells Solomon that each of them bore a child and that the other woman smothered hers in her sleep. Then she exchanged the dead infant for the live one and now claims him. The woman with the child denies this. The king calls for a sword and suggests that the child be divided and half given to each woman. The true mother, in anguish, cries out that the child should live and gives up her claim to him. Solomon gives the child to that woman, who revealed her motherhood in her desire to save the child's life.

Read 1 Kings 3:16–28.

Genuine justice

This story, probably the best-known one about Solomon, appears in folklore all over the world. Whether history or legend, the story offers a wonderful example of fairness without regard to age, position, or importance.

Solomon's Bureaucracy

Solomon, ignoring tribal boundaries, divides the land into twelve new districts and appoints an officer for each region. Then he forms an elite group of administrators and introduces forced labor and taxation to provide supplies for the palace and for government officials.

Read 1 Kings 4:1–7.

The rich are always with us

The peasants in Central and South America have long been exploited by corrupt governments, by wealthy landowners, and by foreign investors. Solomon's glory was built on income raised by oppressing his people in the same way.

Solomon gained his wealth through heavy taxes and slavery—and perhaps through commercial ventures.
Left: Ships carrying Solomon's trading goods may have landed at Pharaoh's Bay, at the northern tip of the Gulf of Aqaba.

Find an item on television or in a newspaper or a magazine that describes how the poor and needy continue to be exploited today. Write a brief note exploring your personal feelings about the situation described. Have you found the same kind of exploitation in the scriptural stories? Where? In what circumstances?

Farmers and shepherds had to provide palace supplies from their own crops and herds and take time from their work to hunt wild game for officials. The prophet Samuel had warned about these things long before, when the people clamored for a king. With the reign of Solomon, the injustice came to pass.

Solomon's Wisdom

Solomon's reputation grows until "all the kings of the earth" know of his wisdom (5:14). He utters three thousand proverbs, writes one thousand and five—that is, numberless—songs, and discusses plants, beasts, birds, reptiles, and fishes.
Read 1 Kings 5:9-14.

Wisdom is not merely knowledge

The biblical writers might have been indulging in satire as they listed Solomon's accomplishments. Familiarity with the lore of nature is not the wisdom that makes a ruler compassionate, self-disciplined, or just. In the end, Solomon's reign will be a disaster to his people, although now all is glory.

The Temple

Rich and powerful, Solomon is now ready to build the Temple in Jerusalem. He asks a Phoenician king to send not only materials but also architects. Because Israel has never built a temple, a Canaanite model must be used. Solomon conscripts thirty thousand workers from his own people in addition to foreign labor.

God agrees to be present in the Temple, adding that if Solomon observes the Law and carries it out, Israel will not be forsaken. In a long prayer, Solomon himself wonders if his great accomplishment is futile: Can any building contain God?

When the Temple is dedicated, God repeats the promise made to Solomon and adds a warning: If Solomon and his descendants forsake the Covenant, the Temple will become a heap of ruins. These words must have pierced the hearts of the exiles in Babylon as they listened and remembered their own story.
Read 1 Kings 5:15-20; 6:11-13; 8:27-30; 9:1-9.

A historical high point

Israel's Temple, enthroning the ark of the Covenant and centralizing worship, becomes a source of pride and joy. Yet its building marks the beginning of Israel's downfall. With

Marvelous though it was, Solomon's Temple marked the beginning of Israel's downfall.

Solomon's Temple

The Bible devotes several pages to the construction, furnishings, and dedication of the Temple at Jerusalem. Indeed, Solomon is probably best known the world over for building his Temple. Financed by taxes, the building was a marvel of cedar beams, bronze pillars, ivory-paneled doors, golden vessels, and carved stonework. Its magnificence rivaled the monuments of Egypt.

The Temple had three chambers, as did the Canaanite temples. The people were relegated to the outer court, the priests and nobles to the inner court. The high priest entered the sanctuary, called the holy of holies, only once a year.

Solomon not only designed the Temple on Canaanite models but also adopted temple practices from his neighbors. In the end, Solomon's Temple became a symbol of wealth at the price of justice and a symbol of arrogance at the price of faith.

the growing splendor of Solomon's reign will come oppression such as the people have never known before.

The Queen of Sheba

Solomon is visited by the queen of Sheba, seeking to discover if he is as wise as reputed. The queen asks Solomon some subtle questions—probably traditional riddles, a number of which survive in collections of tales about Solomon. Observing his wisdom and his wealth, the queen is breathless.
Read 1 Kings 10:1–10.

If you're so good, why aren't you rich?
In this story, the biblical writers linked virtue with wealth. The belief that faith in God is rewarded by "health and wealth" remains a popular notion today. But how is Solomon building up his wealth?

The Sin of Solomon

As Solomon adds to his wealth and his harem, his love for God diminishes. He tolerates shrines where his pagan wives offer sacrifice, and he even joins in their worship. Finally, unable to distinguish right from wrong, Solomon prefers strange gods to the one God. Then God speaks: Solomon's line will lose the throne and all the tribes but Judah!
Read 1 Kings 11:1–13.
By now, Solomon's failure is a foregone conclusion.

Solomon's Foes and His Death

After forty years of harsh rule, the discontent of Solomon's people lures his enemies back from exile to harass him. One of these, Jeroboam, is chief of the labor force fortifying the Jerusalem walls. Disenchanted, Jeroboam leaves Jerusalem to go north and meets the prophet Ahijah, who tears his cloak into twelve pieces, one for each tribe. He gives ten of them to Jeroboam and promises him the throne of Israel in the north if he will follow the ways of God.

Solomon orders Jeroboam killed, but he escapes to Egypt to await Solomon's death. When at last Solomon dies, the golden age of Israel comes to an end.
Read 1 Kings 11:26–35,40–43.

An inheritance of idolatry
In forty years, Solomon has led Israel from a union of freedom-loving tribes under David, loyal to the Covenant,

Read Matthew 6:25–30. Write a brief reaction to Jesus' teachings about wealth.

to subjection and near slavery. Although oppressed by taxes and forced labor, idolatry is the worst of the burdens that Israel has inherited from this golden ruler. The nation, whose identity rests on its fidelity to God, has been led to the worship of false gods.

For Review

1. What do the Books of Samuel tell us about?

2. In their battle with the Philistines, how do the people of Israel use the ark of the Covenant?

3. What does Samuel say will be the consequences of choosing a king?

4. How does the story of David repeat the theme of God's choosing the weakest and lowest?

5. What responsibility does David bear for the destruction of the city of Nob?

6. Describe the contrasting motives behind David's marriage to Abigail and remarriage to Michal.

7. Name the two major themes of the Books of Samuel.

8. Explain why David's choice of Jerusalem for his capital was a stroke of genius.

9. What sort of "house" will God build for David?

10. What biblical promise led to the belief in the Messiah?

11. Who is Solomon's mother? Whose wife was she first?

12. What two never-to-be-forgotten events in Jewish history are described in this chapter?

13. What did the Deuteronomists think of outdoor sanctuaries? Why?

14. Explain how Samuel's warnings to Israel became reality.

15. What burdens does Israel inherit from Solomon?

7

The Kings
of Israel and Judah—
and the Prophets

THE prophets were people called by God to warn Israel when it strayed from true worship and forgot its role of witness to the LORD before the nations. Because they were faithful to this call, the prophets became the conscience of Israel, risking their life to condemn the moral laxity of kings and the decadence of their people. Their harsh criticism of greed and idolatry endeared them to only a few followers. But their ringing accusations and pleas for fidelity and goodness have become a literature ranked among the noblest writings of the ancient world and among the most useful for the modern.

We have already met two of the **former,** or nonwriting, prophets: Samuel, who rejected Saul's flawed kingship, and Nathan, who denounced David's adultery. In this chapter we will meet two more of the nonwriting prophets, Elijah and Elisha. Their tales, a combination of history and legend, are some of the most appealing stories in the Bible and were probably collected and passed along by their disciples.

Although both Elijah and Elisha were fiercely opposed to the wicked kings of Israel, their stories tell more about the wonders they worked than about their political involvement. They have left their mark in music, art, legend, folktales—and in the teachings of Jesus.

We will also meet for the first time some of the **latter,** or writing, prophets. Among them are Amos, a herdsman; Hosea, a betrayed husband; Micah, a devotee of the poor; and the great Isaiah of Jerusalem, a confidant and counselor of kings.

Lastly, there are the remaining kings of the northern and the southern kingdoms. To them the prophets addressed impassioned pleas to turn from idol worship and injustice to Israel's true God. That the kings refused to listen and, together with their people, continued on the path of self-serving inevitably led both kingdoms to exile.

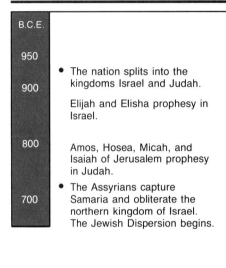

B.C.E.	
950	
900	• The nation splits into the kingdoms Israel and Judah.
	Elijah and Elisha prophesy in Israel.
800	Amos, Hosea, Micah, and Isaiah of Jerusalem prophesy in Judah.
700	• The Assyrians capture Samaria and obliterate the northern kingdom of Israel. The Jewish Dispersion begins.

When the nation of Israel divided into two kingdoms, the northern one possessed fertile farming lands, but the southern one did not.
Facing page: Rich, terraced fields in the region that was once the prosperous northern kingdom called Israel

The Olmecs claimed the fearsome jaguar among their ancestors.
Right: A stone Olmec ceremonial mask, combining the features of both human and cat

Historic Happenings
Between 900 and 600 B.C.E.

Africa
As the Saharan region in North Africa dries up, the inhabitants shift from horses to camels as mounts and beasts of burden. In this same region, the Phoenicians found the city of Carthage and establish a trading empire in the western part of the Near East.

America
Earlier worship of jaguars as fierce and powerful totems develops into widely successful jaguar cults. Among the Olmecs of Mexico and the Chavín of Peru, these beasts are worshiped at great ceremonial centers.

China
Under the Chou dynasty, an aristocracy rules fiefdoms and presides over the practice of ancestor worship.

Europe
The Iron Age arrives and with it come the Celts, who use iron tools and weapons to hew and hack their way through Central Europe.

India
Hindu priests become the most powerful caste within the social order. Wandering sages, disenchanted with religious rituals, practice yoga and meditation as a means of discovering wisdom.

The Near East
The Assyrian Empire reaches the height of its glory, then disappears when its capital, Nineveh, is destroyed in 612 B.C.E.

The Breakup of the Kingdom

The Kings of Israel and Judah

The story of Israel continues, following Solomon's death, when the people of the south accept his son Rehoboam as their king. But the northern tribes set forth a condition: Rehoboam must not oppress them as his father did. The elders of the court agree and advise the young king to be a servant to his people, not a slave driver. But Rehoboam heeds the counsel of his young comrades, who call for more brutality, not less, and the northern tribes reject him. Thus "all Israel" is divided into two kingdoms—Israel in the north, Judah in the south—and the work of David is destroyed in the space of two generations.

When the rebel Jeroboam is declared king in the north, he immediately breaks the Law of God and enshrines two golden calves, one at Dan and the other at Bethel. In spite of the warnings of the prophet Ahijah, Jeroboam raises up non-Levite priests in order to keep his people from going to Jerusalem to worship—and when he dies his dynasty soon comes to an end.

Read 1 Kings 12:1-20,25-33; 13:1-10,33-34.

The world-changing word

God's word runs contrary to conventional wisdom. Rehoboam could not believe that being a king meant being a servant to anyone.

Read John 13:12-15.

Jesus' instruction to his Apostles seems to violate every sensible role of business management. The word of God always turns things upside down.

The Wicked Kings of the North

The history of the northern kings of Israel reads like a police blotter: Jeroboam's son Nadab is assassinated by Baasha, and when Baasha dies, his son Elah becomes king. Elah is on a drinking spree when he is murdered by Zimri, who rules for seven days, is besieged by Omri, and commits suicide. Omri does "evil in the LORD's sight" and is succeeded by his son Ahab, the worst of them all. Ahab marries the Phoenician princess Jezebel, a fiendishly wicked woman, and they become the villains in the stories about the prophets Elijah and Elisha.

Read 1 Kings 15:25-34; 16:1-4,8-13,23-33.

Capable—but evil

Although ignored by the biblical authors, who had no use for the northern kings, Omri was the real founder of the northern kingdom and the builder of its capital, Samaria. He and Ahab were the kingdom's most capable, even if most evil, kings.

The Prophets Elijah and Elisha

How could the people of Israel become what God had called them to be when each king was worse than the last? Who could speak of God to them?

The answer to these questions was the prophets. Among the Israelites, they alone had no interest in power, money, or any approval but God's. They saw, heard, and spoke nothing but God. Moses, Eli, Samuel, and Nathan have been called prophets, and now we meet Elijah and Elisha.

Prophesying is often seen as a kind of crystal ball gazing that foresees the future, but the prophets of Israel based their oracles on the will of God. When the kings became obsessed with power and wealth and led their people into idolatry, God called upon certain individuals to warn Israel of the consequences, and those individuals were the prophets.

The purpose of the stories about Elijah and Elisha—especially when told to the exiles in Babylon—was to show that when God spoke through the prophets, God expected Israel to listen—or else. Elijah and Elisha were historical figures who, without a doubt, tangled with Ahab and Jezebel. Their period was the reigns of the kings of Israel from Ahab to Joash—about 874 to 796 B.C.E.

The Elijah Stories

1. The stories about Elijah open with God's sending Elijah to tell Ahab that he will be punished by a drought, because apparently Jezebel has ordered the slaughter of all the prophets of Israel. Elijah is next sent to hide by a stream, where ravens will feed him. When the stream goes dry, he is sent to a village in Sidon (Phoenicia), where a widow will care for him. Upon his arrival, Elijah sees the woman and asks her for water and a crust of bread. But she has only enough flour and oil, she says, to make a barley cake for herself and her son before they die of starvation. Elijah promises God's help if she will divide the cake with him. The widow does, and afterward, until the drought is over, her jar of flour and jug of oil are never empty.

Read 1 Kings 17:1-16.

Saying yes

The obedience of Elijah is contrasted with the disobedience of the king. The prophet goes on a dangerous errand, entrusts his survival to ravens, and asks a starving woman for her last bit of bread. The woman, a pagan like Jezebel, hears the word of God and also obeys. It is a simple tale about saying yes to God.

God's way is risky—but rewarding. Do you know the story of Dorothy Day? In 1933, when she was in Washington, D.C., for a hunger march, she prayed with anguish that she might be led to use her gifts for her fellow workers and the poor. Later, as co-founder of the Catholic Worker Movement, she became the most powerful advocate for the poor in the United States.

Jesus told his own people in Nazareth that the pagan widow of Zarephath had more faith and heard the prophets more clearly than they did. They confirmed this by immediately trying to push him off a cliff!

Read Luke 4:20-30.

2. Elijah remains with the widow of Zarephath until God sends him back to the court of Ahab. When Ahab blames him for the drought, Elijah challenges the priests of Baal to a contest to see whose god can produce rain. The priests call to Baal in vain. Elijah taunts them to call louder—perhaps Baal is meditating (some translations say "relieving himself"), napping, or on a journey. They slash themselves in an ecstatic frenzy—but no rain.

Then Elijah builds an altar to the LORD. He digs a trench around it, arranges wood for a fire, kills a bull for sacrifice, and has the people—who have been shilly-shallying between Baal and God—drench it with water. He calls for a show of God's power, and fire (perhaps lightning) comes down to consume the bull, the wood, and the stones, even lap up the water. The unfaithful people fall to the ground and worship the God of Israel.

Read 1 Kings 18:1-46.

In this story, Elijah accuses the people of halfheartedness in their faith: They must make up their mind! Biblical

What are your dreams for the future? Think about ways of helping to heal the world. Then respond in writing to this question:
• If *anything* were possible, what would you do to heal the world?

Dorothy Day co-founded the Catholic Worker Movement and became the most powerful advocate for the poor in the United States.

Baal, depicted **above,** was the storm god of the Canaanites and the Phoenicians. The prophet Elijah's experience of God in a tiny breeze suggests that Elijah's god was a very different sort of god.

faith calls for commitment, not standing on the sidelines being careful.

Read Luke 11:23.

3. Angry at Elijah's victory over the priests of Baal, Jezebel threatens his life, and he flees to the desert, where an angel tells him to journey on to Horeb (Sinai). There he takes shelter in a cave, and when God asks why he has come, Elijah, filled with self-pity, pours out his woe. There is no point in going on, he mourns; all Israel but he, Elijah, has abandoned God.

God bids Elijah to stand outside the cave. First Elijah hears a powerful wind, then he feels an earthquake, then he sees a fire, but God is not in them. At last a tiny breeze speaks to Elijah of the presence of God, and Elijah hides his face in shame at his own disbelief and in gratitude for the patience of God. God sends Elijah back to work, reminding him that he is *not* the only one who cares, that seven thousand Israelites have remained faithful.

Read 1 Kings 19:1–18.

Quaking with doubt

Have you ever put all your energy into a project and felt that no one seemed to care? That was Elijah's experience at Sinai. He had also bought the notion that God's power was to be seen only in big, showy successes.

4. Elijah starts back and on the way meets a young man named Elisha plowing in tandem with eleven other farmers behind pairs of yoked oxen. Elijah puts his cloak on the lad's shoulders as a sign of transferring his prophetic call, and Elisha joins him.

Read 1 Kings 19:19–21.

5. In the fifth story of Elijah, Ahab wants a vineyard belonging to a man named Naboth, but Naboth refuses him because it is ancestral land, which is always kept in the family. Ahab returns to his palace, lies down, and frets.

When Jezebel asks what is wrong, he tells her, and she replies in effect, "No problem." She instructs the elders in Naboth's town to proclaim a fast for some local calamity and, with Naboth present, to have false witnesses—probably bribed—accuse him of cursing God and the king. The penalty for this crime is death by stoning.

The plan is carried out, Naboth is killed, and because the property of a condemned person reverts to the king, Ahab gets his vineyard in a neat but nasty operation.

Read 1 Kings 21:1-16.

Windup toys?

"Where is God?" is our cry when we see such villainy—in history or today. But people are free to choose either good or evil. Unfortunately, when someone chooses evil, it often destroys the innocent. The answer to "I can't believe in a God who would let this happen!" is "God didn't; people did." The alternative to free will is to be like windup toys with God turning the key.

6. God sends Elijah to curse Ahab. Elijah tells the king that as dogs licked the blood of Naboth, they will lick Ahab's blood, Jezebel they will devour, and Ahab's line will disappear. The king is wildly contrite, and God reserves the bloody death for the king's son, Joram. But when Ahab dies in battle and attendants wash his chariot, dogs lick the blood that rinses out.

Read 1 Kings 21:17-29; 22:29-38.

The story of Naboth's vineyard tells how humans' free will can lead to villainy and injury to innocent persons.
Left: A vineyard in Israel

The storytellers may have chosen the image of a fiery chariot and horses to describe the fiery prophet Elijah.

Reflect on your life and list the people who have handed down their faith to you. In a brief statement, explain why these people felt that it was important to pass on their faith.

The good live on

Evil is often self-destructive, while good is usually fruitful and multiplies. Heinous villains like Ahab can be forgotten, while saints who lived as unknowns have emerged to be known all over the world. For example, the funny-looking little fat man who became pope in 1958 had everyone asking, "Cardinal who?" But when he died, the whole world, people of all faiths, called him "Good Saint John" (Pope John XXIII).

Similarly, a young French girl entered the Carmelite order at age fifteen, kept a journal of her spiritual life, and died at twenty-four. She was unknown except to her community, but she came to be heralded as one of the great modern saints—Saint Thérèse de Lisieux.

7. Elijah, aware that his life is over, goes to the Jordan River with Elisha. There he parts the water with his cloak, and the two cross over. In their last moments together, Elisha asks for a double portion of Elijah's spirit. Suddenly a flaming chariot with fiery horses comes between the two, and Elijah disappears in a whirlwind. Elisha watches, crying out. He tears his own cloak in half, strikes the Jordan's water with Elijah's cloak, and returns across the riverbed. For three days the fifty guild prophets of the region search for Elijah but fail to find him.
Read 2 Kings 2:1-17.

Because the two Books of Kings are really one narrative, the story of Elijah continues from one to the next without interruption.

Guild prophets

Many of Israel's prophets belonged to professional groups called *guilds* and worked for the court. These prophets were the king's messengers, not God's—and their messages were patriotic and nationalistic. Exceptional guild prophets like Samuel and Nathan were not afraid to oppose the kings—but they were the exceptions.

A flaming chariot?

Did the fiery chariot really appear and take Elijah to heaven? The storytellers had Elisha alone witness this event. The fiery chariot image may have been chosen to describe the fiery Elijah, who spoke out so fearlessly before the most powerful of the land—Ahab, Jezebel, the priests of Baal, and the entire court.

Eventually this tale gave rise to the belief that Elijah would return to announce the coming of the Messiah. This tradition was the basis for references to Elijah in the gospel stories of Jesus and John the Baptist. In Luke, the priest Zechariah announces that John the Baptist has " 'the spirit and power of Elijah' " (Luke 1:17). In the Gospel of John, John the Baptist is asked if he is Elijah. Later, Elijah appears at the Transfiguration of Jesus.

Read Luke 1:13,17; John 1:19-21; Luke 9:28-33.

The Elisha Stories

1. Elisha crosses the Jordan, returns to Jericho, and from that time on his story is an unbroken succession of wonders. He purifies Jericho's water supply, which has been causing deaths and miscarriages. He helps Israel win a war against Moab. He helps a widow avoid selling her children to pay her debts. He blesses a childless couple, and they beget a son. Later he raises this child from the dead in a manner that strangely suggests artificial respiration. He purifies poisoned stew and multiplies loaves.

Read 2 Kings 2:19-22; 3:13-25; 4:1-44.

The multiplication of loaves

The multiplication of loaves by both Elisha and Jesus were signs of God's loving concern for people. To see Elisha's act as a divine trick or Jesus' as proof of his divinity is to miss the point. Elisha's concern was for the people, not raising eyebrows; Jesus' identity as Son of God rests on his Resurrection, not on miracles.

In our own times, saints and prophets have multiplied food, healed people, and raised them from the dead. Thousands of people have "multiplied" food for the starving population in Africa. The sick have been healed by doctors, nurses, prayer groups, and spiritual healers. The dead have been "raised" by medics in ambulances, emergency rooms, and intensive care units in hospitals. Are these deeds less miraculous than the miracles in the Scriptures? Are the hungry less fed? the sick less healed? the dead less revived?

2. Naaman, the commander of the armies of Aram (Syria), is a leper. A young Jewish slave who belongs to Naaman's wife suggests that he go to Israel to see Elisha and be cured. When Elisha hears of Naaman's arrival, he sends for him and has a servant bid him to bathe in the Jordan seven times.

In a paragraph, respond to the following questions:
- Have you ever used the word *miracle* for an event you witnessed or for a solution to a situation you thought was unsolvable? Describe the event.
- Was the event a suspending of the natural order? Or did you use the word simply to say that the event was wonderful beyond expectations? or for lack of another word to describe a spooky experience?
- Did the event have anything to do with faith?

The prophet Elisha's multiplication of loaves was a sign of God's loving concern for people.

Respond in writing to one of the following sets of questions, related to the story of Naaman:
1. Who is the key figure in this story—without whom Naaman would not have been cured? Is every good thing that we do—no matter how small—sacred? Explain.
2. Do you agree with Elisha's approval of Namaan's need to attend worship in a pagan temple? Explain.

Naaman is insulted because he expected Elisha himself to perform a healing ritual. He starts home, but his servants protest: If he had been told to do something extraordinary, like fast or scourge himself, he would have done it. Why not give this simple request a try? Naaman does and is cured. A grateful and humbler Naaman returns to Elisha, believing in Elisha's God. He offers Elisha gifts, but the prophet refuses them. Then Naaman asks for earth from Israel to take home so that every day he can stand and pray to God on Israel's soil.

When Naaman leaves, Elisha's servant Gehazi—who considers Elisha foolish to reject the gifts—follows him. Pretending that Elisha has changed his mind, he trumps up a story, accepts the gifts, and returns home. Elisha questions Gehazi, who lies. But Elisha is aware of his misdeed, and the leprosy from which Naaman was cleansed now afflicts Gehazi.

Read 2 Kings 5:1-27.

A sensible convert

Naaman's humble conversion and request for earth from Israel on which he will pray is enormously moving. His embarrassed confession—that although now worshiping God, he will have to go to the pagan temple with his king—is sensible. Elisha understands and approves.

3. Because Ahab's son Joram, now the king of Israel, is exceedingly corrupt, God chooses Jehu, the commander of the armies, to replace him. At Elisha's instruction, Jehu races to the town of Jezreel, assassinates Joram, and has his body thrown into Naboth's vineyard—which is certainly poetic justice.

Told that Jehu is headed for the palace, Jezebel puts on her eye makeup, arranges her hair, leans on the palace windowsill, and as Jehu arrives, taunts him, "Murderer!" Three servants push her out the window, Jehu's chariot runs over her body, and the remains, as Elijah predicted, are eaten by dogs. Thus ends the story of Jezebel, the murderer of Naboth and the prophets of Israel.

In a horrendous bloodletting, Jehu kills Ahab's descendants and all the Baal worshipers in Samaria—and, the scriptural text says, God commends Jehu.

Read 2 Kings 9:1-37.

We must assume that here the writer simply accepted Jehu's bloody deeds as the custom in war and *presumed* that

A stone carving shows King Jehu of Israel prostrating himself before an Assyrian monarch. Historians prize this artwork from the ninth century B.C.E. because it is the oldest known portrait of an Israelite.

God was pleased. In time, the word *Jezreel* became a synonym for *butchery*, based on Jehu's bloodletting there.

In the history of the church, many horrendous deeds done in God's name were also thought to be justified. The Crusades, once praised, today have few defenders for the spilling of Jewish and Muslim blood.

4. Elisha dies and is buried, but even in his death the wonders continue. Some people burying a man spy a band of Moabite raiders, fling the body into Elisha's tomb, and flee. As the dead man's body touches Elisha's bones, it springs to life again.

Read 2 Kings 13:20–21.

This tale, like many about the early saints, is probably a legend that grew out of the loving embellishments of Elisha's story.

Many legends grew up around Elisha. Has this happened with our national heroes? In writing, briefly retell a couple of such legends from our national history.

The Prophets
Amos, Hosea, and Micah

If, at first glance, the prophets all seem alike, it is for a good reason: they were concerned about the same things. They called Israel and Judah to remember the God who saved them, who made a Covenant with them, who wanted them to return to it and be a blessing to the nations. The prophets' language and symbolic actions said long ago what still needs saying today. Reading about them can be exciting if we listen to pick up the clues for *now*. However, in other ways the prophets were not alike. Their personalities, backgrounds, ways of speech, and actions were very different—as we shall see.

The Prophet Amos: Israel—Guilty!

The time is about 750 B.C.E., and Jeroboam II is king in prosperous Israel. Amos, a farmer, is tending sheep when he hears God's call. His home is in Tekoa, a harsh, inhospitable place south of Jerusalem in Judah, but it is to Israel he is sent to preach. Like the land he comes from, Amos is harsh, blunt, and angry—a prophet who is said to roar like a lion. Four episodes and one famous passage will help us remember Amos.

1. Amos first appears at Bethel where, after the breakup of David's kingdom, Jeroboam I set up a golden calf. Amos's rustic garments are a sharp contrast to the worshipers' rich attire, but they recognize the voice of a prophet when he speaks. He names six of Israel's enemies who will fall because of their own evil deeds, and the people wait complacently to hear the name of the seventh. It is Israel!
Read Amos 1:1; 2:6–8; 3:1–2.

Religion reduced to ritualism
Amos is not some disgruntled yokel who resents the rich. He is angered by Israel's disregard for God's Law, so lovingly designed to protect the people—both the poor from going hungry and the rich from becoming greedy. The Law was given to Israel when it was called to be God's nation, but now Israel has become like other nations: wealth is in the hands of a few, justice has been corrupted, poor people are oppressed, and religion has been reduced to empty ritualism.

2. Amos goes to Samaria, the capital of the kingdom, and there he condemns the rich women of Samaria, comparing them to the fat cattle for which the region of Bashan is famous. He describes a scene like a movie set: Lying on their couches and ivory beds, the Samaritan women loll about and call to their husbands, "Bring us drinks!" They eat lamb and veal from the flocks, drink wine from bowls, and anoint their skin with perfumed oil—all at the expense of the poor! Amos warns that it will not last; the day will come when, like dead animals, they will be dragged away with hooks through their noses and deposited on the refuse heap outside the city.

Read Amos 3:9b–11,15; 4:1–3.

3. In an eloquent passage said to have been the favorite of Dr. Martin Luther King, Jr., Amos says that the LORD hates and abominates processions, sacrifices, and hymn singing that do not come from hearts out of which justice surges "like water, and goodness like an unfailing stream" (5:24).

Read Amos 5:21–24.

Ways of worship

God condemns not formal worship but empty worship. In the gospel story of the Samaritan woman at the well, Jesus further explains the difference.

Read John 4:19–24.

False worship continues to be a problem in modern times. Before the civil rights laws and desegregation, widespread discrimination existed in many Christian churches in the United States—with black people unwelcome in white churches and on occasion, in some Catholic churches, refused the sacraments.

4. Amos has visions of Israel's final fate, insights that come to him while he works. Watching locusts eating the crops, Amos sees that Israel is helpless to survive the fate it has brought upon itself. Seeing fire ravage the land during the dry season, he sees Israel being destroyed by the people's sin. Amos sees God measuring a crooked wall, about to collapse, with a plumb line, and he sees that Israel is also about to collapse. Referring to Israel as "Jacob," Amos pleads for Israel to God, who at first relents but finally says that Israel has *chosen* evil; God will leave it to its own destruction.

Read Amos 7:1–9; 8:4–12; 9:8b–15.

The prophet Amos envisioned Israel's fate in the image of a swarm of locusts destroying the crops.

Writing the Hebrew Scriptures

Many of the books of the Hebrew Scriptures were derived from earlier oral versions going back to the time when Israel was a people but not yet a nation. The written versions began later, when a simple system of writing Hebrew became available around 1000 B.C.E.—the time of David's and Solomon's reigns. The story of writing systems and the Bible is a fascinating one.

Picture writing

In a limited form, writing has been used for over thirty thousand years. In picture writing, realistically drawn figures represent an object, an event, or an idea. For instance, a picture of a hunter, a spear, and a bear can mean "The hunter killed the bear."

Many ancient societies developed writing systems based on picture writing. Over time, the written characters became simpler, but each one still represented a word or a phrase. Ancient writers had to learn hundreds, even thousands, of written characters in order to record even brief reports or letters.

Hieroglyphics

We associate the written characters called **hieroglyphics** with the Egyptians, who carved them on their temples and tombs beginning around 3000 B.C.E. Actually, the term *hieroglyphic*, meaning "of holy carvings," can refer to any system of highly stylized pictures—such as those once used by the Cretans in the Mediterranean or the Mayans in Central America.

The Egyptians added a special feature to writing by using some of their pictures to represent sounds. We will see in a moment what an important change that was!

Above: A cave painting dating from about 4500 B.C.E., found in the Saharan desert of North Africa
Right: An Egyptian hieroglyphic representing water
Facing page: This statue of an Egyptian scribe dates from about 2400 B.C.E. Because the ancient kings usually were not literate, their scribes could advance to positions of royal administrators and advisors.

Object represented	Canaanite, 1500 B.C.E.	Phoenician, 1000 B.C.E.	Hebrew, 700 B.C.E.	Greek, 600 B.C.E.	Modern English
ox head					A
house					B
palm of hand					K
water					M
human head					R

Alphabetic writing

Egyptian writing influenced the system that the Canaanites invented sometime before 1550 B.C.E.. The Canaanites also used pictures, but eventually they adopted a set of simply written characters—all of which represented consonants.

Think about what that meant: The written characters were linked to sounds, not words. Relatively few characters were needed; a couple of dozen could represent most of the sounds of speech. Now anyone who could learn a simple alphabet could write. Suddenly many more people could become professional writers, or scribes.

Hebrew writings

After the Israelites entered Canaan, they adopted both the language of the Canaan-

ites and their alphabetic writing system. The ease of using an alphabet made it possible to preserve the ideas of common people, not just royalty. In the Hebrew Scriptures, then, the words of unpopular prophets stand alongside those of powerful kings.

The Greek alphabet

The alphabet moved toward completion when the Greeks borrowed it from the Phoenicians, descendants of the Canaanites, around 800 B.C.E. Soon after, the Greeks took the final step of using some of the characters to represent vowel sounds. Hundreds of years later, the early Christian writers used the Greek alphabet and language to record the Gospel.

List some prophetic messages from our time. In writing, respond to these questions:
- Do people listen to modern prophecies?
- Why or why not? Give examples.

5. The prophets instill such awe that people usually tolerate them, even when the things they say are unpleasant. But at last Bethel's high priest, Amaziah, has had enough of Amos. " 'Off with you, visionary,' " he cries, accusing Amos of prophesying for money (7:12). Amos furiously denies this, delivers a stinging prediction of the fate of Amaziah and his family—and leaves. How long he stayed at Bethel is not certain, possibly two weeks, possibly two years.

Read Amos 7:12-17.

The Prophet Hosea and God: Betrayed!

A line of corrupt kings makes the last years of Israel (786 to 722 B.C.E.) a sordid tale. During this period, toward the end of Jeroboam II's reign, the prophet Hosea appeared. Hosea was from the northern kingdom and may have been a priest, but little is known about him save for his unhappy marriage. Gomer, the wife he loved, deserted Hosea for other lovers—as Israel deserted God for the Canaanite god Baal—and out of his experience Hosea found the words for his oracles to unfaithful Israel.

When Hosea speaks of himself and Gomer, he is telling Israel a parable of its own betrayal of God. If we keep this in mind, we will understand him clearly. The first three chapters of the Book of Hosea deliver his message. The remaining eleven chapters are fragments of oracles condemning Israel's sin.

1. As the book opens, God commands Hosea to take an unfaithful wife. That is, he is to take a wife who later will be discovered to be unfaithful. Looking back, Hosea sees his call to marry Gomer as prophetic. Without his own heartbreak, he could never have understood the magnitude of Israel's betrayal of God.

Hosea and Gomer have three children, to whom Hosea is told to give strange names. They probably have other names in actuality, but these names serve God's purpose as Hosea tells his story to the Israelites. The first child is named Jezreel—after Jehu's savagery at Jezreel. It is a synonym for "shameful butchery." This shakes Israel with revulsion and horror—just as naming a child Hiroshima or Auschwitz would shake us.

The second child is called Lo-ruhama, meaning "She is not pitied." Israel now begins to get the point of Hosea's

In the prophet Hosea's canticle of joy, God promises to bring peace and security to Israel, and to make a covenant for Israel even with the beasts and the birds.

message and is alarmed to hear these words from God, who has loved it so tenderly in the past.

Finally, the third child is named Lo-ammi, meaning "Divorce"! God will break the Covenant! A more threatening image could not exist. No matter how it sinned, Israel has always presumed that God's Covenant with it would stave off punishment.

Read Hosea 1:1-9.

> If Hosea were to name his children to symbolize corruption in our time or in our country, list what names you think he might choose.

2. Chapter 2 takes place in a divorce court, where Hosea testifies to Gomer's unfaithfulness and ingratitude. He is angry, and his plans for her punishment are harsh. She has forgotten that he gave her everything she ever had—grain, wine, oil, silver, and gold. He will take these things away! She has even credited her lovers with the gifts Hosea gave her! He will punish her until at last she is abandoned and forlorn and returns to him.

As Hosea's story proceeds and he speaks of his longing to forgive Gomer and be reunited with her, he fantasizes of days to come. Strangely, his voice seems to be replaced by the LORD's, as though God is speaking now without the pretext of the parable. God speaks hopefully of the future with Israel. God will lead Israel out into the desert and touch her heart again. God will remind her of their young love, and they will remarry. In a canticle of joy, God promises to make up for every deprivation Israel has suffered. Every good gift will be restored, and their children (the Israelites) will be renamed.

Read Hosea 2:4-25.

> Rewrite the language of Israel's punishment and restoration.
> * When will God take Israel into the desert?
> * What was the time of their young love?
> * How will they remarry?

Hosea is the first book to feature the relationship between God and Israel as a marriage and to use the language and images of marriage in describing it. To God, "infidelity" means betrayal of justice, compassion, integrity, or true worship. Gomer has merited the sentence of death for her adultery. What does this punishment foretell for Israel?

A loving husband

The puzzling verses 18 and 19 are based on a Hebrew wordplay. The Hebrew noun *baal* means "lord and master." Hosea is saying that when reunited, Israel will call God her loving husband, not her lord and master, and certainly not *Baal,* or "false master," which is used for the Canaanite god.

Read Luke 11:9-13.

God's capacity for love and forgiveness far exceeds our own.

> Respond in writing to the following questions:
> * Is the knowledge of God's willingness to forgive an encouragement to laxity and sin? Or does it inspire deeper love and gratitude?
> * What about the opinion that "a little fear never did anyone any harm!"—meaning that the fear of hell and damnation is an inducement to avoid sin. Is it? Explain your view.

3. As chapter 3 opens, God tells Hosea to seek out Gomer and pay a bride-price for her again—or a ransom should she be a slave or in the hire of Baal's priests as a temple prostitute. Then, after she has been through a period of waiting and faithfulness, he is to take her back.

Read Hosea 3:1-5.

The Prophet Micah: Ruin!

Micah is a minor prophet about whom little is known other than his birthplace, Moresheth, a town twenty miles southwest of Jerusalem. That nothing is recorded of his family suggests a humble origin, perhaps a family of farmers and artisans. His language is like Amos's, blunt and uncompromising, and his passionate condemnation of those who oppress the poor reveals an intimate knowledge of their sufferings. A contemporary of Amos, Hosea, and First Isaiah, Micah prophesied during the reigns of the last kings of Israel, Pekah and Hoshea, and the reigns of Jotham, Ahaz, and Hezekiah of Judah—around 750 to 700 B.C.E.

Micah's book has only seven chapters, not in chronological order, but it contains two passages that have become universally known: "They shall beat their swords into plowshares" (4:3) and the prophecy of Bethlehem as the birthplace of the Messiah (5:1). These passages are a good reason—and a good way—to remember Micah.

Respond in writing to these questions:
- Why does Micah call both kingdoms Jacob?
- Can you think of a similar nickname for our country?

1. Micah mourns the crimes of both kingdoms. Calling them both Jacob, he describes their sins, the ruin in store for them, and how he goes about the city lamenting them.

Read Micah 1:1-8.

Find and summarize in writing two news stories about scheming and manipulation that have, in the end, turned into complete ruin.

2. The rich, says Micah, lie in bed at night concocting schemes for depriving the poor. But the day will come when they will meet their undoing and say, " 'Our ruin is complete!' " (2:4).

Read Micah 2:1-4; 3:9-12.

3. Micah calls for Israel to repent and return to God, and believes that it can happen. He writes hopefully of the time when the nations will walk in the way of the LORD, a time of justice and peace when "they shall beat their swords into plowshares, and their spears into pruning hooks," and there will be no more training for war (4:3).

Read Micah 4:1-4.

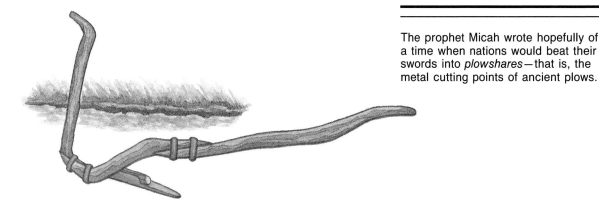

The prophet Micah wrote hopefully of a time when nations would beat their swords into *plowshares*—that is, the metal cutting points of ancient plows.

4. Micah foresees a day when a descendant of David's line will rise up and lead Israel to the reign of peace and justice. He will shepherd his flock by the strength of the LORD, and "his greatness shall reach to the ends of the earth; he shall *be* peace" (5:3–4a, emphasis added).

Read Micah 5:1–4a.

Some scholars consider Micah 6:8 the most powerful passage in his book. Write a one-paragraph response to this question:
- Is Micah 6:8 a complete statement of what God requires of Christians?

Israel in Exile

Even with Micah's warnings, nothing changes. Assyria strips Israel of territory, Pekah is murdered by Hoshea, and this last king of Israel refuses to pay tribute to Assyria. In retaliation, Assyria takes Samaria, deports its inhabitants to what today is Iraq, and installs foreign colonists. In the Second Book of Kings, the scriptural text describing the dismantling of the northern tribes ends tersely: ". . . the LORD put them away out of his sight. Only the tribe of Judah was left" (17:18).

Read 2 Kings 17:1–18.

Back to Judah: More Bad Kings and Isaiah

Now let us go back about 210 years to the death of Solomon, the ascent of his son Rehoboam to the throne, and the breakup of the united nation Israel. The southern kingdom of Judah loses control of the rich farmlands and the trade routes in the north and is left with little but hills, olive groves, and desertlike pasture. But hardship can be a deterrent to extravagance, and for a while the southern kingdom remains true to God.

The Kingdoms of Israel and Judah

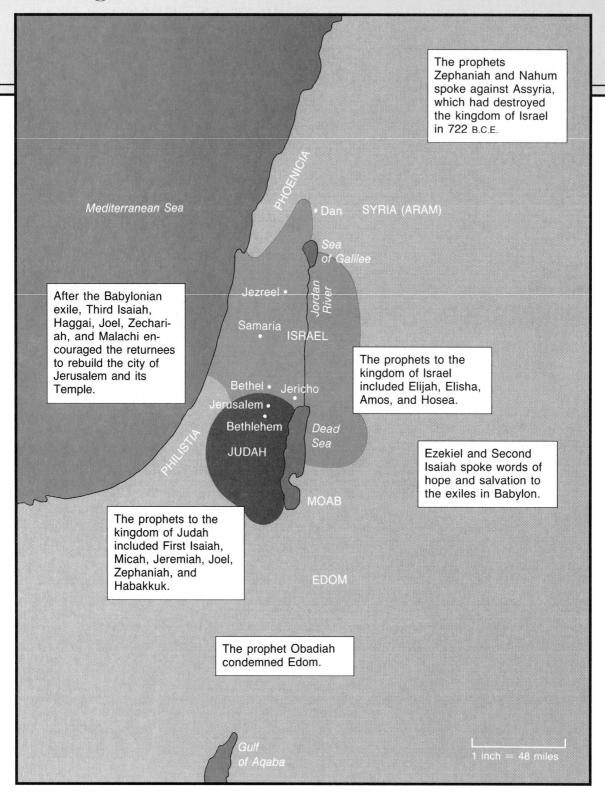

The prophets Zephaniah and Nahum spoke against Assyria, which had destroyed the kingdom of Israel in 722 B.C.E.

After the Babylonian exile, Third Isaiah, Haggai, Joel, Zechariah, and Malachi encouraged the returnees to rebuild the city of Jerusalem and its Temple.

The prophets to the kingdom of Israel included Elijah, Elisha, Amos, and Hosea.

Ezekiel and Second Isaiah spoke words of hope and salvation to the exiles in Babylon.

The prophets to the kingdom of Judah included First Isaiah, Micah, Jeremiah, Joel, Zephaniah, and Habakkuk.

The prophet Obadiah condemned Edom.

Mediterranean Sea

PHOENICIA

Dan SYRIA (ARAM)

Sea of Galilee

Jezreel

Jordan River

Samaria ISRAEL

Bethel Jericho

Jerusalem

Bethlehem

JUDAH

Dead Sea

PHILISTIA

MOAB

EDOM

Gulf of Aqaba

1 inch = 48 miles

Rehoboam and Abijam, his son, are unfaithful, but grandson Asa and great-grandson Jehoshaphat are reformers. Unfortunately, Jehoshaphat marries into the Ahab-Jezebel clan, and his son Jehoram marries one of their daughters, Athaliah, and *their* son Ahaziah is killed when he is visiting in the north. Athaliah succeeds him on the throne. She kills all the royal heirs but one, a princeling named Joash, who is hidden by the Temple priests until he is seven. He is then produced and crowned, and the traitorous Athaliah is executed.

Joash grows up to reign but is murdered. His son Amaziah is also murdered, and *his* son Azariah, also called Uzziah, succeeds to the throne. In the year of Uzziah's death, the prophet Isaiah has a vision of God in the Temple at Jerusalem.

Read 1 Kings 14:21-24,30-31; 15:1-3,7-15,23-24; and 22:41-47,51.

A few good kings

Judah's dreary tale of sacrilegious and murderous kings is hardly different from Israel's—with the exception of a few good kings. And the failure of Judah's kings is, like the failure of Israel's, due to a lack of faith and commitment.

The Prophets Isaiah

Isaiah of Jerusalem, or First Isaiah, is mentioned in only thirty-nine of the sixty-six chapters of his book, and of these only twelve chapters are from his hand. Why, then, is it called the Book of Isaiah? Is Isaiah the only inspired author? Are the other "Isaiahs" inspired prophets also? They are indeed.

The Book of Isaiah is the longest and most influential of the prophetic books, covering from two hundred to two hundred and fifty years, and some say that its contributors may number as many as seventeen. It is usually recognized as falling into three parts, the work of three principal authors: First Isaiah, or Isaiah of Jerusalem, who pleaded with Judah's kings and people before the Babylonian exile; Second Isaiah, who spoke during and at the end of the exile; and Third Isaiah, who was with the people when they returned. The entire collection is named after Isaiah of Jerusalem because he was the first and most important contributor. All the others shared his vision and seem to fall into the category of disciples.

Some of the Isaiahs wrote their own oracles, others had them recorded by scribes, but all shared a passionate desire to bring Israel back to God. The Book of Isaiah is a story of infidelity, suffering, repentance, and consolation for the people and of threats, condemnations, promises, and comfort by the prophets. This story is told not so much in events as in oracles and poetry. Isaiah contains some of the most beautiful language in the Bible, spoken by men who were geniuses and saints.

First Isaiah, Isaiah of Jerusalem

Isaiah ben Amos (*ben* meaning "son of") was probably a lad when the prophet Amos (no relation) preached in Israel. He lived in Jerusalem during the reigns of the kings Uzziah (Azariah), Jotham, Ahaz, and Hezekiah. He was married and the father of at least two sons, and he was familiar with the court and a counselor to kings. His Hebrew, the best in the prophetic writings, suggests a high-placed, well-educated—perhaps priestly—family background.

In the year of Uzziah's death, 742 B.C.E., the young Isaiah had a vision of God in the Temple at Jerusalem and answered God's call. Israel, to the north, had not yet been exiled, and Judah and Jerusalem, prosperous at last, had become idolatrous, self-serving, and greedy.

The threat of Assyrian invasion sets the scene for the forty years of First Isaiah's career. Israel and Judah, fearful of Assyria, are in danger of invasion, and Israel joins a coalition of neighboring states to stave it off. But Judah refuses to participate and tries to solve the problem by becoming a vassal of Assyria and paying tribute—all the while dreading the day when its "landlord" might want more.

"Sinful Nation"

The Book of Isaiah starts with five chapters of savage condemnation of Judah and Jerusalem for their infidelity and corruption—chapters broken briefly by a hope-filled passage about a day of reconciliation.

1. The prophet decries the greed and injustice of Jerusalem's leaders and warns that God will punish them if they do not change. Judah's business is to trust in God, he says—not to plot ways to avoid invasion. God will protect the people of Judah—but if they ignore the LORD, no treaty or alliance will be able to save them. Yet Judah and Jerusalem turn a deaf ear to Isaiah's warnings.
Read Isaiah 1:1-4,24-31.

Getting to the point

These first passages illustrate why God is angry and a prophet is needed. But why do five chapters precede the description of Isaiah's vision in the Temple, when God called him?

Isaiah's oracles are not in chronological order because the editors wanted the material to accent the message rather than set forth a calendar of events. Today's scriptural readings for the liturgy are similarly combined to give emphasis to a message.

Majesty and goodness

Characteristic of Isaiah's message is his insistence on the majesty and glory of God. He calls God the One to whom all nations and creatures owe existence and, therefore, obedience and honor. Seeing Judah and Jerusalem ignore God's majesty and goodness is the cause of his rage.

To illustrate this point, in Isaiah 1:2–3 the fidelity of the ox and the donkey is contrasted with the infidelity of the people. The dumb ox and the stubborn donkey, Isaiah says, recognize their master—but Judah does not. This passage is probably the source of the ox and the donkey in the Christmas manger scene; the Gospels do not mention them.

2. The LORD is a forgiving God, no matter how grave the sin. In one of the most familiar passages from Isaiah, God

In a passage reminiscent of the story about Balaam and his donkey, Isaiah says that even the stubborn donkey recognizes its master—but Judah does not.

promises forgiveness if Judah and Jerusalem will turn from injustice and idolatry. God can make sin that is as red as scarlet to be as white as snow, sin like bloodstained garments to be as white as new wool. A change of heart can show Judah and Jerusalem new ways to solve the dilemma with Assyria. Repentance and prayer can open them to the wisdom of God, who knows how things work.

Read Isaiah 1:18-20.

3. Isaiah describes the coming fall of Judah and Jerusalem and the people's deportation, first to Assyria and later to Babylon. Hero, warrior, judge, prophet, elder, captain, nobleman, counselor—all will be taken. Only the poor and the weak will be left in the land. Judah and Jerusalem "deal out evil to themselves," says God (3:9). Their leaders have devoured God's "vineyard," wresting loot from the poor, grinding down the helpless.

Read Isaiah 3:1-15.

Here God clearly states that Judah and Jerusalem are the authors of their own punishment.

4. Isaiah's language concerning the "daughters of Zion," or Jerusalem, makes Amos in his berating the women of Samaria sound as mild as Mary Poppins.

Read Isaiah 3:16-24a.

The wardrobe and beauty aids of the women of Jerusalem in the eighth century B.C.E. were not much different from today's except for the nose rings—and we may see them yet.

5. The Vineyard Song is like a country music ballad telling of a brokenhearted lover lamenting betrayal by a faithless sweetheart. It starts with Isaiah telling the story of a friend, but soon that text changes to the first person and the betrayed lover is revealed to be God, the unfaithful lover to be Judah.

Read Isaiah 5:1-7.

Isaiah's Vision: "Here I Am—Send Me!"

The five opening chapters of Isaiah are like a view from a wide-angle lens. They show us the broad picture of how things

Read Matthew 21:33–41. Jesus frequently quoted from the Book of Isaiah. In writing, compare the symbols and message of this parable with those of the Vineyard Song.

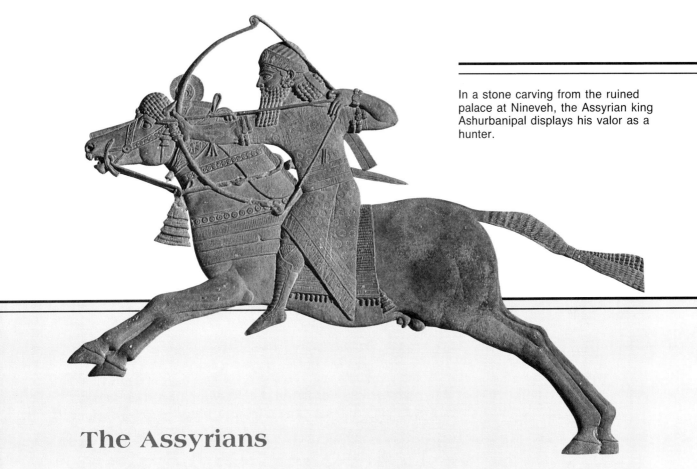

In a stone carving from the ruined palace at Nineveh, the Assyrian king Ashurbanipal displays his valor as a hunter.

The Assyrians

Sometime after 2000 B.C.E., history began to hear from the Assyrians, a Semitic group that took its name from its major city, Assur. The story of Assyria tells about alternating periods of domination and decline and about the struggle for leadership of the region against the rulers of Babylon, a city about two hundred miles southeast of Assur. Assyria was located in the area now belonging to northern Iraq.

While the Babylonians are best remembered as culture lovers, the Assyrians have a reputation as warmongers. They often tried to negotiate disputes with their neighbors, but more frequently their kings adopted tactics of terror that made the Assyrians feared and despised throughout the Near East.

The height of Assyrian domination came in the seventh century B.C.E. In the reign of Ashurbanipal (668 to 627 B.C.E.), the Assyrians ruled the largest empire in the world—including all of Iraq, Syria, Lebanon, and Jordan; much of Egypt; and some of Turkey.

Historians compare the Assyrians to the Romans. Like these later empire builders, the Assyrians became efficient administrators and war tacticians. They were one of the first nations to train a professional army and to deploy it in formal lines of battle. And just as the Romans borrowed much of their culture from the Greeks, the Assyrians embraced the Babylonians' language, literature, and religious, economic, and legal concepts. The Assyrians' lasting achievement was Ashurbanipal's library in his capital city, Nineveh. It contained twenty thousand tablets on such topics as history, astronomy, and mathematics.

At its peak, the Assyrian Empire was overextended, undefendable, and doomed to collapse. Fifteen years after Ashurbanipal's death, Nineveh fell to the Babylonians.

Seraphim, or angels, symbolized the divinity and mystery of God in the prophet Isaiah's vision in the Temple.

were. Now chapter 6 focuses on specific events and the people taking part in them: Isaiah's vision in the Temple, his status as a counselor to kings, and his efforts to make them listen to God.

1. In the Temple, probably on a feast day, Isaiah has a shattering experience of the All-holy One and sees God enthroned, surrounded by chanting angels (seraphim), with the divine presence filling the Temple. Overwhelmed by his own sinfulness, Isaiah fears that he will die because he has seen God. But an angel descends and with tongs picks a live coal from the altar and cleanses Isaiah's lips. When a voice cries out, " 'Whom shall I send?' " Isaiah answers, " 'Here I am, . . . send me!' " (6:8).
Read Isaiah 6:1-8.

"Holy, holy, holy!"
The angels' hymn in Isaiah 6:3 is sung daily in the Jewish morning service and is known to Catholic Christians as the Sanctus of the Mass. Seraphim with wings covering themselves have become a traditional symbol in religious art.

What you get is what you expect to see
God does not sit on a throne, nor do angels use tongs to pick up coals, but things appearing to visionaries seem to conform to their expectations—for Isaiah, the splendor and language of Temple worship. Saint Bernadette's "beautiful lady" at Lourdes dressed just as a little French Basque peasant would expect the Blessed Virgin to dress, and she spoke in Bernadette's dialect. Our Lady of Guadalupe appeared to Juan Diego in Mexico as a Mexican woman and spoke in his native tongue.

2. God has a strange errand for Isaiah. He is to make the hearts of the people sluggish—dull their ears and close their eyes to the message of God. The prophet asks how long this will continue and is told that it will be until exile.
Read Isaiah 6:9-13.

The heart grows harder
We always find biting irony in the passages that bid the prophets—and Moses in Exodus—to make the people blind, deaf, and hard of heart. God does not deny light and grace to anyone who seeks it, but hearts already hardened may only grow harder when the prophets speak.

The Immanuel Prophecies

God tells Isaiah to find the young king Ahaz outside of Jerusalem, where he is preparing for the siege by Syria (Aram) and Israel (Ephraim), who are in league against him. Isaiah tells Ahaz that faith in God, not elaborate preparations, will overcome these enemies and bids him to ask for a sign. But with a great show of false humility, the young king refuses. He has already abandoned God, and before the crisis is over, Ahaz will sacrifice his son by fire and become a vassal of the Assyrian king in return for protection. To curry favor, he will eventually replace God's altar in the Temple with one to an Assyrian god!

Isaiah angrily replies that Ahaz will get a sign, like it or not: a virgin will bear a son named Immanuel, meaning "God is with us." Assyria comes at Ahaz's invitation and seizes Judah's enemies, Israel and Syria. Again Isaiah's prophecy of a child uses words that describe more than some future Judaean king: This child will be given titles belonging only to the greatest of all kings, one who will rule forever.

Read Isaiah 7:1-14; 9:1-6.

The future king

Isaiah's oracle about the birth of Immanuel has been interpreted in various ways but never, at the time, as a messianic passage because belief in a messiah had not yet developed. The prophecy seems to have referred to the future birth of a perfect Davidic prince who would rule Judah in an age of peace and justice—thus "God with us."

Another interpretation sees the child as Hezekiah, Ahaz's son and successor, who was truly a religious king. The Hebrew word translated as "virgin" is, more correctly, "young woman," married or single. The word might refer to a young girl whom Ahaz married and added to his harem.

Christians have always believed that Isaiah's longing for the ideal king, through whom God would be revealed fully, was accomplished in Jesus' *Incarnation*—God united with them in Jesus.

Read Matthew 1:22-23.

Hezekiah: A Faithful King

Ahaz dies, and surprisingly, his son Hezekiah is faithful to God. He destroys the pagan shrines and even the bronze serpent of Moses (Numbers 21:8-9), which the people have begun to worship.

Read Isaiah 10:1-2. Like that of all the prophets, Isaiah's language condemning the sins of the greedy who victimize the poor can begin to sound like "the same old thing." In writing, answer these questions:
- Why do the prophets keep repeating themselves?
- Do you sometimes feel this way about today's prophets when they speak out about the poor and the homeless again and again?
- How can we overcome this hardening of sensitivity in ourselves?

In 722 B.C.E., the Assyrians obliterated the kingdom of Israel, exiling its leading citizens.
Above: An ancient stone carving shows an Assyrian warrior guarding a procession of exiles.

Consider Hezekiah's contentment that disaster will not strike until he is dead. Today some people are equally unconcerned about the danger to our planet. Respond to this question in writing:
• What is our obligation to future generations?

In the sixth year of Hezekiah's reign, the northern kingdom of Israel falls to Assyria, and its upper class, intellectuals, and artisans are deported into exile. When Hezekiah flirts with the idea of revolting against Assyria, Isaiah is told to warn him by walking around Jerusalem in a loincloth, as a symbol of how Judah will be stripped if it revolts.

In the fourteenth year of Hezekiah's reign, Assyria sacks the Judaean cities north of Jerusalem. Although Hezekiah sends Assyria the gold from the Temple in a bid for mercy, Assyria's army nevertheless camps outside of Jerusalem. When its general taunts God, the king at last turns to Isaiah to pray to the LORD for help, and Isaiah assures Hezekiah that the city will be saved. The invaders are struck by a plague and retreat—although a passage in Isaiah implies that a battle takes place first.

Read 2 Kings 18:1–12; 19:20–23a,32–36.

Several years later, when Hezekiah is visited by envoys from the princes of Babylon, he impulsively shows them the royal treasures. Isaiah is exasperated and predicts that after Hezekiah's death, Babylon will return to take Jerusalem, its wealth, and its people. Appallingly, Hezekiah contents himself with the knowledge that it will not happen during his lifetime!

Back to the wilderness

For all the praise heaped upon Hezekiah by the court historians, he is a disappointment, and Isaiah knows now that his ideal king will not appear until Jerusalem's greed and infidelity are purged. Only exile will force his people to remember their Covenant with God, their call to be a blessing on the nations.

First Isaiah in Conclusion

The remaining chapters of First Isaiah contain oracles against the pagan nations, an *apocalyptic* passage (concerning the end of the world), a passage taken from the Second Book of Kings, and further condemnations of Judah and Jerusalem. Then Isaiah prophesies of a time when everything will be changed. The deaf will hear, the blind see, the lowly find joy, and the poor rejoice. And "the tyrant will be no more" (29:20). First Isaiah ends with the prediction of Babylon's capture of Jerusalem and the removal of its people and its wealth into exile.

Then Isaiah disappears from sight. A legend tells of his martyrdom at the hands of King Manasseh, Hezekiah's wicked son, to whom Isaiah's daughter is supposed to be married, but scholars call it unfounded. Isaiah leaves as his heritage a passion for God and an unquenchable hope that Israel will one day reclaim its role as a light to the nations. The Isaiahs who follow him continue his work—begging Israel to be Israel.

Read Isaiah 29:17–24.

Answer the following in writing:
- What kind of person do you think Isaiah was?
- Would you have liked him? been afraid of him?
- Who in literature, film, or theater would you liken to him?
- Who would you cast in the role of Isaiah in a film or play?

For Review

1. Who were the prophets?

2. How does Israel's king Jeroboam break the Law of God? Why does he do so?

3. Against what dangers did the prophets warn Israel?

4. In the stories about Elijah, the obedience of the prophet is contrasted with what?

5. Where does Elijah meet God? What form does God take?

6. How does the author describe the prophet Amos?

7. In the Book of Amos, does God condemn formal worship? Explain.

8. Out of what experience does the prophet Hosea find words for his oracles?

9. What two passages is the Book of Micah remembered for?

10. How many writers may have contributed to the Book of Isaiah?

11. Explain the image in Isaiah that is probably the source of the ox and the donkey in the Christmas manger scene.

12. Describe the strange errand that God has for Isaiah. Explain the reasoning behind it.

13. What is the meaning of the name *Immanuel?*

8

Exile:
Losing Jerusalem, Life in Babylon

THIS chapter is like a weaving with many threads that meet and cross one another to form a great plaid. The warp threads—going up and down—are the books of the prophets, who spoke the word of God to the kings. The woof threads—going across—are the stories of the kings, who (with one exception) rebuked the prophets, ignored God's word, and led Judah into exile and Jerusalem to destruction. The books of the minor prophets add to the chapter's pattern, and in the account of the Babylonian exile, still other prophetic voices are heard. To think of these books and stories as interweaving in this way may help to make them all of a piece, rather than seeming hopelessly haphazard and confusing.

What does each of the books tell us?

- The Second Book of Kings tells of the remaining kings and of Judah's two journeys into exile, ten years apart.
- The Book of Jeremiah recounts that prophet's call, his futile struggle to make the kings listen to God's message, his persecution, and the fall of Judah and Jerusalem—followed by exile.
- The Book of Lamentations is a group of five poems expressing Judah's suffering in exile.
- The books of the minor prophets Zephaniah, Nahum, and Habakkuk speak briefly on other issues of the time.
- The Book of Ezekiel tells of the call of another major prophet, his pantomimes of God's message, and his struggles to lead the Israelites to repentance and renewal.
- The Book of Baruch, although set in Babylon, was actually written four centuries later, during the Greek occupation of Palestine between the first and second century B.C.E., and purports to be an encouragement to the Babylonian exiles to keep faith and to live in hope of eventual freedom.
- Second Isaiah is filled with hope and expectation of the return to Jerusalem from Babylon and of the reign of peace.

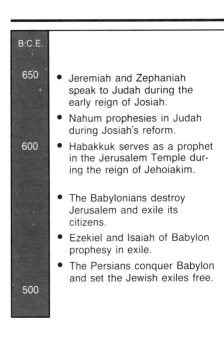

B.C.E.

650
- Jeremiah and Zephaniah speak to Judah during the early reign of Josiah.
- Nahum prophesies in Judah during Josiah's reform.

600
- Habakkuk serves as a prophet in the Jerusalem Temple during the reign of Jehoiakim.

- The Babylonians destroy Jerusalem and exile its citizens.
- Ezekiel and Isaiah of Babylon prophesy in exile.
- The Persians conquer Babylon and set the Jewish exiles free.

500

The people of Judah found themselves exiled in Babylon, the major cultural and commercial city of the Near East in the sixth century B.C.E. *Facing page:* The sun sets on the Euphrates River, on which the ancient city of Babylon lay.

The Last of the Kings

King Manasseh—who rules Judah from about 692 to 642 B.C.E. and is hopelessly enslaved by Assyria—abandons God, puts pagan shrines in the Temple, offers his son as a sacrifice, and drenches Jerusalem in blood. His son Amon, who succeeds him, is assassinated, but his grandson Josiah, who becomes king around 640 B.C.E. at the age of eight, grows up to be one of Judah's great reformers. The prophets Jeremiah, Zephaniah, Nahum, and Habakkuk are all contemporaries of Josiah.

Josiah: The Reformer-King

During Josiah's repair of the Temple, a copy of "the book of the law," probably part of Deuteronomy, is found. When the king hears it read, he is appalled that Judah has abandoned the Law of God so shamelessly. After leading the people in a renewal of the Covenant and a celebration of the Passover, Josiah commences his reforms. First he destroys pagan altars and executes pagan priests and temple prostitutes. Then, driving north, he reclaims territory lost to Judah for a hundred years—and Israel, it seems, will be its old self again! Assyria, now past its zenith, is fighting for its life far away.

Unfortunately, the reform does not touch the hearts of the people, and it is clear that Isaiah's prophecy was right—only suffering will make them repent and turn again to God.

Read 2 Kings 21:1-6,16-24; 22:1-20; 23:15,19-25.

Sin deafens

Josiah's reforms fail because the people are too deeply immersed in greed and idolatry to heed his call to return to God. When Jeremiah later rebukes one of Josiah's sons, the wicked king Jehoiakim, he will cite Josiah's integrity and contrast it with Jehoiakim's self-indulgence.

Read Jeremiah 22:13-17.

Jeremiah: A Reluctant Prophet

Jeremiah is one of the great tragic figures of the Bible. He agrees to God's call only reluctantly, because God promises to help him. But when all his missions fail, when his enemies multiply and his life is threatened, he accuses God of tricking him. Torn between despair and the belief that Israel will one day return to God, Jeremiah is a figure of monumental faith. In spite of repeated failures, he loves and serves God all his life—even as he is dragged off to Egypt to an unrecorded death. He lived from about 650 to 570 B.C.E.

The Book of Jeremiah is a combination of poetry, prose, and biographical material combined by the editors in thematic rather than chronological order. This means that writings treating similar themes are found together, even if they describe events that occurred at different times.

Jeremiah ben Hilkiah was born in the village of Anathoth, just north of Jerusalem. He came from a priestly family, possibly descended from David's trusted priest Abiathar. We are not told where he is when God calls him, but it is an interior experience, profound and frightening, and he is probably about twenty years old. Unlike First Isaiah, Jeremiah is not eager to respond. When he cries out, "I am too young!" God tells him not to fear: God will put the right words into Jeremiah's mouth. And Jeremiah gives in.

Jeremiah has two visions: He sees a branch of a "watching-tree"; God is watching to see if Judah and Jerusalem will change. He also sees a boiling cauldron tipped on a hearth in the north; God will summon kingdoms from the north to be poured out over Judah if it does not change. These warnings, says God, will outrage people and create enemies, so Jeremiah must stand fast!

Read Jeremiah 1:1–19.

Try to enter into Jeremiah's reluctance to receive God's call. In writing, describe a call to action or a decision about which you were uncertain. How did you respond and why?

The almond tree is the first fruit tree to blossom in the spring, a fact that may contribute to its being called "the watching-tree," suggesting that it does not sleep during the winter.
Left: A grove of almond trees blossoms in the hills between Bethlehem and Hebron.

The watching-tree

The watching-tree passage is based on an untranslatable pun on the Hebrew words for *almond tree* and *watching*, which are similar. This pun must have occurred to Jeremiah when his eyes fell on an almond tree. An example in English would be a pun on the words *write* and *right*. If Jeremiah were to see God penning a message of warning to Judah, he might say, "I see that you are *writing* [a message]," to which the answer would be, "Yes, I am *righting* [a wrong]."

Josiah Dies—
Enter the Detestable Jehoiakim

When Josiah rides off to foil an Egyptian invasion, he is killed, and his body is brought back to Jerusalem amid great mourning. The victorious Egyptians exile his eldest son and rename another of Josiah's sons Jehoiakim, who becomes the contemptible monarch whom Jeremiah despises and confronts.

Early in Jehoiakim's reign, the Babylonian king Nebuchadnezzar II challenges Egypt for control of the eastern Mediterranean. Jehoiakim sides with Egypt, but Jeremiah is convinced that God will use Babylon to punish Israel for its unrepentant heart.

Read 2 Kings 23:28-30,34-35.

1. Jeremiah sees the coming destruction of Jerusalem as the reverse of the Creation. Where once a formless waste was transformed into a garden, his vision now is of an "uncreation"—at the hands of "the boiling cauldron from the north," Babylon.

Moreover, God warns, Judah and Jerusalem are building their punishment into their crimes. When God bids Jeremiah to search the city for an honest person, he can find none. The people have filled their houses with loot taken from the poor and have grown rich and fat—all the while winking at evil. Their time is coming!

Read Jeremiah 4:11-12,23-26,18 (in that order); 5:1-5, 26-29.

When all else fails, read the instructions

To ignore God's instructions for how things work is to ask for the consequences. Similarly, every car manual tells us that driving a car without oil in it will ruin the engine. Yet every day, car engines burn out from lack of oil, and the carmaker who wrote the manual cannot be held at fault.

Jeremiah's prophecies were not predictions of what was bound to happen but of what *could* happen if people and nations continued to be blind, deaf, and hard-hearted. Furthermore, this was the only language that could have startled Judah and Jerusalem into changing, if they were willing. Alas, they were not.

2. God tells Jeremiah to preach in the Temple, and Jeremiah warns his listeners that even the Temple does not assure God's presence. Unless they stop oppressing aliens, shedding innocent blood, and worshiping idols, unless they treat their neighbors with justice and show mercy to widows and orphans, they will be lost. How can they steal, murder, commit adultery and perjury, worship strange gods—and still believe that they are safe?

Outraged, the priests and court prophets start a riot and call for Jeremiah's death. When the princes and elders come to investigate, they remind the crowd that the prophet Micah warned Hezekiah in his time, but far from condemning the prophet, the king heeded him and the city was saved. Fortunately, Jeremiah is whisked away while the ruckus is being quelled, and he escapes alive.

Read Jeremiah 7:1-15.

In the Gospels, the Temple is again called " 'a den of thieves.' " Who says that?

Read Matthew 21:12-13.

3. Outraged at Jerusalem's infidelity, God ridicules the idols the people honor—gods fastened with nails lest they totter, carried because they cannot walk, and able to do neither good nor evil. They are nothings. By contrast, the one God is true, living, eternal, the maker of the earth, the stretcher of the sky, the mover of the waters. God's inheritance is Jacob, God's tribe is Israel, and the LORD of Moses is God's name; *there is no other God.*

Read Jeremiah 10:1-16.

God is the world's One and Only

The author of this poem, perhaps Jeremiah, perhaps the writer known as Second Isaiah, is witty, imaginative, and lyrical and for the first time in the Bible names the LORD as the one God. To Israel, the LORD has up to now been the only God who mattered, superior to all others, but not the only God. Now the writer denies that other gods exist; those "gods" are powerless pieces of carved wood.

Jeremiah was the first prophet to ridicule the idols that the people too often worshiped.
Above: An ancient mold and a modern casting of a statue of a Canaanite goddess

Respond to one of the following:
1. List some of today's "idols" and write an essay pointing out their limitations.
2. In a crisis—when truth, fairness, character, and compassion are needed—how do we acquire them? Give an example.

4. Next, God sends Jeremiah to a potter's house to watch how, when a piece turns out badly, the potter smashes it. God asks, Cannot God do the same to Israel?

Jeremiah is told to buy a flask and take some of the leaders of Jerusalem to the Potsherd Gate, where broken pottery is thrown away. He must smash the flask and say that just so God will smash the city—unless the people repent and turn from their sins.

Read Jeremiah 19:1–6,10–11.

5. Accusing Jeremiah of blasphemy, a court prophet has him beaten and put in stocks overnight. Jeremiah cries out that God has duped him; he will never mention God's name again! But he cannot hold it in; it becomes like a fire burning in his heart. People whisper against him and try to entrap him, but when Jeremiah realizes that his enemies have failed, he shouts jubilantly, "The LORD is with me!" Just as quickly, his mood plummets, and he utters his most horrific cry of despair and curses the day he was born.

Read Jeremiah 20:1–18.

Who else was sent to teach God's ways? Who else was despised, plotted against, and entrapped? And who else finally cried out to God in near despair, " 'Why have you forsaken me?' " (Mark 15:34).

"In me there is darkness . . ."

A prayer written in prison by Dietrich Bonhoeffer, the Lutheran pastor who was executed by the Nazis in 1945, gives us words for such times of darkness as Jeremiah suffered. On Christmas two years before his death, he wrote these lines, arranging them on paper in the form of a Christmas tree:

Oh God,

. . . .

In me there is darkness,
But with you there is light;
I am lonely, but you do not leave me;
I am feeble in heart, but with you there is help;
I am restless, but with you there is peace.
In me there is bitterness, but with you there is
patience;
I do not understand your ways,
But you know the way for me.

1. Describe in writing the darkest moment of your life. What made it so? Who made it so? Write a note to someone who was involved, telling them how you felt. Or write a note of thanks to someone who helped you through that time.
2. Have you ever been angry at God? Write a letter to God telling why you were angry, how you felt, whether the emotion passed, and if not, why not.

The Lutheran pastor and martyr Dietrich Bonhoeffer, who was executed by the Nazis in 1945

Judah's First Exile

After Babylon defeats Egypt, Jehoiakim has no choice but to become its vassal. But several years later, he foolishly withholds tribute from Nebuchadnezzar, and in retaliation Babylon attacks Jerusalem. Jehoiakim dies, probably assassinated, and is given "the burial of an ass," says Jeremiah—dragged like a dead carcass and thrown on the refuse heap (22:19).

Jehoiakim's son Jehoiachin reigns for three months, until he is exiled to Babylon with his court and many professionals, craftsmen, and soldiers.

Read 2 Kings 24:1-14; Jeremiah 22:13-19.

1. Sometime after the exiles arrive in Babylon, Jeremiah writes a letter telling them to settle down, build houses, plant gardens, and find spouses for their children. They must increase in number and promote the good of the city, he writes, for one day God will bring them home. Exile is for purgation, not annihilation, so they can return to the role God chose for them long ago—God's witness before the nations.

Read Jeremiah 29:1-14.

Jeremiah's use of seventy years as the span of the people's exile means only "a long time."

2. Zedekiah, who succeeds Jehoiachin in Judah, is a weak man, curious to hear Jeremiah but afraid to follow him. He too is a vassal of Babylon, and when he stupidly takes part in a revolt, Babylon again besieges Jerusalem. Zedekiah asks Jeremiah if God will rescue the city as was done in the time of Hezekiah, and the answer is that Jerusalem must go willingly into exile or it will be destroyed. God tells Jeremiah to wear a wooden yoke to symbolize Jerusalem's fate should it refuse. A court prophet, insisting that Jerusalem will break the yoke of Babylon, destroys Jeremiah's. Now, says God, Jerusalem will wear an iron yoke.

Read Jeremiah 27:1-2,6-8,12-15. The first verse contains an error: read the name *Zedekiah* for *Jehoiakim.*

Prophet and traitor?

Jeremiah will be accused of treason and imprisoned, and attempts will be made on his life—which is not surprising for a man who says that surrender to the enemy is better than fighting for king and country. But God wants Judah

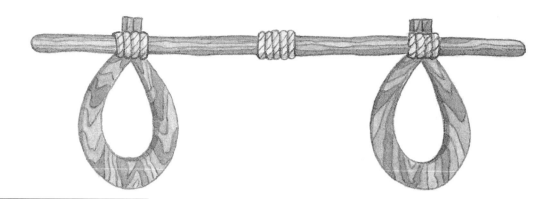

Jeremiah wore a wooden yoke like the one shown above. Ordinarily farmers used a yoke to harness a work animal to the plow—making it an apt symbol of oppression.

to repent, and the purification of exile is the only means left, as Isaiah said long before.

3. On the way to his village, Jeremiah is arrested and accused of deserting to the Babylonians. He is beaten and thrown into prison, and there God speaks to him of the future return of the people from exile. At that time God will make a new covenant with the people, writing the Law on their hearts instead of on stone tablets; God will forgive their evil and remember their sin no more.

Read Jeremiah 31:31–34.

4. When the nobles at court insist that Jeremiah's call for surrender is demoralizing the army, they throw him into a muddy cistern normally used for collecting rainwater. An Ethiopian courtier discovers him there and, with the permission of the wavering king, secretly saves Jeremiah.

When the king asks Jeremiah for God's latest message, he is told to surrender to Babylon or his wife and children will be captured, the city destroyed, and he himself executed. Poor Zedekiah—his response is to make Jeremiah promise not to tell that they have talked! So much for a man who prefers annihilation to doing the unpopular thing.

Read Jeremiah 38:1–28.

Jerusalem Captured

Finally time runs out for Jerusalem, its fainthearted king, and the people. The Babylonians return, breach its walls, and torch its buildings; the Temple is destroyed, and the people are deported. Only the poor of the land and a handful of citizens who favored surrender are left. Zedekiah tries to flee but is captured, brought to Nebuchadnezzar, and forced to see his sons slain, after which he is blinded and sent to Babylon in chains.

Read Jeremiah 39:1–10.

1. Because his efforts to achieve Jerusalem's surrender are known to the Babylonians, Jeremiah is not taken into exile. He joins the temporary governor of Jerusalem, Gedaliah, and when Gedaliah is assassinated, the remaining survivors beg Jeremiah to ask God what they should do. Jeremiah prays for ten days, then gives them God's message: They are to remain in Jerusalem, where they will be safe. "You lie!" they shriek, insisting that this is not God's word but that of Jeremiah's attendant, Baruch, who wants them slain. They flee to Egypt, taking with them Jeremiah and Baruch—whether willingly or by force is unknown.

Read Jeremiah 39:11–14; 42:1–12; 43:1–7.

2. In Egypt, God has Jeremiah tell the refugees that their flight has brought them no safety: Nebuchadnezzar will ravage Egypt and, like a shepherd picking lice from his cloak, through him God will "delouse" Egypt of these stubborn Israelites. And the refugees respond as usual, " 'We will not listen to what you say in the name of the LORD' " (44:16). Few, if any of them, will return to Jerusalem.

With that, Jeremiah disappears. No one knows what happens to him. One tradition holds that he is murdered, which is possible, although there is no record of it. But Baruch returns to Judah as God has promised.

Read Jeremiah 43:8–13; 44:7–10,15–28; 45:1–5.

The gospel of health and wealth

The rationale for the refugees' idolatry in Egypt was the good life; wealth, luxury, and ease were mistaken as signs that they were doing right.

In the story of Saint Lawrence, a third-century deacon and martyr, the Roman emperor Valerian believes the Church to be wealthy and wishes to finance his army with its wealth. He demands that Lawrence turn over the Church's treasure to him. Lawrence replies that the Church indeed is rich but that he will need three days to collect its treasure. At the end of the three days, Lawrence leads the emperor's official to where he has gathered together the blind, the lame, and the crippled, the lepers, orphans, widows, and maidens. "Here are the treasures of the Church," he says. Needless to say, Lawrence is martyred for his little joke.

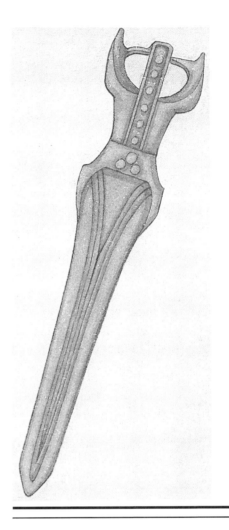

The slaying of king Zedekiah's sons and the assassination of the governor Gedaliah suggest the high level of violence in biblical times.

Write a character sketch of Jeremiah.
* Is he like a person you know or know about?
* What is his most outstanding trait?
* Whom would you cast as Jeremiah in a movie?
* What will you remember about him?

Zephaniah: The Remnant

For almost a century after First Isaiah, there is no prophetic voice in Judah. Then Zephaniah speaks in about 630 B.C.E., during the early reign of Josiah, a few years before Jeremiah. Zephaniah's book is probably only a small part of the total works written by him and his disciples.

Zephaniah's three short chapters tell of "the day of the LORD," a time of judgment not only for Judah's enemies but for the unfaithful of Judah and Jerusalem as well. On that day, the guilty will be judged for their deeds, not for their religious affiliation.

Zephaniah introduces an idea only briefly touched on by Isaiah and Hosea: The unfortunate and impoverished of the land will become God's **remnant**, a new kind of "chosen" from whom God will build the new Israel.

Read Zephaniah 2:3; 3:11-13.

The humble remnant

Zephaniah's words would have sounded like heresy to the upper-class citizens of the time. The poor were considered sinners because of their poverty. It made it impossible for them to keep the laws about washing, contributing money, and offering sacrifices—because they could not buy animal offerings. If reduced to begging, people were outcasts; if ill, they were considered unclean. To the respectable Temple-going citizens, the poor were beyond the reach of God.

Such words were as shocking to the self-satisfied citizens of Jesus' time as they were to the people in the days of Zephaniah—and as they are to some people today.

Read Luke 6:20-26.

The prophets Zephaniah and Nahum spoke about the fall of the Assyrian capital, Nineveh. Zephaniah declared that the city would become a lair for beasts.

Nahum: Nineveh Will Fall!

Nahum, a little-known prophet, probably prophesied around 612 B.C.E., a few years before Nineveh, the capital of Assyria, fell to the Babylonians.

As Nahum's book opens, Josiah's reform is in full swing, Nahum is jubilant because God is about to destroy Judah's fiercest enemy, and he assumes that all will be well in Judah. Assyria has bathed the Near East in blood for three hundred years, devising unspeakable butchery for its captives. Nahum—rejoicing that God will use Babylon as the instrument to punish Assyria—gloats over his vision of its vanquished soldiers, their shields scarlet with blood, and Assyria's queen and her ladies moaning with grief. Little does Nahum dream that Judah will also become corrupt and that

God will use the same Babylon as an instrument for its purification.

Read Nahum 2:2-10.

Habakkuk: Why, God, Why?

Habakkuk was probably a professional prophet in the Jerusalem Temple during the reign of Jehoiakim—609 to 598 B.C.E. Beyond this, details are missing. But he had a marvelous way with words and wrote his short book at God's bidding after a vision in the Temple.

In chapter 1, verses 2 to 4, Habakkuk complains to God that he has prayed endlessly that Judah, corrupted under the contemptible Jehoiakim, be punished for its injustice and violence. But his prayer has not been heard. Now he wants to know why. When God replies that his prayer has been heard and Judah will indeed be punished—by Babylon—Habakkuk is appalled. An exchange between Habakkuk and God finally leaves the prophet praising God and humbled by his own ignorance of divine ways.

Read Habakkuk 1:1-17; 2:1-20; 3:16-19.

Why?

Habakkuk's is the first book to introduce the question Why? Why, if God is present, does God seem not to be? Why, when God says that prayer will be answered, does it seem not to be? Why does God not stop human evil? Even Jeremiah did not ask these questions. Habakkuk's questioning was a bold step forward in the people's understanding of God: It is all right to challenge and question God.

Lamentations: Judah Grieves

The Book of Lamentations is a collection of five hymns of grief composed shortly after the fall of Jerusalem. Although not written by Jeremiah, these dirges have been attributed to him because the writer sounds like Jeremiah. Each chapter is a separate poem, perhaps by a separate author. The first, second, and fourth chapters are funeral laments for the lost mother, Jerusalem. The third chapter tells of the author's suffering and of the hope that one day God will bring it to an end. The fifth chapter is the voice of a people admitting their guilt, expressing their hope, and praying for restoration. The Book of Lamentations seems to have been a grieving process for Judah—recalling its agony, lamenting, and asking for healing.

Read Lamentations 1:1-7,10,18-20.

Habakkuk was the first prophet to introduce the question Why? Why do prayers sometimes seem to go unanswered?

Imagine that Habakkuk is a friend of yours who has asked why some misfortune has happened to him. In writing, explain what you would say to him.

The Jews of the Dispersion

Beginning with the eighth century B.C.E., many Jews left Israel, victims of the power games played by the Assyrians, the Babylonians, and the Persians. Jewish refugees and deportees settled in cities around the Near East and became artisans and merchants. Scholars estimate that in Jesus' time, about 10 percent of the Roman Empire's population were Jews—four million living outside Israel.

Some Jewish communities were large, prosperous, and long-lived, like the group remaining in Babylon after the exile, who survived into the Middle Ages. The largest of all the Jewish communities was in the Egyptian city of Alexandria, a cultural and literary hub of the Near Eastern world. In the last centuries before Christ, its Jewish population grew to nearly one million.

In Alexandria, in the third century B.C.E., Jewish scholars began work on the *Septua-gint*, the Greek translation of the Hebrew Scriptures and today the oldest version in existence. According to legend, seventy-two scholars worked independently on separate translations for seventy-two days—and this resulted in seventy-two identical texts. The name of this version comes from the Latin term *septuaginta*, meaning "seventy."

Within the Alexandrian community, as elsewhere, many Jews chose to abandon the Law and adopt the local lifestyle. Others kept the Sabbath and the dietary laws, continued to regard Jerusalem as their spiritual capital, contributed to the upkeep of the Temple, and made pilgrimage there.

At the same time, Jewish communities built *synagogues*, where worship, education, and traditional celebrations could take place. The synagogue, a prominent part of life for Jews, also played a vital role in the origin of Christianity. In the Gospels we find Jesus

attending synagogue services and teaching there.

But the Jews of the Dispersion often paid a heavy price for their clannish ways and unusual customs. Mob attacks on Jews—called *pogroms* in modern times—were reported in the records of Alexandria and Rome.

As the gods of the ancient world lost their attraction, people hungered for a more spiritual and moral religion, and many were attracted to Judaism. The growth of a large Jewish population in Roman times suggests that Jews earnestly pursued their mission to reveal the one God to the world and that they actively sought—and received—converts.

Potential believers could not always make a full commitment to Judaism, however—perhaps because of the stigma of circumcision or the fear of persecution. Such seekers became an eager audience for the early Christian missionaries, who did not demand compliance with the Jewish regulations. Saint Paul gained many converts with his teaching that salvation depended on faith in Jesus Christ, not on obedience to the Law.

The Dispersion continued to be the determining element in Jewish history for many centuries, until the modern state of Israel was formed in 1948. As the ancient prophets saw it, the infidelity of the Jews caused the Dispersion, but in time it proved the durability of their faith—which survived the destruction of both nation and Temple and became one of the most creative and moral forces in history.

Baruch: Keep the Faith!

The Book of Baruch was written by several authors sometime between the second and first centuries B.C.E.—although its setting is the Babylonian exile several hundred years earlier. In the tradition of attributing late works to Israel's famous men—for example, the Book of Proverbs to Solomon, the Psalms to David, Lamentations to Jeremiah—this book is attributed to Baruch. The details of life in exile were probably taken from the authors' familiarity with the Book of Jeremiah. Evidently meant to be read at liturgical gatherings, the purpose of the book was to encourage the faith of the Jews of the Dispersion and to nourish their hope for return.

Three chapters constitute a prayer for forgiveness of the sins of Judah and Jerusalem and a reminder of God's promise that the people will return. Another section praises the wisdom of the Law and personifies Jerusalem as a mother, first consoling her children and then promising them reunion with God in a time of peace and tranquility.

The letter from Jeremiah in chapter 6 is not the one from the Book of Jeremiah (Jeremiah 29:1–23) but a powerful and amusing ridicule of the idols that surround the Jews in these far-off lands. These idols have tongues smoothed by woodworkers and covered with gold and silver, but they cannot speak. They are decked out in garments like men, wrapped in purple, but are not safe from moths or corruption. Lamps are lighted for them, but they cannot see. If they fall to the ground, they must be picked up. They need dusting; their faces are black from the smoke of candles, and when the bats and the swallows light on them . . . ! The point is this: Do not be duped, you faraway sons and daughters of the one God; there is no other God but the LORD!

Read Baruch 6:1–22.

The Exile and Its Prophets

Ezekiel: Prophetic Pantomimes

Ezekiel was born in Jerusalem during the last years of the city's independence. Jehoiakim was king, and the threat of invasion by Babylon was ever-present. When the city fell for the first time, in 597 B.C.E., Ezekiel is thought by some scholars to have been one of the exiles to Babylon. Others believe that he stayed in Jerusalem, predicted the city's ruin, and was taken away in the second exile, ten years later, following the capture of Zedekiah. The text of the Book of Ezekiel is one of the most difficult in the Bible, and both opinions about his exile find support, but we will assume that he stayed in Jerusalem until the second deportation.

Unlike the other prophets, Ezekiel's gifts were not writing and poetry but drama, symbol making, and storytelling. With one bizarre performance after another he tried to convince the Jerusalemites that their rescue was *not* at hand, Jerusalem would *not* be saved, and exile would last a long time. But they continued to believe that because they were the chosen people, God would come charging in to save them. Repentance came only when, much later, they recognized that their sins had brought about the loss of the city and the Temple, that *they* had been the enemy—not Babylon. The last chapters of Ezekiel's book are a message of hope for the exiles—after they have come to true remorse.

1. The call of Ezekiel seems to have had two parts. Surely he was called by God in Jerusalem, but chapter 1 describes another episode, in Babylon. Scholars believe that both events occurred.

Ezekiel sees a bright light in a chariot drawn by four winged creatures, each with four faces—those of a lion, an ox, an eagle, and a man. Each chariot wheel has a hub—a wheel within a wheel—and on a throne above the creatures is a being of light resembling a man.

Read Ezekiel 1:1-28.

Calling versus career

At the time of his calling, Ezekiel was probably around thirty—the age for induction into the priesthood. Because his father was a priest, that was probably the career that Ezekiel planned to follow.

The cherubim

The symbolic faces of the cherubim, the winged creatures, represent divine attributes: the human's face, intelligence; the lion's, aggressive courage; the ox's, strength; and the eagle's, swiftness. These creatures could not be more different in appearance from the way we think of angels, or *cherubs,* today.

2. A voice instructs Ezekiel to tell the people of the LORD's displeasure with them, and it bids him to eat a scroll on which God has written, "Lamentation and wailing and

This carved ivory image of a cherub is from a palace in Samaria. Similar to the cherubim in Ezekiel's vision, it combines the features of a human, a lion, and an eagle. Cherubim were divine beings, but they themselves were never worshiped. Divine beings like cherubim were also part of other Near Eastern religions.

woe!'' (2:10). When he does eat the scroll, the taste is as sweet as honey. Ezekiel is warned: The people will be stubborn, so he must be equally stubborn. The vision fades, and Ezekiel awakens and is himself again.

A week later, God says that Ezekiel is to be watchman over the house of Israel, to warn the wicked to repent and the good to avoid evil. God tells Ezekiel to be silent until he is bade to speak—and Ezekiel is no longer his own man; he is God's.

Read Ezekiel 2:2-10; 3:1-27.

3. God tells Ezekiel to draw a map of Jerusalem on an un-baked clay brick and to set it in front of his house. Around it he is to model—as children do with bits of sticks and pebbles—a siege with battering rams, towers, and ramps. Then he is to wedge a large iron griddle into the ground behind the "city." He is to lie down and gaze at the griddle—to signify God watching Nebuchadnezzar's siege of Jerusalem but doing nothing. Daily for 390 days—the number of years of the kingdom Israel's sin—Ezekiel is to lie there, then 40 more days to signify the years of Judah's sin.

Ezekiel must also eat the food of besieged people—coarse bread made from the grain scraped from the bins—and drink only a quart of water a day. Finally, when he is told to bake his bread over a fire of dried human excrement, Ezekiel is so horrified at the prospect of ritual impurity that God substitutes dried cow dung—a common fuel in the Near East.

Read Ezekiel 4:1-15.

Number games

The 390 days may represent the years from the dedication of the Temple in Solomon's time to its destruction—yet to come—in 587 B.C.E. The forty years, the span of a generation, may signify the length of the exile in Babylon or the time from the destruction of the Temple to its restoration.

Ezekiel says that the scroll describing God's mission for him tastes as sweet as honey. Write a half page about your own discovery that doing what is right, even if it is difficult, could be said to taste sweet.

The prophet Ezekiel drew a map of Jerusalem on an unbaked clay brick and then placed bits of sticks and pebbles around it to signify a siege with battering rams, towers, and ramps.

Their total of 430 recalls another long and painful exile—Israel's years in Egypt.

4. Next, God tells Ezekiel to cut off his hair and his beard and to weigh them on a scale. He burns a third of the hair within his "city," strews a third around the city and strikes it with a sword, and tosses the final third in the wind. A few hairs are to be kept in the hem of his garment until finally even some of these are to be burned.

Bald and clean-shaven—a totally inappropriate appearance for an adult Israelite male—Ezekiel says that the hair is a symbol of the Jerusalemites, who will be cut down. A third will die of pestilence after invasion, a third will be slain, and a third scattered in exile. Only a few will become the remnant who will return.

Read Ezekiel 5:1-2,11-12.

5. The people *still* do not believe that Jerusalem will fall.

God suggests one more role-play, hoping that Judah will yet see itself for the "rebellious house" it is. Ezekiel packs his baggage, leaves his house, and goes through an elaborate pantomime of escaping from the city. In the morning he explains that his actions represented King Zedekiah in disguise escaping the city. But Zedekiah will be caught, taken to Babylon, and blinded, and he will die there. God then tells Ezekiel to stand in front of the people and tremble as he eats bread and drinks water—as they will when they are captives.

For all this, the people are unconvinced. They respond with a proverb about prophetic visions that never come to anything. In other words, "Talk! Talk! Talk!" God angrily says that their proverb has run itself out; the fulfillment of Ezekiel's vision is at hand.

Read Ezekiel 12:1-28.

A glimpse of love

Verse 3b, giving the exiles another chance to repent of their sins or face the inevitable, is a glimpse of the compassion of the God we know from Exodus and the Gospels. Here—in a text that so often shows God raging, condemning, and punishing—is the Father who wants to forgive, the God who has always been this way. But forgiving needs someone who wants to be forgiven—and the exiles answer Ezekiel's parable in the same old way: "Okay, okay, we heard you the first time!"

Create a list of symbolic actions—like Ezekiel's—that people might take to get across a message about one of these issues:
- nuclear waste disposal
- air pollution
- endangered life-forms
- destroying water supplies

6. Still the false prophets of Jerusalem insist that peace, not invasion, is at hand, and God condemns them. They are like people who build a shoddy wall and cover it with whitewash. When the rains come, the paint washes off, and the wall crumbles.

Read Ezekiel 13:1–12.

7. In a last effort to make the people realize the enormity of their sin, Ezekiel offers a series of allegories that dramatize the coming fall of Jerusalem, the exile of its people, and the restoration of those who turn to God.

One such comparison is a love story, reminiscent of Hosea's, in which Jerusalem proves to be a vain and faithless spouse. Only when she has shamed herself entirely—taking countless lovers, paying for their services, destroying her beauty, and behaving worse than her sisters Sodom and Samaria—only then will God forgive her and renew their marriage.

In another figure, Ezekiel compares Jerusalem to a cooking pot and its people to the stew meat in the pot. Babylon is the fire under the pot. Even when emptied, the pot is left on the fire to be purified of rust—read *corruption*—which is so great that even fire cannot remove it!

Finally comes the most tragic allegory of all. God tells Ezekiel, "I am taking away from you the delight of your eyes," and orders him not to show his grief (24:16). That evening, Ezekiel's wife dies of a stroke. The people recognize in his silence another message and ask what it means. He an-

When Ezekiel's wife died, God ordered the prophet not to show grief.
Below: Grief is perhaps the most powerful human emotion.

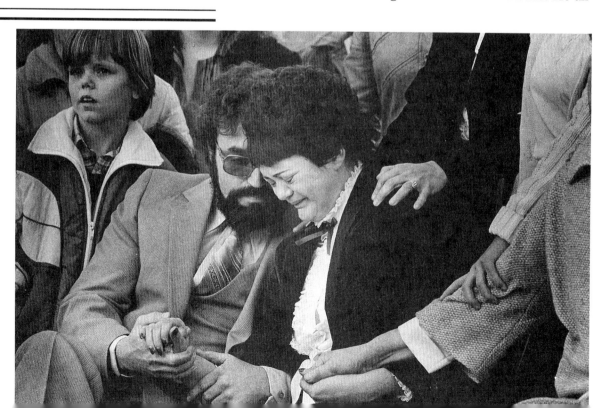

swers that the delight of *their* eyes—the Temple, Jerusalem, and all its people—will also be taken away.

Read Ezekiel 16:1–63; 24:1–27.

Ezekiel's grief

Ezekiel's prophetic role has exacted a terrible price—his reputation, his public respect, his success, and in the end his need to mourn his wife. Ezekiel's not mourning his heart's dearest symbolizes the exiles' not mourning the loss of their relationship with God. Their belief that "we haven't been all that bad" has insulated them from remorse.

8. Jerusalem falls. Ezekiel is at last vindicated. The people whom he has been warning all this time now flock around him as the man of the hour, but God warns him that this popularity will be short-lived. It is not inspired by conversion but by the shallow impulse to jump on the bandwagon. The people will not really hear God's word, nor will they do it.

Read Ezekiel 33:27–33.

9. God condemns the unfaithful "shepherds" of Israel, who have led their sheep (the people) astray. Instead of feeding their sheep, the shepherds have taken away their wool and killed them for their fat. Because they did not seek the lost sheep, the flock is scattered, and now God will be the shepherd and bring the sheep back to the land.

Speaking to the sheep, God promises to separate the good from the bad—those who have trampled the grass, fouled it, and muddied the streams so the weak cannot eat or drink. In a passage that Christians interpret as referring to Christ, God promises to appoint a new David to protect and guide Israel.

Read Ezekiel 34:7–24.

10. Having arrived at long last in Babylon, the exiles are without hope. " 'Our bones are dried up,' " they moan (37:11). Ezekiel has a vision of a plain filled with dry bones, and when God asks him, "Can these bones come to life?" (37:3) Ezekiel replies that only God knows. With this, he is told to say, "Dry bones, hear the word of the Lord!" (37:4). As he speaks there is a rattling sound, the bones come together, sinew and flesh covering them, but the bodies have no life. Ezekiel is told to call forth spirit for the bones; he does, and suddenly standing before him is a vast array of living people. This is the whole house of Israel, whose grave of exile God will open to

The Babylonians and the Exile

The city of Babylon dates from before 2000 B.C.E. but did not achieve notoriety until the time of King Hammurabi (1792 to 1750 B.C.E.), famous for his code of laws. For the next twelve hundred years, the rulers of Babylon withstood the sieges and sackings of, and were sometimes governed by, the Amorites, the Elamites, the Kassites, the Assyrians, and the Aramaeans.

Babylon had inherited from its predecessors a rich cultural and religious tradition going back to 4000 B.C.E. The Babylonians themselves produced extensive literature, including the famous *Gilgamesh Epic*. Cities under Babylonian rule were governed by law, with courts and police, contractual business arrangements, and the guarantee

of private property. Among their other accomplishments, the Babylonians designed the Hanging Gardens, famous as one of the Seven Wonders of the Ancient World. Because Babylon heard and often acted upon the will of its people, some scholars refer to it as a primitive democracy.

In the eighth century B.C.E., a neighboring group called the Chaldeans took Babylon from the Assyrians. Twice the Assyrian kings retaliated by destroying Babylon, and twice the Chaldeans rebuilt it. Finally, in 612 B.C.E., the Chaldeans demolished the Assyrian capital, Nineveh. Twenty-five years later, the Chaldean king Nebuchadnezzar II destroyed Jerusalem and carried the citizens of Judah into exile in Babylon—a tactic of-

ten used to destroy a people's will to resist foreign rule.

In biblical writings, Nebuchadnezzar is represented as a tyrant—a portrait that may owe more to the Jews' experience with Greek and Roman oppression than with that by the Babylonians. Although the Jews came to Babylon as captives, they were not slaves. In fact, during the exile there, they played an important part in the empire's economy and became farmers, bankers, merchants, artisans, contractors, and land-owners. Some Jews felt enough at home to take Babylonian names.

The biblical view of Babylon as a symbol of paganism has more validity. Jews who could not stomach the worship of Marduk and other Babylonian gods were not allowed to build their own temples or practice their religious rituals. But they carefully preserved the words of the prophets and the sacred writings of the Torah, and probably gathered together as families or in community to read the Scriptures, pray, and chant their hymns and psalms.

In the centuries that followed the exile, many Jews remained in Babylon and were true to Judaism. They trained exceptional scholars in the Mosaic Law and in the sixth century B.C.E. produced the Babylonian Talmud—the most influential Jewish writing other than the Hebrew Scriptures.

lead them back to their land and to give them a new spirit, and there they will turn to God once more.

Read Ezekiel 37:1-14.

A disheartened nation

Probably the most familiar of the Ezekiel stories, his vision of the dry bones is often thought, incorrectly, to be about resurrection. Rather, it is about the raising up of a nation—now disheartened and hopeless. Israel has tried to manipulate its own fate and has failed lamentably; now it is God, whom they have ignored, betrayed, and rejected, who alone can—and will—save them.

11. The last chapters of Ezekiel are a vision of the exiles' journey back to Jerusalem, the rebuilding of the Temple, and the return of the glory of God. The LORD orders Ezekiel to tell the priests and the people how to worship; celebrate feast days; observe the laws of ritual, the rules for nobles, and the laws for division of land—and much more. After that, Ezekiel announces that the name of the city shall henceforth be " 'The LORD is here' " (48:35). But Ezekiel does not live to see Jerusalem again—except in his vision. He dies in exile.

Read Ezekiel 43:1-9; 48:35b.

Ezekiel was the herald of Israel's hope and at long last became its teacher and counselor. One can imagine that when the exiles, filled with remorse, finally asked him, "Why did it happen?" he reminded them not only of their infidelities but, far more eagerly, of their God, a saving God.

Second Isaiah: The Book of Consolation

Second Isaiah, the principal author of the Book of Consolation (Isaiah, chapters 40 through 55), was an anonymous prophet in Babylon around 550 B.C.E. He adapted the spirit of First Isaiah to the years of exile and return. Where Isaiah of Jerusalem had condemned the pagan nations for leading Israel astray, Isaiah of Babylon saw them as instruments that God could use to bring Israel to repentance.

Second Isaiah's writings also marked the beginning of the long march home. Once Cyrus the Persian had overcome the Babylonians and set the exiles free in 538 B.C.E., groups of exiles took this journey over a span of ten to fifteen years. Because almost all the original deportees had died, probably only a few thousand of their offspring, together with some very old people, made the difficult journey back. Many second-generation exiles did not know or remember Jerusalem, and they preferred to remain in Babylon in their comfortable homes and with their prosperous businesses.

Second Isaiah, like Jeremiah, spoke of God as the One and Only. For Israel, the Creation had always been the loving act of Israel's God, but these prophets were the first to say that God was the *only* God, the God of all the nations. That Israel had worshiped only the one God is not the same as saying that God had had no competition at all. After the prophets affirmed that there was only one God, the word *Yahweh*—the name of Israel's God—could be dropped in favor of simply the word *God.*

Second Isaiah begins with chapter 35, skips chapters 36 to 39—most of which is lifted bodily from the Second Book of Kings, chapters 18 to 20—and continues with chapters 40 to 55. Oddly enough, reading chapters 41 to 48 in reverse order makes the most sense. Scholars wonder if pieces of parchment were reversed and unintentionally sewn together in the wrong sequence.

Two themes make Second Isaiah memorable. One is its joyous expectation of the return to Jerusalem, of the Promised One, and of the day when all nations will gather to worship God in justice and peace. The other is the Servant Songs, which speak of the promise of salvation for Israel. Today the passages of expectation and joy are used as readings for the Advent liturgy, and the Servant Songs for the Lenten liturgy.

1. God sharply rebukes the exiles for their sins, but because they have been refined "in the furnace of affliction" (48:10)—exile—God will summon Cyrus the Persian to overthrow Babylon and to allow Israel to return home. Exile will end with a New Exodus!

God taunts Babylon as it prepares for Cyrus's invasion. God had turned the people of Jerusalem over to Babylon because they needed chastisement, but the brutal leveling of Jerusalem was merciless, as was the treatment of the prisoners. Now Babylon herself will become a widow without children, with no one to save her.

God also ridicules the gods of Babylon, wobbling on the backs of oxen as they are carted to cities where they can be saved from destruction. They cannot save anyone, not even themselves! But Israel's God has carried Israel since birth and will do so forever. Let Israel compare Babylon's gods to God! "I am God, there is no other . . ." (46:9).

Cyrus the Persian overthrew the Babylonians and allowed the exiles to return home.
Above: A marble head of an Iranian king, dating from about the time of Cyrus

Second Isaiah pictures Cyrus subduing nations and kings, thanks to Israel's God, who calls Cyrus by name—although Cyrus does not know God. God joyously bids nature to let justice descend from the heavens like dew and salvation bud forth from the earth.

Read Isaiah 48:1-22; 47:5-10; 46:1-9; 45:1-8.

God's anointed liberator

Unlike other conquerors, Cyrus does not resort to rape, genocide, or the deportation of populations. He allows conquered peoples to return home, asking only that when they worship their gods, they pray for him as well. God calls Cyrus "the anointed" out of respect for his kingship. Among his mercies, this Persian warrior frees a tiny group of captives (the exiles from Jerusalem) whose descendants will survive long after Persia and will bring forth in the fullness of time one who will change the world.

2. As if watching a scene in a play, Second Isaiah sees God present with the heavenly court and hears God say to the angels, "Comfort my people!" A voice cries out, "In the desert prepare the way of the LORD! . . . Every valley shall be filled in, every mountain and hill shall be made low" (40:3-4). Another voice says, " 'Cry out!' " and the prophet asks, " 'What shall I cry out?' " (40:6). He is to cry out that God is coming to lead Israel—like a shepherd who leads his flock and carries his lambs in his bosom.

The exiles, who are about to return home, need reassurance from God. After fifty years in Babylon, they have begun

The prophet Isaiah of Babylon saw God coming to lead Israel like a caring shepherd leads a flock. **Below:** A flock in Israel

to wonder if the local god Marduk has not outperformed their LORD. God reminds them of who created all things. Do they think that God has forgotten them? Why?

> They that hope in the LORD will renew their strength,
>   they will soar as with eagles' wings;
> They will run and not grow weary,
>   walk and not grow faint.

(40:31)

Second Isaiah says that a new age will emerge for Israel as the exiles make their way home. The desert will bloom, the travelers will sing, and the sick and the lame will be healed.

Read Isaiah 40:1–11,27–31; 35:1–6.

In reply to a question put by John the Baptist's disciples, Jesus answered with the words of Second Isaiah about the dawning of a new age.

Read Matthew 11:2–6.

3. Isaiah of Babylon may have written the Servant Songs, or they may be a second book by another poet and prophet, mistakenly inserted piecemeal into Isaiah. Equally uncertain is the identity of the servant in the songs. Often he seems to be Israel, sometimes the prophet, and sometimes a composite portrait of Israel's great men. Christians have always seen a prophetic image of Christ in the suffering servant.

In the first song, God speaks of a chosen one, one set above others. He has been given God's spirit, and his mission is to bring justice to the nations. He will not raise his voice in noisy authority but will speak with gentleness and act tenderly toward the "bruised reed"—hopeless Israel.

In the next song, the speaker is the prophet. He likens himself to a sharp-edged sword, a polished arrow that God had hidden in a quiver. He was called from his mother's womb to restore Israel as a light to the nations—so that the salvation of the LORD can reach to the ends of the earth.

In the third song, the servant is subject to insults and derision, he is beaten, his beard plucked, his face spat upon. Patiently he endures this abuse, certain that God will uphold him. His tormentors will wear out, he says, like moth-eaten clothing.

In the fourth song, the suffering servant seems to be Israel, who, before finally being exalted, is first spurned and avoided and so disfigured as to seem inhuman. The people think that he is being punished for his sins, but in reality

According to Isaiah of Babylon, God would renew the strength of the exiles; they would "soar as with eagles' wings" (Isaiah 40:31).

Among your acquaintances, family members, and neighbors, identify someone who is a "bruised reed." Write a note to that person, expressing your concern.

he is chastised for the nation's wrongdoing. Like a lamb led to slaughter he is taken away, "cut off from the land of the living" (53:8), and buried in a criminal's grave, although he has done no wrong. But because he has "surrendered himself to death and was counted among the wicked" (53:12), he will win pardon for the sins of many.

Read Isaiah 42:1-4; 49:1-6; 50:4-9; 52:13-15; 53:1-12.

Jesus as the Suffering Servant

Today the Song of the Suffering Servant (52:13-15; 53:1-12) is used in the Good Friday liturgy. It is easy to see why Christians would interpret the suffering, death, and triumph of the servant as a prophetic image of Jesus.

We need to reflect deeply on the fact that the Bible offers images of God as Mother as well as Father.

Write down your thoughts about God as Mother, reacting to the scriptural passages from Second Isaiah where the female image is used for God (49:15 and 42:14).

4. When Jerusalem complains that God has forgotten it, God responds with one of the most beautiful passages in the Scriptures. Even a mother might forget her infant or be without tenderness for the child of her womb, but God will never forget Israel.

In another passage, God becomes a woman in labor, "gasping and panting" as she struggles to bring forth Israel as a reborn nation (42:14).

Read Isaiah 49:14-15; 42:13-14.

God as Mother

Many people today are offended at the suggestion that we call God Mother as well as Father. We need to reflect deeply on the fact that these passages, written long ago in a male-oriented culture, were accepted into the canons of both the Hebrew and the Christian Scriptures.

5. A joyful poem bids Jerusalem to prepare for the return of the exiles. God calls to the once-faithless city, like Hosea called to Gomer, in the language of a spouse reunited to his or her beloved. God invites the people to a life-giving banquet, and the faithful offspring of Jacob are included in the invitation.

Second Isaiah closes in a hymn of joy, with God promising peace, mountains that break into song, trees that clap their hands, cypresses instead of thornbushes, myrtle instead of nettles. No wonder the returning exiles leave Babylon with high hearts and visions of another Eden!

Read Isaiah 55:1-6,12-13.

For Review

1. Who is Judah's reformer king, and what discovery is made during his reign that inspires him to action?

2. How does Jeremiah's response to God's call differ from First Isaiah's?

3. What outrage moves Jeremiah to state that Israel's God is the one God?

4. Which of Jerusalem's people are taken into exile the first time?

5. Why is Jeremiah accused of treason by his own people and thrown into prison?

6. When the Babylonians capture Jerusalem, why is Jeremiah free to remain there instead of being forced into exile, and what happens to him?

7. Which minor prophet reveals that the remnant, about whom God speaks with such love, will be the poor and the lowly, the unfortunate and the impoverished?

8. What question does the minor prophet Habakkuk ask of God that none of the other prophets have asked before?

9. How are Ezekiel's methods different from those of the other prophets? Give examples.

10. Describe Ezekiel's pantomime of the siege of Jerusalem. What does it mean?

11. In Ezekiel's allegory of the love story, what does the faithless spouse represent?

12. In Ezekiel's vision of the dry bones, what is the significance of the bones' rising up and becoming living people?

13. Why did many second-generation exiles remain in Babylon after the exiles had been freed to go back?

14. Why does God call the Persian king Cyrus "the anointed"?

15. Describe two passages from Second Isaiah in which God is portrayed as a mother.

9

The Remnant:
The Return from Exile

THIS chapter tells the rest of Israel's story up to the year 100 B.C.E. as it is written in the Hebrew Scriptures. The two Books of Chronicles present a review of Israel's history, not the way it was but the way it should have been. The Books of Ezra, Nehemiah, Third Isaiah, Haggai, and Zechariah tell of the exiles' return to Jerusalem and fit together like the pieces of a jigsaw puzzle. This means that we must move about a bit in the biblical text in order to put the events in chronological order.

For example: The story of the priest Ezra dates from the time of the exiles' return, starting in 538 B.C.E., when the Persian king Cyrus issued his decree setting them free. Chapters 1 through 6 of Ezra tell of that event. The writers known as Third Isaiah also belonged to that period, and their works treat the lamentable state of the Jerusalem community in its early years after the return. Then closely follows the prophet Haggai, who goaded the Jews into rebuilding the Temple after a long delay, and Zechariah and Malachi speak shortly after Haggai. Then come Nehemiah (the governor who journeyed to Jerusalem to organize its restoration), the rest of Ezra, and the prophets Joel and Obadiah. The two Books of the Maccabees bring the historical material to a close.

The Jews

After the exile, the term *Jew*—from *Judah*—came into common use along with *Jewish* and *Judaism.*

B.C.E.	
600	• Third Isaiah, Haggai, and Zechariah write after the return to Jerusalem. The returnees begin work on the second Temple.
500	• Malachi speaks to the Jews after the second Temple has been completed.
	• Nehemiah rebuilds the walls around Jerusalem. Obadiah condemns Edom.
400	• Joel calls the people of Judah to return to God.
	• Ezra brings the Torah to Jerusalem.
	• Greece conquers Persia.
300	• A Greek ruler of Egypt orders a Greek translation of the Torah, called the Septuagint.
200	
	• The Maccabees revolt against their Greek rulers.
100	
	• The Roman general Pompey takes Jerusalem.
C.E.	• Jesus is born.

Facing page: The ruins of a palace at the ancient Persian city of Persepolis give us a glimpse of its splendor—and that of the Persian Empire.

Chronicles:
History as It Should Have Been

The two Books of Chronicles, once a single volume with Ezra and Nehemiah, were written—possibly by Ezra—sometime after the rebuilding of the Temple. Estimates of when the Chronicles were written vary from 520 to 350 B.C.E., although the more recent dates are most likely. The books retell Israel's history in terms of its meaning in God's unfolding plan, rather than in factual, chronological events. They are a valuable prologue to the Books of Ezra and Nehemiah, which are the key to the development of modern Judaism.

Why are we told still another version of Israel's history, one that skips over large chunks of it, puts the emphasis on David and Solomon—omitting all their sins—and still claims to be inspired scripture?

The Books of Chronicles were the writer's effort to put things in focus. They reminded the Jews that they were called to be a priestly people and a holy nation, not an empire. The Chronicler was not concerned with Israel's scandals, wars, or wealth. Israel's political greatness was over, but that did not matter because by holding to the ideal set forth by David, Israel would keep on course to the greatness that was its destiny. So the Chronicler made David and Solomon the key figures in his saga and retold their story the way it should have been. He recalled how David took Jerusalem, rebuilt it, made it the capital of the twelve tribes, and brought the ark of the Covenant there. David dreamed of a house for God, purchased land for it, drew plans, provided materials, wrote regulations for the Temple, trained choristers and musicians, and even wrote music for Israel's worship. Much of this information appears for the first time in Chronicles.

The story of Solomon is told the same way, with emphasis on his wealth, his building and dedication of the Temple, and his wisdom. Only when the Chronicler got to the stories of the kings who led Israel into infidelity, idolatry, and exile did he criticize and condemn. He ended with the Edict of Cyrus, which at last freed Israel to return from exile to Jerusalem to start again.

The Deuteronomists portrayed David as a great warrior-king and a repentant sinner. The Chronicler, however, presented David as a liturgist and leader in worship, in order to inspire the Jerusalem community to return to a vibrant religious life.

Read the summaries of 1 and 2 Chronicles that introduce the two books in your Bible.

The Chronicler rewrote Israel's history the way it should have been. Try doing the same: rewrite an incident in your life to make it come out as you wish it had.

Going Home

Ezra: Is This Jerusalem?

Ezra is a priest and scribe who resides in Babylon and whose book opens with the decree of Cyrus giving freedom to all the exiles in the Persian Empire who wish to return to Jerusalem. Cyrus suggests that the exiles remaining behind in Babylon contribute supplies to those who are returning and that all artifacts taken from Solomon's Temple be restored. The travelers are led by Sheshbazaar, the son of Jehoiachin, who was released from prison and allowed to live as a king in exile.

The exiles start out from Babylon full of hope and excitement, buoyed by Second Isaiah's prophecy of a new Jerusalem—which, we should remember, foretells a time in the *distant* future. When they arrive in Jerusalem, they find nothing but a miserable little village perched on a pile of rubble—its wall and Temple in ruins—and ahead of them a future promising nothing but hardship. Judah is an impoverished land spanning a mere twenty-five miles from north to south, and the residents of Jerusalem, left behind after the deportations to Babylon, resent the newcomers. To the north, the Jews of Samaria observe them with suspicion.

The exiles resettle in their ancestral towns and several months later gather in the city to offer sacrifice. Led by Zerubbabel (also of the Davidic line) and the high priest Joshua, they lay a foundation for a new Temple and commence work. News of this enterprise travels to the north, and the Samaritans come down to help, saying that they have worshiped Israel's God since the days when they were transported to Israel by the king of Assyria. But to the former exiles, who consider themselves the remnant, the true Israel, these hybrid Jews are not Jews at all, and their offer is rebuffed. The angry Samaritans return to the north and report the project to their Persian rulers as rebellion. Because Cyrus is dead and the present king is unfamiliar with the decree permitting the Jews to rebuild their Temple, the work is halted—for eighteen years.

Read Ezra 1:1-4; 4:1-24.

The bad Samaritans?

The Judaean-Samaritan hatred began when Jeroboam, the first king of the northern kingdom, erected golden calves at Dan and at Bethel and appointed non-Levite priests to keep his people from going to Jerusalem to worship.

When the exiles returned to Jerusalem, they immediately laid the foundation for a new Temple. But their work was halted for eighteen years by order of their Persian ruler.

Are you surprised to find so much prejudice in the Bible? Write a one-paragraph answer to this question:
- Is there more prejudice today than people faced in biblical times?

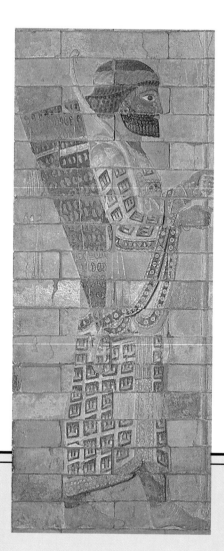

When the northern kingdom's elite were exiled to Assyria in 722 B.C.E., foreign settlers were brought in to colonize Israel. They were ordered by the Assyrians to marry with the local people and to worship Israel's God as well as their own gods. The result was a weakening of tribal identity and religious fidelity.

Third Isaiah: Alas, the Same Old Thing

Because the last ten chapters of Isaiah comment on the state of affairs in Jerusalem after the return of the exiles, both lamenting the people's laxity and sin and calling them to renewal, this is an appropriate place to hear about them.

Called Third Isaiah, this collection of writings is by several disciples of Second Isaiah, probably dating around 540 to 510 B.C.E.. It speaks of the far-from-glorious state of affairs in the Jersualem community, painting a melancholy picture of human behavior—which so quickly falls into old ways.

Cyrus the Persian

By the age of thirty, the Persian king Cyrus II had gained a reputation as a wise man, a religiously tolerant man, and a conquerer —among whose conquests was Croesus, better known as the fabulously rich King Midas. Cyrus next looked toward Babylon and in 538 B.C.E. took the city, according to legend, by diverting the city's river and using the dry riverbed for his attack. The Babylonian king was notoriously disliked not only by his vassals but by his own people as well, so Second Isaiah was not alone in praising Cyrus as a great deliverer.

Respectful of the Babylonians' worship, Cyrus restrained his army from plunder, ordered them instead to restore the city's temples, and dubbed the god Marduk king of Babylon's gods. In addition, he returned to neighboring peoples the statues of their gods that the former king had confiscated, and—most important for our story— allowed the Jewish exiles in Babylon to return to Jerusalem.

By winning Babylon, Cyrus had gained the world's greatest business center, extensive and productive farmlands, and even a

Third Isaiah sees things going downhill rapidly after the arrivals' shock at the ruin in Jerusalem, followed by the obstruction of their Temple project. Laxness and religious apathy settle over the community like a blight. The poor are reduced to hopelessness, the rich care only for themselves, the leaders are faithless, and infidelity and idol worship are rife.

When the rich ask why God ignores their fasting and prayer—and because they alone have enough food, they alone can fast—the answer is that God desires *true* fasting. True fasting is working for the release of the unjustly imprisoned, freeing the oppressed, sharing bread with the hungry, sheltering the homeless, and clothing the naked.

After harshly rebuking them for their sins, God answers the people's plaintive wail for forgiveness and help. Again God uses maternal language to describe a new Jerusalem: Would God allow such a child to be conceived in the minds and hearts of this people without letting it be born? Would God bring a mother to the moment of birth and not let her

Facing page: Enameled tile depicting a Persian warrior, from the sixth century B.C.E.
Left: A carved image of the Zoroastrian god of wisdom

navy. Among his subjects was Phoenicia, whose fleet made the Persians a sea power. Cyrus administered these immense territories until his death in battle in 529 B.C.E., and his successors built upon his conquests. By 500 B.C.E., the Persian Empire stretched from Greece to India and from the Black Sea to the Sudan, in northern Africa.

The story of the first Persian Empire is not complete without a mention of *Zoroastrianism*, a radical religion dating from the sixth century B.C.E. The teachings of a Persian religious reformer named Zoroaster included now-familiar doctrines: One true God served by angels engages in a cosmic battle between the spirit of the truth and the spirit of lies—both spirits constantly seeking to win over the people. After a person dies, the one God either rewards the person with eternal ease or punishes her or him with everlasting torment—depending upon which spirit the person chose to serve in life. Zoroastrianism may have contributed to Jewish, Christian, and Muslim belief such concepts as heaven, hell, angels, Satan, free will, and a final judgment.

The collection of writings called Third Isaiah tells about the new heaven and new earth, where all people will worship God.

child be delivered? The new heavens and the new earth will come to pass, and all the world will worship the LORD.
Read Isaiah 58:1–11; 64:1–11; 66:1–14,18–23.

The end of Isaiah

Here ends the Book of Isaiah, a masterpiece of the Hebrew Scriptures. First, Second, and Third Isaiah have different authors, moods, and historical settings, but together they weave a single theme: God's love for Israel.

- In prosperous Jerusalem, First Isaiah is anguished by the people's pettiness and sin and explodes with prophetic wrath, tempered here and there by glimpses of a golden promise—a king who will rule the nations in justice and peace.
- During the end of the Babylonian exile, Second Isaiah rejoices in God's forgiveness and the call to return to God and be faithful. God promises not only a new Jerusalem but a shepherd who will lead the people—and, as a servant, will suffer and die for them.
- When the people return to Jerusalem, Third Isaiah faces up to Israel's continuing sinfulness, goads it in the painful struggle to reform, and assures the people that God's promises will be kept. One day Israel and all the nations will gather in Jerusalem to worship the one God together.

Rebuilding the Temple

After Jerusalem has languished in apathy for eighteen years, the prophets Haggai, Zechariah, and Malachi appear. They are appalled that God's people have forgotten their calling and realize that the Temple is crucial if the Jews are to keep their religious identity. They waken the people with powerful oracles.

Haggai: No House for God?

Haggai, a speaker with a concise, humorous style, would probably be a political organizer today. He sees the delay in rebuilding the Temple as not entirely the fault of the Samaritans. Poverty, and the powerlessness that goes with poverty, is widespread in Jerusalem, and the rich care only for getting richer—so who is surprised that the leaders are halfhearted and the people religiously lax? or that all agree on one thing only: there are more important things to do than rebuild a temple that has been in ruins for over fifty years.

Without the Temple, however, the Jerusalem community will lose its faith, and Haggai rails at the people for ceasing work on God's house when they have found time to build their own. His eloquence is so effective that they hasten to the site and begin work!

Read Haggai 1:2-4,12-15.

Later in the same year, God asks the people if they are discouraged with their efforts. In truth the rebuilt Temple does not remotely compare with Solomon's great Temple. God tells them to take courage, "for I am with you" (2:4). But their fervor is centered on the building project, not on the state of their lives or their worship, and they fail to understand.

Read Haggai 2:3-5.

Creating a sacred space

God makes a stunning point about the appearance of the rebuilt Temple: The Jerusalem community needs the Temple in order to focus their faith on God's presence among them, worship together, and renew their commitment to God's call. The Temple's size and furnishings should be a minor concern.

Dating to the day

The two chapters of Haggai give dates, so we know to the month and day when the prophet spoke—an unusual advantage in biblical dating. Going by our current calendar system, his exhortations from chapter 1 took place on 29 August 520 B.C.E. The passage cited from chapter 2 was on 17 October of the same year.

Why was there no reason for the Jews to feel ashamed of the second Temple? Imagine an ideal building for worship. Explain in writing what it looks like and why.

In the Book of Haggai, God tells the people not to worry about the second Temple's size and splendor.
Left: God can be with us anywhere we worship—be it a storefront church or a cathedral.

Zechariah: The Days of the Messiah

Zechariah was a visionary whose language and message were concerned with the coming of the Messiah, a Davidic king who would rule in peace and justice. The New Testament contains over seventy references to Zechariah, mainly in the Book of Revelation. The two halves of his book are so different that some scholars, assuming two different writers, call the parts First and Second Zechariah. First Zechariah spoke shortly after Haggai; Second Zechariah was written about two hundred years later.

1. The first eight chapters of the Book of Zechariah tell of eight visions that come to Zechariah as he walks in a quiet valley outside the city at night. Five of the visions speak of the moral corruption of Jerusalem, and three of things to come. One of the latter visions shows the new Jerusalem with only God for its walls, meaning that enemies will become a thing of the past and that Jews and Gentiles will live in peace together. The Messiah on the throne is Zerubbabel. (This does not come to pass, of course. In fact after Zerubbabel disappears, ruling power among the Jews rests with the high priest.)

First Zechariah concludes with a description of messianic times: Jerusalem will be a city where the elderly enjoy their leisure and where children play in safety. People will speak the truth, and days of fasting will be occasions for joy.

Read Zechariah 8:1–8.

2. The focus of Second Zechariah is also messianic; however, now the expected Messiah is not a rich and powerful king but a peaceful Messiah of the poor. We know this from the images the prophet uses. Warrior-kings always ride horses; the messianic king of peace will ride a white donkey—a symbol of peace. The horse, the chariot, and the bow—all symbols of war—will be banned by the messianic king.

Read Zechariah 9:9–10.

3. Zechariah, chapter 11, provides an allegory of a shepherd: the people wander like sheep without a shepherd until the prophet becomes the true shepherd. In chapter 12, the prophet shows Jerusalem grieving for someone they have apparently murdered and, stricken with guilt, seeking forgiveness. It is easy to understand why the early Christians adapted these images to Christ.

Read Zechariah 11:4-5,7; 12:10; Mark 14:27.

4. The conclusion of Zechariah is a vision of an *apocalypse:* the end of the old world and the appearance of the new. On that day, horses, once beasts of war, will be consecrated to God, and their bells, once used in superstitious rituals, will be engraved with "Holy to the LORD." There will be no more commercializing by priests in the Temple, and the worship of God will be universal.

Read Zechariah 14:1-9,20-21.

Jesus and Zechariah

The shepherd passages in Zechariah, together with those in Ezekiel, may have been the source of Jesus' perception of himself as the Good Shepherd. Also, Jesus acted out the part of the peaceful king when he rode into Jerusalem on the back of a donkey on the Sunday before his death.

Read John 10:7-15; Matthew 21:1-5; John 12:12-15.

About apocalyptic texts

We must avoid reading apocalyptic texts such as that in Zechariah as interpretations of the events of our times. Endless groups of people have done so, prepared for the end of the world on their hilltops or in their sanctuaries, and have been left standing there asking, "What happened?" To find a portrait of ourselves in the story of God's people is a good way to profit from the Hebrew Scriptures, but to assert that the signs of the Second Coming are there to be decoded and announced is unwise and, so far, in vain.

Malachi: A Sacrilegious Community

The next piece of the puzzle is supplied by the minor prophet Malachi, who spoke sometime after 515 B.C.E., when the Temple was rebuilt, but before the coming of Nehemiah (445 B.C.E.). His book reveals the dismal conditions in Jerusalem. Malachi is a pen name meaning "my messenger."

1. In Jerusalem, faith is at its lowest. The sacrifices offered in the Temple can only be called sacrilegious—with blemished, lame, and blind animals offered instead of the perfect

Passages in the Books of Zechariah and Ezekiel may have been the source of Jesus' perception of himself as the Good Shepherd.

ones required by the Law. God, through the prophet Malachi, suggests that the priests try giving such gifts to the governor and see what he says! All over the world, says God, the Gentiles worship with pure offerings, but God's own people profane the altar and call worship a burden.

The people are as guilty as the priests. Returning from exile, they have divorced their Jewish wives and married rich pagan women in order to live more prosperously. They have not only broken vows to God and to their wives but have deprived the community of its rightful children. Indeed, they now believe that " 'every evildoer is good in the sight of the LORD' " (2:17) and claim that it is unjust of God not to agree.

Read Malachi 1:6-8,10-14; 2:7-8,17.

2. Malachi announces that God will send a messenger to prepare the people for the coming of judgment. He will be like a refiner's fire that burns the impurities out of gold or like the fuller's lye with which the new wool is cleansed. The people ask, "How shall we return to the LORD?" and Malachi tells them to *tithe*—that is, donate a tenth of their income. Evidently the storehouses in the Temple are empty because the offerings have been stolen. Shallow faith has led the people to admire the successful as the blessed, to approve even prosperous evildoers who hold God in contempt. But, says Malachi, God is keeping a record. Only repentance will save the people.

Read Malachi 3:1-5,7-10; Mark 1:1-2.

According to Malachi, the Jerusalemites believe that successful people are blessed. Write a half page on contemporary attitudes toward material success:
• Is it seen as a virtue today?
• Do you see it that way?
• Who does?

Rebuilding the Walls, Restoring the Law

Nehemiah: A Model Public Servant

Much of the Book of Nehemiah, written beginning in 445 B.C.E., was taken from Nehemiah's private journal and was meant for God alone. It reveals to us one of the most admirable people in Israel's history—a model public servant.

1. Nehemiah is cupbearer to Artaxerxes I in the Persian court, a privileged position. When his brother Hanani comes from Jerusalem and tells of the city's walls still in ruins, gates gutted, and people demoralized, Nehemiah grieves and fasts for several days. The king asks why he is sad, and Nehemiah

The Return of the Exiles

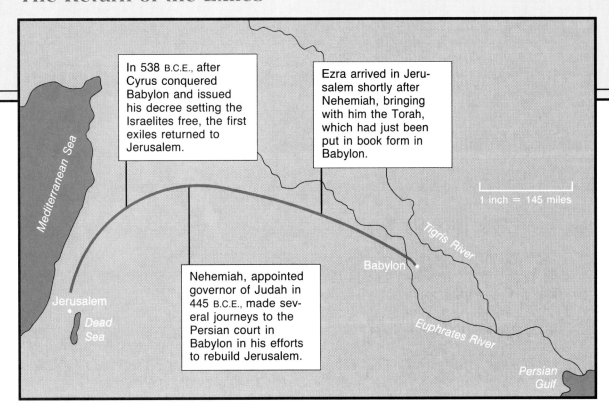

In 538 B.C.E., after Cyrus conquered Babylon and issued his decree setting the Israelites free, the first exiles returned to Jerusalem.

Ezra arrived in Jerusalem shortly after Nehemiah, bringing with him the Torah, which had just been put in book form in Babylon.

1 inch = 145 miles

Nehemiah, appointed governor of Judah in 445 B.C.E., made several journeys to the Persian court in Babylon in his efforts to rebuild Jerusalem.

Mediterranean Sea

Tigris River

Babylon

Euphrates River

Jerusalem

Dead Sea

Persian Gulf

tells him and asks if he might go to Jerusalem to rebuild the city. Both king and queen consent, and Nehemiah leaves with an escort and letters of safe passage through the lands of Judah's resentful neighbors.

On a moonlit night shortly after his arrival, with only a handful of companions, Nehemiah rides around the city's walls to inspect the ruins, so devastated that at times he has to dismount and walk his horse through the rubble.

In the following days Nehemiah calls everyone in the city to rebuild the walls of Jerusalem in order to protect it, and also to recover its former status in the eyes of neighboring peoples. Impressed with his words, the Jerusalemites want to start work immediately. Neighboring governors accuse the Jews of rebellion and try to frustrate the work, but Nehemiah promises that God will help the people and the task gets under way.

Read Nehemiah 1:1-4; 2:1-18.

2. A long list of workers rebuild the walls and gates of the city. The high priest and his staff build the Sheep Gate, the

A marble bust of Socrates (470 to 399 B.C.E.), a Greek philosopher who lived in the same century as Confucius, Siddhārtha Gautama, Zoroaster, and Ezra—none of whom knew of the others' existence

Historical Happenings Between 600 and 1 B.C.E.

Major religious and philosophical movements arise in the period preceding Jesus' life—movements that shape our ideas about God and goodness today.

China

The teacher K'ung Fu-tzu, better known as Confucius (551 to 479 B.C.E.), promotes social ethics, stressing traditional values, courtesy, and good government. His contemporary Lao-tzu writes the *Tao-te Ching,* which prescribes living in joy and harmony with nature. Their complementary systems —Confucianism and Taoism—guide Chinese culture and politics into modern times.

Greece

In the Athens of the fifth and fourth centuries B.C.E., democracy blooms, and thinkers such as Socrates, Plato, and Aristotle lay the foundations for Western philosophy, emphasizing a systematic search for wisdom.

India

The monk Vardhamāna (599 to 527 B.C.E.) establishes Jainism, a religion based on equality and nonviolence. (India's present-day dominant religion, Hinduism, eventually adopts nonviolence as part of its own teachings.) About the same time, the prince Siddhārtha Gautama (563 to 483 B.C.E.) has a spiritual awakening and, as *the Buddha,* teaches the principles of meditation and moderation. Although unpopular in India, Buddhism spreads throughout the rest of the Eastern world.

The Near East

The prophets of Israel and Judah preach monotheism and justice—religious and social ideas that become core beliefs in the great Western religions.

The reformer priest Ezra revives the Jewish community in Jerusalem, teaching the obligations and restrictions set down in the Torah. Later tradition acclaims Ezra to be a second Moses.

In the sixth century B.C.E., the reformer priest Zoroaster revolutionizes Persian religion with his teachings on free will and the afterlife.

gate closest to the Temple. The guilds of goldsmiths and perfumers build; fathers and sons build; and a certain Shallum, who has no sons, builds with his daughters. The list recorded in the book is a tribute to Nehemiah's record keeping and to how an inspired leader could get the people to roll up their sleeves and get to work lifting rock out of decades of debris to rebuild Jerusalem.

The Jerusalemites' enemies try to attack them, but Nehemiah posts guards, arms whole families, and stations a trumpeter to blow an alarm. He writes in his journal that in readiness for an attack, neither he nor his attendants take off their clothes, even at night.

Read Nehemiah 3:1–2,12,33–38; 4:5–17.

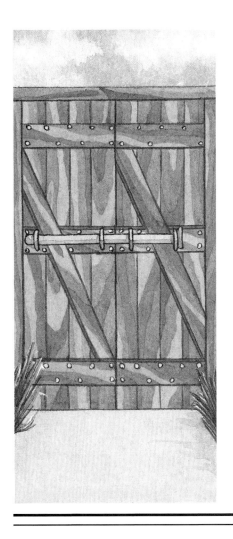

Nehemiah, a diplomat and public servant, called the people together to rebuild the walls of Jerusalem in order to protect the city.

3. Before the walls are completed, Nehemiah hears the common people cry out against the affluent Jerusalemites to whom they have had to pawn their fields, vineyards, homes, and even sons and daughters in order to buy grain to eat. Reduced to poverty, now some of their daughters are even being molested by wealthy kinsmen.

Nehemiah is outraged and orders the wealthy to return everything to the people they have cheated and to repay any interest they have charged. He and his friends and family loan money and grain to the poor without charge. The wealthy people agree to do as he says, and Nehemiah makes them swear to it in the presence of the priests.

Read Nehemiah 5:1–13.

4. As governor of Judah, Nehemiah refuses to use an expense account, to benefit from taxes, or to take land for himself. During the rebuilding of the walls, he sets a table with food and wine for the workers, at his own expense.

But even a model public servant can have enemies, and Nehemiah's—especially two named Sanballat and Tobiah—try to ambush him, start a smear campaign, and even try to lure him into the Temple and arrest him. He avoids their schemes, and at last the walls are finished. He orders that the gates never be opened before the sun is hot and always be closed before sundown, and he has a watch kept at all times.

The Jewish leaders take up residence in Jerusalem, and lots are cast among the people to decide who will live there; the rest of the Jews must reside in the other cities. The wall is finally dedicated with great ceremony, and after the religious rituals are celebrated, a gigantic feast is held for all.

Read Nehemiah 5:14–19; 6:1–19; 11:1–2; 12:27–30,43.

5. Nehemiah journeys back and forth between the Persian court and Jerusalem several times. Returning to Jerusalem for the last time, he finds that his archenemy Tobiah is living in the Temple and that the tithes of grain, wine, and oil for the Temple attendants have been stolen or given away. He has Tobiah thrown out, the chambers purified, and the supplies restored. He calls back the Levites, who have gone home to grow food, and appoints trustworthy administrators.

But there is worse. The Jerusalem farmers and merchants are not keeping the Sabbath—they are trading in the city—and the people are shopping on the Sabbath! Nehemiah reminds them that it was such contempt for the Law that led to Israel's downfall in the past and orders the gates sealed before the Sabbath and opened only when it is over.

Next, Nehemiah condemns the Jews who have married foreign women and whose children cannot even speak Hebrew. He curses those Jews and has them beaten—so dangerous does he believe this mixing of blood to be for the future of Israel. He warns the other Jews not to give their children in marriage to these half-breeds—as they appear to him. He reminds the people of how Solomon married foreign wives and dissipated the blood of the Davidic line, causing the nation to be divided. He conducts a rite of cleansing so they might be free of all foreign contamination, and with a brief summary of the provisions he has made for the Temple, his book abruptly comes to a close.

Read Nehemiah 13:4-13,15-19,23-30.

Nehemiah's last reforms

The two final reforms of Nehemiah pose tricky questions. To understand his motives, we must put ourselves in his time.

Buying and selling on the Sabbath was forbidden by the third commandment, and in Moses' time, the penalty for doing so was death (Exodus 35:1-2). In Nehemiah's time, people were not, as they are today, working three shifts or on rotating schedules—sometimes on Sunday. The prophets loudly condemned the attitude that put money and profit before religious commitment, as did Jesus (Matthew 6:24).

The second reform had to do with the divorce of foreign wives and sending them away with their children. In Nehemiah's time, intermarriage was the quickest way to weaken a people's religious commitment. That was why the Assyrians had demanded that the settlers in the northern kingdom marry the local people. And as Nehemiah knew, all the years in Babylon had led many Jews to wonder if the Babylonian god Marduk was not the equal of, or even superior to, Israel's God. The threat of divided loyalties was real.

Ezra Concludes: Commitment Renewed

Because it would seem to be impossible for Ezra to do his work before Jerusalem was restored to some kind of order by Nehemiah, we assume that Nehemiah came to Jerusalem first—in spite of the confusing order given in the biblical text. However, Ezra could have visited Jerusalem with Nehemiah around 445 B.C.E., and it makes sense to keep this in mind when we read about him in chapter 8 of the Book of Nehemiah.

1. Nehemiah, chapter 8, opens with the people gathered at the Water Gate, where Ezra is reading aloud the book of the Law, probably the Torah, to the men, the women, and all the children who can understand. When he concludes, they fall to their knees weeping. Both Ezra and Nehemiah bid them to rejoice, not weep, and they celebrate the event as a time of renewal.

The following week, the people celebrate the Feast of Booths—another name for Sukkoth—and twenty-four days later, dressed in sackcloth and covered with ashes, they confess their sins. Ezra reads the history of Israel to the people and calls them to make a new pact with God. Once again, they commit themselves to the Law and reject the sins of their past.

Read Nehemiah 8:1–3,9–12; 10:1–2,29–32.

2. Ezra evidently returns to Babylon, but he has his heart set on teaching the Law in Judah. When he asks Artaxerxes II to let him return to Jerusalem, the Persian king gives Ezra permission and the freedom to take any Jews who wish to go with him. He is given gold and silver to be used in Temple worship, with the request that there be prayers to Israel's God for the protection of the Persian king and his sons. The king forbids taxes to be levied on anyone who serves in the Temple. Ezra and his company set forth, and arriving in Jerusalem, they offer sacrifices of thanksgiving. The date is around 398 B.C.E.

Read Ezra 7:1–24; 8:21–23,31–33.

3. Ezra now turns his attention to reports that in spite of Nehemiah's warnings, the Jews have continued to marry foreign women. He tears his cloak, pulls out his hair and beard, and in a retelling of Israel's past infidelities, begs God

Ezra and Nehemiah celebrated Sukkoth with the people of Jerusalem to mark a renewed commitment to the Law.
Above: In Israel, youths gather roofing materials to be used in building a Sukkoth booth.

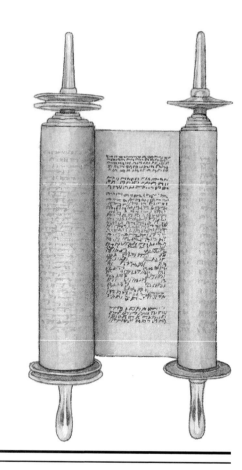

Ezra rooted his teaching—and the lives of his people—in the Torah.

to pardon its wickedness now. Weeping, the people offer to put aside their foreign wives and children, and after Ezra has prayed, he announces that they must do so at once! But it is the rainy season, and the people, shivering in the cold rain, beg for more time. They are given two months to complete the arrangements, and Ezra's book ends with this forlorn statement: "All these had taken foreign wives; but they sent them away, both the women and their children" (10:44).

Read Ezra 9:1-7; 10:1-17,44.

Reformer, priest, editor

Ezra helped reform and unify the Jewish community at a time when it was disintegrating. By preaching the Law of Moses, which had just been put in book form in Babylon, Ezra may have provided a constitution for the Jews—rooting their lives in a common faith and a common code of behavior.

Joel: Locusts!

The Book of Joel is thought to have been written around 400 B.C.E., after the rebuilding of the Temple. It opens with the prophet's calling the people to fast and pray after a plague of locusts has attacked the land. Everyone is weeping and wailing. Wheat, barley, fig trees, pomegranates, date palms, and apple trees have dried up. Barns have collapsed; cattle and sheep have perished. Joel bids the people to don sackcloth, proclaim a fast, and beg God to spare them. After the people have fasted and prayed, God promises plenty and peace again.

Read Joel 1:1-12; 2:15-18; 3:1.

Joel contains one of the most familiar passages in the Scriptures: ". . . I will pour out my spirit upon all mankind. Your sons and daughters shall prophesy, your old men shall dream dreams, your young men shall see visions . . ." (3:1). Saint Peter would use these words in his sermon on the first Pentecost.

Read Acts 2:14-17.

Obadiah: Woe to Edom!

Obadiah, the shortest book in the Bible, is a one-chapter attack on Edom (a small state in what is now Jordan), possibly for its part in the Babylonians' sack of Jerusalem. Because Esau, the founder of Edom, and Jacob were brothers, Obadiah accuses Edom of fratricide—gloating over its brother's ruin, looting his goods, and selling his survivors.

Obadiah is a great believer that the punishment is built into the crime.

Read Obadiah 1:10–15,17,21.

Rebuilding the Empire

Maccabees:
Civil War, Rebellion, and Rights

The two Books of Maccabees were written by two anonymous authors around 100 B.C.E.—but are set about two hundred years after the stories of Ezra and Nehemiah. First Maccabees is a history of the revolt of the Jews under the domination of Greek rulers. It tells of the struggle of Judas Maccabeus and his brothers to free the Jews from Greek control, confirms that God is with the people, exalts the Jews who remain faithful to God, and condemns the *apostates,* those who have renounced their faith.

Second Maccabees, part of a lost five-volume work, tells in detail of a cruel persecution of the Jews. It confirms belief in the resurrection of the dead, the intercession of the saints, and the offering of prayers for the dead.

The question arises, What happened during the time between Ezra (about 398 B.C.E.) and the Maccabees? There is no existing history of Israel's colonial years, but a bit of world history can help to put the Maccabees in place:

The Persian Empire fell in 330 B.C.E. to the young Greek conqueror Alexander the Great. After Alexander's death in 323 B.C.E., his empire was parceled out among his generals, two of whom founded dynasties affecting the Jews. The *Ptolemaic* dynasty in Egypt was started by a general who took the name of Ptolemy. The *Seleucid* dynasty, also named after a general, was given the rest of what had been the Persian Empire. Originally, the Ptolemies controlled the corridor between the two empires, which was inhabited by the Jews and the Phoenicians. But eventually the Seleucids seized it, and our story tells of the Jews' struggle for independence under the rule of the Seleucids.

The problem at the time of the Maccabees was how to live with the rapid introduction of Greek language, philosophy, and customs yet remain faithful to the God of Israel. Some Jews opted for adaptation to things Greek as the realistic method of survival. Others, like the Maccabees, would brook no change in Jewish life. Thus a schism grew in the Jewish community that soon mushroomed into full-scale civil war.

The Persian Empire fell to the young Greek conqueror Alexander in 330 B.C.E., beginning almost three hundred years of Greek domination. ***Above:*** A bust of Alexander the Great, who is known in Persian history as "the Vandal" because he burned down the Persian Empire's royal palace

Antiochus's Persecution of the Jews

The First Book of Maccabees opens when the Seleucid king Antiochus IV comes to the throne in 175 B.C.E., calling himself *Epiphanes,* meaning "God made visible." His subjects soon change this name to *Epimanes,* meaning "madman." In Jerusalem, the pro-Greek Jews, led by a corrupt high priest, build a gymnasium where young men participate in athletic events naked—a practice that the traditional Jews condemn. When Antiochus takes the treasures from the Temple to pay for his military adventures, animosity among the faithful Jews mounts. Two years later he sends a military force to Jerusalem to control the anti-Greek Jews. The soldiers burn houses, kill people, and build a citadel or fortress—called the Acra—for housing a continuing military presence and for the protection of the apostate Jews.

When these measures fail to counter Jewish resistance, Antiochus orders that everyone in his realm must embrace his religion. Under penalty of death, the Jews must abandon their Law, destroy their scrolls, offer sacrifices to Greek gods, cease circumcision, and ignore their dietary rules. The Temple is defiled, the altar profaned with sacrifices of swine— and most horrible of all to the Jews, an altar to the god Zeus is erected on the altar of holocausts!

Read 1 Maccabees 1:1-9,20-24,29-35,41-50,54-62.

At this time, an elder named Eleazar has been arrested for his refusal to eat pork. In charge of his execution are

The soldiers of the Greek ruler Antiochus IV burned homes and killed people in Jerusalem.
Right: A bronze illustration of a Greek infantry soldier

young Jews who have known him all their life, and they are deeply disturbed at the thought of his death. They propose to bring him meat that is not pork but looks like pork. He can eat it without breaking the Law yet dupe the king by seeming to eat pork. Eleazar replies to their scheme in effect, "If you think that to save my life for a few short years, I would scandalize all the young who are watching me, you are quite mistaken." And he dies, "an unforgettable example of virtue not only for the young but for the whole nation" (2 Maccabees 6:31).

Also at this time, a mother and her seven sons are arrested for refusing to eat pork. When torture fails to persuade them, the mother is forced to watch all her sons, from the eldest to the youngest, endure unspeakable torments and be put to death, after which the mother is also slain. It is a horrible story of the king's depravity and of the magnificent faith and courage of the Jerusalem Jews.

Read 2 Maccabees 6:18–31; 7:1–42.

Jewish faith, Greek culture

All through the Greek world the Jews were considered strange and exclusive because of their religion. Many Jews who lived in the Greek-speaking culture continued to preserve their Jewish traditions by downplaying the issues, living *in* the Greek culture but not being *of* it. But to the Maccabees this tactic had built-in dangers and was not to be tolerated.

Actually, the king's edict about worship was probably not a genuine attempt to make converts. More likely, it was merely a response to the civil dispute between the two factions of Jews: no evidence exists that anyone but Jews were its target, and of course the pro-Greek Jews had already abandoned their religious customs.

Mattathias and His Sons

We first meet the Maccabees in the town of Modein, where the priest Mattathias and his five sons—John, Simon, Judas, Eleazar, and Jonathan—are mourning the slaughter of the Jerusalem Jews. When the king's men arrive and order them to sacrifice to the Greek gods, Mattathias is so outraged that he slays one of them and races through the town warning the people to flee and hide.

Mattathias and his sons are joined by the *Hasideans,* a rebel group famed as warriors, and together they form a guerrilla army to tear down Greek shrines and kill pro-Greek Jews.

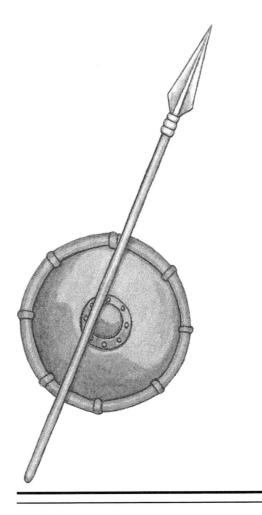

The priest Mattathias, his sons, and their allies formed a guerrilla army to fight against Greek rule and customs. **Above:** A shield and a spear like those of ancient Israel

The biblical Jews wanted to preserve their heritage—a desire we can all share. Write a paragraph detailing your ethnic background and describing any family customs and stories associated with it.

Later, as he is dying, Mattathias bids his sons to live for the Covenant. He then appoints Judas—a warrior also called Maccabeus, meaning "the hammerer"—as commander of the army and Simon as father to the clan.
Read 1 Maccabees 2:1–70.

The first challenge to Judas is from a king's officer who has slaughtered many Jerusalem Jews. Judas defeats the officer, and Antiochus pays the Seleucid army a year's wages in advance to march to Samaria and destroy Judas. Judas defeats this army as well and, now holding the upper hand, returns to Jerusalem to repair and purify the Temple.
Read 1 Maccabees 3:1–2,27–36,38–40,42–54; 4:6–14,34–35.

Judas and his men find the Temple forlorn and abandoned—its altar desecrated, the gates burnt, and weeds growing in the courts. First they mourn; then they get to work. They purify the sanctuary and the courts, remove the profaned altar and build a new one, make new sacred vessels, light a new lampstand, hang curtains, and place fresh loaves on the altar of holocausts. A year from the day of its defilement, the Temple is consecrated again. The people celebrate for eight days, and Judas decrees that these days be celebrated on the anniversary every year. This is the event celebrated by our Jewish brothers and sisters on their feast of *Hanukkah.*

When Judah's neighbors hear of the restored Temple, they attack on every front, but Judas and his brothers defeat them. On one occasion when the Maccabees return to the battlefield to gather the bodies of the fallen, they find pagan amulets about the necks of their dead. Judas takes a collection from among his soliders and sends monies back to Jerusalem to provide for sacrifices of atonement.
Read 1 Maccabees 4:36–59.

The Festival of Lights

On the celebration of Hanukkah, Jews tell a much-loved legend not found in the Bible:

When the priests, led by Judas Maccabeus, were about to light the *menorah*, the seven-branched candelabra, they were alarmed to find that the specially prepared oil was gone. Jugs of this oil were always kept sealed by the high priests, but there was only one small jar left—barely enough oil for one night. To their delight, the oil miraculously lasted for eight full days while the people celebrated and prepared more oil.

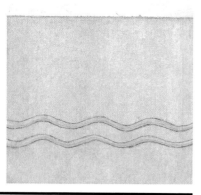

The menorah, a seven-branched candelabra, is lighted at the Jewish festival of Hanukkah to recollect the reconsecration of the Temple, which was defiled by the Greeks.

Hanukkah, which takes place in early December, is also called the *Festival of Lights* and is celebrated for eight days with prayer and praise. Tiny candles or oil lamps are lighted, one each day, in Jewish homes, and gifts are given to the children.

Restoration of Jewish Rights

Soon after Antiochus IV dies and his son Antiochus V ascends to the throne, Judas and his army besiege the pro-Greeks in the Acra, who call to the king for help. A large army, complete with thirty-two elephants, marches south from Antioch to attack Judas and defeat him, and he must retreat. His brother Eleazar is killed when he fearlessly attacks an elephant that he thinks is carrying the king.

Antiochus besieges Jerusalem, but unsuccessfully. Instead, a peace treaty is made to repeal the decree refusing the Jews' right to worship, and Antiochus's army withdraws.

Read 1 Maccabees 6:5-14,18-30,42-47,55-59.

Antiochus V is murdered by his brother Demetrius, who sends a peacekeeping group to Jerusalem, headed by a corrupt high priest named Alcimus, a descendant of Aaron. Judas is suspicious of him, and in no time Alcimus renews the persecution of the Jerusalem Jews. Judas is stirred to fight, and in battle once more, many of Judas' men become fearful and desert him—and Judas is killed.

Read 1 Maccabees 9:1,4-10,12-22.

Now Jonathan, Judas's youngest brother, takes Judas's place. After many victories, during which time his brother John is killed in ambush, Jonathan and the Seleucids declare a truce, and peace reigns—for a while.

Rival Seleucids court Jonathan, but another son of Epiphanes, Alexander, makes him high priest and wins his loyalty. This action is widely disapproved by many Jews. A Seleucid king has no right to appoint a high priest, nor is Jonathan's obscure Aaronite ancestry deemed desirable—but there is no other solution. When Jonathan is finally made governor of his province as well, his enemies withdraw.

When, in time, Jonathan is tricked and captured by a Seleucid strongman named Trypho, the people assume that he is dead, and his enemies rejoice that now the Jews have no one to lead them: " 'Let us make war on them and wipe out their memory from among men' " (12:53).

Read 1 Maccabees 9:23-31,54-57,65-73; 10:9,15-20,59-66; 12:39-48,53.

Assuming that Jonathan is dead, his brother Simon steps forward to be the Jews' leader. Learning that Jonathan

The Maccabees served as models of courage and integrity for their people. Write one hundred words about someone who inspires you in these ways.

is alive, Simon agrees to Trypho's bargain for his return. But Trypho murders Jonathan and the young Antiochus VI as well, and puts the Seleucid crown on his own head.

Simon continues to fortify Judah, occupying the fort himself and making his son John Hyrcanus commander of the army. When the people honor Simon for his service, he is granted full hereditary rights—the highest priestly, military, and civil office. Thus, the *Hasmonean* dynasty is born, named for the father of Mattathias.

Read 1 Maccabees 13:1-10,14-24,31-32,49-53; 14:4-19.

The young Antiochus VII, wanting to recover his family's kingdom, goes to war with John Hyrcanus, but he is defeated. Another plot—hatched by Simon's son-in-law, Ptolemy (no relation to the Greek general), who wants to rule Judah—is more successful. Ptolemy invites Simon and two of his sons to dinner and has them murdered. When he sends men to Jerusalem to seize Hyrcanus, word of the plot precedes them, and the men are caught and executed.

The Bible's story of the Maccabees ends by stating simply that John remained in charge and that his history and brave deeds were recorded in the chronicles of his reign, which was from 135 to 104 B.C.E.

Read 1 Maccabees 16:1-24.

How Does It All Turn Out?

To stop the story here is unsettling, and we want to know how it all turns out. The time is only one hundred years before the birth of Christ. Is there a connection?

Rome Takes Over

Two Hasmonean princes battle for the throne in vain and finally ask the Roman emissary Pompey—Judah has kept its Roman connections—to choose for them. When Pompey delays, the aggressive brother, Aristobulus II, attacks his brother, Hyrcanus II, and Pompey deports Aristobulus to Rome. Pompey then seizes Jerusalem, appoints Hyrcanus high priest, strips Judah of all its territory except for Galilee and the region across the Jordan River—and in 63 B.C.E. Jerusalem is under Roman domination. This is how the Jews became subject to the Romans.

The Arch of Titus, in Rome, contains a scene celebrating the fall of Jerusalem in 70 C.E.

Athens and Rome— and Jerusalem

The golden age of Greece, before the rise of Alexander the Great, was dominated by the city-state Athens, whose highly developed culture rapidly spread throughout the Aegean. Twice in the fifth century B.C.E. Athens led a military alliance of smaller Greek cities against invasions by the Persians. At peace again, Athens acquired wealth, produced magnificent architecture— such as the buildings of the Acropolis—and nurtured the concept of a democracy, which allowed its male citizens to vote and to judge cases in courts of law.

The genius of Athens' politicians, philosophers, poets, dramatists, and artists produced works held in the highest esteem all over the world, works that have given "the classical period" and "the classics" their name.

Even after the death of Alexander in the second century B.C.E. and the conquest of Greece by Rome, Greek culture continued to dominate the eastern Mediterranean. Its language became an international tongue that even found its way into the Gospels and the Epistles. Greek culture continued to inspire the art and literature of the Romans, although its democratic form of government, and Rome's republican model, began to disappear. By the time of Jesus, emperors and not the senate ruled the Romans—among whose captive peoples was a rebellious province called *Judaea*.

The first Jewish revolt, which was crushed by Titus—son of the emperor Vespasian— cost a reputed one million Jewish lives. In 70 C.E., Titus destroyed Jerusalem and the Temple, which was never rebuilt, and in the year 135 C.E., following a second rebellion, Jews were forbidden to enter Jerusalem.

Enter the Herods

Several years later, Julius Caesar himself appoints an Edomite half-Jew named Antipater governor of Judah. He rules until 43 B.C.E., when he is poisoned. Antipater leaves as his heir a son whom we know as Herod the Great.

In 37 B.C.E., Herod receives from the Roman Senate the title "king of the Jews." He returns to Judah and becomes a builder and warrior—and later the murderer and madman who instigates the slaughter of the Innocents in Bethlehem (Matthew 2:16–18).

News of Herod's death in the year 4 B.C.E. moves Joseph to return from Egypt with Mary and Jesus. Joseph avoids Bethlehem and goes north to live in Nazareth in Galilee because Herod's dangerous son Archelaus rules in Jerusalem.

Enter Jesus of Nazareth

Herod Antipas, another son of Herod the Great, is governor of Galilee, and he is the one who, at his birthday party, has John the Baptist beheaded. A year and a half later, Herod Antipas is in Jerusalem for the Passover, and because Herod has jurisdiction over Galileans, Pilate sends Jesus to be ques-

Herod the Great built a new temple in Jerusalem, beginning in 19 B.C.E. *Right:* A portion of a scaled model of Jerusalem showing Herod's temple

tioned by him. Herod, filled with curiosity, meets Jesus and hopes to see a miracle.

So the story of the Maccabees leads to the Hasmoneans, and the Hasmoneans lead to the Herods, and the Herods lead to the story of Jesus of Nazareth.

For Review

1. Why did the Chronicler write a history of Israel that is so different from the history we have read in earlier books of the Bible?

2. Why do the Jerusalem Jews refuse the help of the Jewish Samaritans?

3. What is true fasting, as mentioned in Third Isaiah?

4. In addition to the Samaritans' interference, what are the other reasons that the Jerusalemites delay rebuilding the Temple?

5. What is the symbolic meaning of the messianic king riding a donkey, not a horse?

6. The prophet Malachi tells the people to tithe. Define *tithe* and explain why tithing was needed.

7. Give two examples of how Nehemiah acts as a model public servant.

8. How might Ezra be said to have provided a constitution for his people?

9. Why does Obadiah accuse Edom of fratricide?

10. Who are the Seleucids, and how do the Jews come under their dominance?

11. Who are the Maccabees, and how do they enter the Jewish history?

12. Explain how the Jews become subject to the Romans.

13. What biblical incident is associated with each of the following: Herod the Great, his son Archelaus, and Herod Antipas?

10

Wisdom and Wit: Finding a Way to the Future

THIS chapter introduces the wisdom and the story books, most of which came late to the Bible. The **wisdom books** were written by Jewish sages to help Israel pray, love the Law, and live righteously. The **story books,** one of which you have already read in the Book of Ruth, are among the most memorable biblical tales.

The Wisdom Books: How to Live a Good Life

The seven wisdom books grew out of an ancient scribal tradition in the Near East, especially in Egypt, that instructed court administrators on how to act. These earlier writings contained maxims on the acquiring of virtues and, often, on the problem of good versus evil—although they were not religious texts. But Israel's wisdom writings gained a character of their own because of Israel's belief that God was the source of all wisdom. Israel's wisdom books speak to the individual about the wholeness and integrity of a good life, and about the personal disintegration caused by sin.

When Saint Luke says in his Gospel that Jesus "advanced [in] wisdom and age and favor before God and man" (2:52), he is saying that Jesus became a whole person—thoughtful, knowledgeable, and loving in his relationships with his family, friends, village, world, and God. Inspiring moral integrity was the goal of the biblical teachers of wisdom.

Over two thousand years ago, the writers of the wisdom and the story books wondered about how to survive while living in submission to foreign cultures.
Facing page: In Jerusalem, Jews celebrate "the blessing of the priests" at the Western Wall, which dates back to the destruction of the second Temple by the Romans.

Job: Whom Do We Trust?

The Book of Job is based on a folktale perhaps five thousand years old. Job was written sometime after the Babylonian exile by an unknown Jew, who is the most-learned writer in the Bible and, above all, a brilliant poet. His work is one of the world's literary treasures.

The first two chapters of Job and chapter 42, verses 7 to 17, tell the original folktale. Although this book is not a historical piece, Job was apparently a historical person, mentioned in the Book of Ezekiel as a model of integrity and justice (14:13–14).

The message of Job is that suffering is not punishment from God nor is prosperity a sign of God's approval. The mystery of evil is too big to understand, and to trust in God is the only way to live. The author has inserted, between the beginning and the end of the tale, a series of disputes about these issues between Job and his friends, who rebuke Job for questioning God.

1. Job is praised by God, who permits an angel to test him with terrible disasters. Job accepts them in faith.
Read Job 1:1–22; 2:1–13.

Notes on the Book of Job

Satan: The Hebrew word for *Satan* is often translated as "the Satan," meaning "the adversary." The Satan mentioned in Job is not the familiar devil who appears later in Jewish and Christian theology but, rather, a heavenly prosecutor whose job is to test the genuineness of human virtue.

The message of the Book of Job is that suffering is not punishment from God nor is prosperity a sign of God's approval.
Right: In Soviet Armenia, family members mourn the loss of loved ones killed in an earthquake.

The angel: The author of Job used God's permitting the angel to test Job simply to get the story moving. We are not to understand that God ever initiates human suffering.

2. When finally Job cries out, "Why?" his friends insist that his own sin is the reason for his misfortune. But Job disagrees.

   Read the following passages from Job:
- *3:1-6 (Job's complaint)*
- *4:7-9 (the words of Job's friend Eliphaz)*
- *6:8-10,24-25 (Job's reply to Eliphaz)*
- *8:3-7 (the words of Job's friend Bildad)*
- *11:1-6 (the words of Job's friend Zophar)*
- *13:1-5,15-16 (Job's reply to Zophar)*
- *27:3-6 (Job's words to Bildad)*
- *33:1-6,8-13 (the words of a young man named Elihu)*

3. God speaks—and Job admits that the mystery of life is too great for him to understand. At last he believes this truth and accepts what has happened.

   Read Job 38:1-30; 39:19-30; 42:1-6.

What was Job's experience like? In a one-page essay, relate it to the tough times you have faced.

Psalms: Who Is the Enemy?

The *Psalter*, or the Book of Psalms, is a collection of one hundred and fifty religious songs written by poets and musicians from early history through the postexilic period. "David's" psalms (noted as such in the Bible) are David's in the way that many of the wisdom books are credited to Solomon: written to, for, or in the mode of—rather than by—David. We can find many styles of poetry among the psalms and a multitude of themes: praise, lament, petition, thanksgiving, love, sorrow, hope, and anger. Some psalms were written to praise the king, some for religious celebrations, and some for individual prayer. The psalms that review Israel's history recall virtues and sins like our own.

   Some of the psalms fit easily into our life—like the twenty-third psalm, ". . . I fear no evil; for you are at my side . . ." (23:4)—but others are puzzling.

   The masculine nouns and pronouns used for God and all humans throughout the psalms are disturbing to some people. In reading, they can be substituted whenever the meaning of the psalm is not changed. The words *humanity* and *humankind* are substitutes for *man* and *mankind*. Feminine pronouns, the word *one*, the plural *people* or *persons*,

Take an experience in your life and tell about it in the style of a psalm of love, petition, lament, or praise.

The Psalms condemn the evils in the world that keep people hungry, homeless, imprisoned, and tortured. **Below:** A child in a farmers' market in Detroit

the collective *sisters and brothers,* and the word *others* are substitutes for other masculine terms.

The psalms should be read slowly, aloud if possible, even to yourself. Explore their meaning phrase by phrase, allowing each word to speak for itself. Too often we scan a psalm, assume we have grasped it, and miss all but the most obvious message. To read a psalm and discover fresh meaning that touches life at school and with peers is to read it for the first time. The psalms were written for people who had the same needs as we do and lived in a world as good and as evil as ours. To pray the psalms is to talk to God in some of the most beautiful language and with some of the most eloquent voices in the world.

Read the following passages from the Book of Psalms:
- *18:2–7,17–20:* How is God a rock?
- *6:2–5,9–11:* Who or what are the evildoers in your life?
- *25:4–7,16–18:* This is a beautiful prayer for forgiveness, guidance, and help.
- *28:1–2,6–9:* To what would this prayer apply?
- *14:1–7:* For whom would you pray this prayer?
- *10:1–6,11–18:* This psalm repeats the old lament, Why do the evil prosper?

Enemies—inside and outside

The enemies that the psalms berate can be the oppression and the evil in the world that keep people hungry, homeless, imprisoned, and tortured: the terrorists, the racists, the tyrants, the greedy arms merchants, and the industrialists who despoil the planet. Or the enemies can be our own crippling fears of mugging, rape, bullies, exploiters, or betrayers of age, weakness, and insecurity. Or the enemies can be the evils in ourselves: our jealousy, vengeance, lust, greed, anger, or self-pity. Wherever such evil is present, we can say with the Psalmist, Smash it in the teeth! (3:8).

Proverbs: Where Is Wisdom Found?

The Book of Proverbs, appearing sometime after the Babylonian exile, responded to a lapse in Israel's religious practice. Immorality, greed, and exploitation of the poor were rife, and the need to keep the heart and spirit of early Judaism alive inspired the scribes who put this book together. If Israel were to lose its spirit entirely, it would lose its faith.

But Proverbs is not a book of spirituality. Like the other wisdom writings, it is concerned with how to live life well.

Full of practical advice, Proverbs also contains moving passages about helping the poor and revering the elderly, and although it does not go as far as Jesus' forgiveness of enemies, it reaches beyond vengeance. Riches and worldly success, rightly gained, are seen as the reward for the good life—there is no hint of an afterlife—and honor, dignity, and a good name are a person's memorial.

The role of the good wife is exalted in the famous passage about "The Ideal Wife" (31:10–31), while the adulteress and the nagging wife are condemned. Proverbs also warns against the evils of alcohol and counsels on the disciplining of children—once translated as the "*beating* of children"—and the avoidance of bad company. In this book, wisdom, an attribute of God, speaks in a feminine voice. We cannot be good without her, she says.

Read the following passages from the Book of Proverbs:
- *1:1-6:* This passage explains the purpose of the book.
- *1:10-19:* Wisdom speaks about keeping dangerous company.
- *1:20-23:* Wisdom says that she roams the streets and is found everywhere.
- *8:22-31:* Wisdom existed before all other things.
- *31:10-11,25-31:* "The Ideal Wife" praises a valiant woman.
- *3:11-12:* Like a loving parent, God disciplines us.

God's reproof

We can learn much from God's reprimands, but that does not make them easier to accept. Once, while journeying to visit her convents, Saint Teresa of Ávila was riding her donkey across a stream when the saddle slipped and she ended up head-down under the belly of the beast. After complaining to the LORD about such treatment, she heard, "Teresa, who the LORD loves, the LORD chastises. This is how I treat all my friends." And Teresa replied tartly, "No wonder you have so few!"

Ecclesiastes: Is Life Lived in Vain?

Ecclesiastes is Greek for the name *Qoheleth,* which is Hebrew for "teacher," and Qoheleth's pupils thought of him as *the* teacher. He lived around 250 B.C.E., during the Greek period, and at first glance seems to have been impossibly pessimistic about life. Where Habakkuk and Job asked God why, Qoheleth's response to life's inconsistencies was, Who's surprised? On the other hand, he may have been the kind of man who

Write three proverbs for our age.

Write a reaction to Qoheleth's "What's new?" attitude toward life. Do you agree or disagree with him? Why?

According to the teacher Qoheleth, life is a mysterious cycle of birth and death that only God understands. *Below:* In the Judaean desert, swimmers enjoy an oasis pool. *Right:* In Maryland, students mourn the death of a classmate who was killed in a car accident.

liked to startle his students with unexpected questions and provocative comments—just to make them think. For example:

- In his book, Qoheleth says that nothing makes a difference—people are born, die, and are forgotten, and there is nothing new under the sun: ". . . Vanity of vanities! All things are vanity!" (1:2).
- Then he reverses this dour comment with his famous poem (3:1–8): "There is an appointed time for everything . . . under the heavens"—familiar today as the folk song "Turn, Turn, Turn."
- He concludes that although everything repeats itself, it is always in God's time.

Qoheleth worried about injustice and wickedness and about their victims, who were doomed, he believed, to a dead end in earthly life. As for eternity, he knew nothing of a heaven hereafter. But in the end he came to the conclusion that life was a mystery he could not solve. The sensible thing, he says in his book, is to accept it from the hand of God and enjoy it as well as one can. So Qoheleth was not, after all, the world's greatest crank.

Read Ecclesiastes 1:1–11; 2:18–26; 3:1–22.

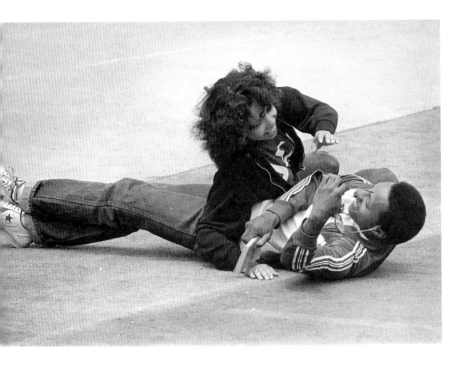

The Song of Songs is a collection of poems celebrating love and sexuality as a powerful and holy bond.

The Song of Songs: Human and Divine Love

The Song of Songs is a collection of love poems written by unknown authors sometime after the Babylonian exile, about 450 B.C.E. It is a dialog between a bridegroom and a bride, who speak of their love and longing for one another, with now-and-again asides from their friends.

Although God is not mentioned in the book, early interpreters saw the work as a religious allegory. For both Jews and Christians, it was an image of God's love for Israel; and for the Christians, it was a figure of Christ's love for the soul or for the Church. Surprisingly, even some modern commentators have found this language of human love and sexuality inappropriate for a sacred book—as though God did not design human love as a powerful and holy bond.

1. The bride describes herself as dark, like the tents of Kedar that are woven from black goat's hair. She wistfully asks where her lover pastures his sheep. It is the kind of yearning all lovers know.

Read Song of Songs 1:5-7.

2. The bride compares herself to a flower of the field, unlike the exotic blooms that grow in the gardens of the rich. But the groom says that compared to the other women, she is a lily among thistles!

Read Song of Songs 2:1-6.

Do young people today see virginity as a virtue? Give your opinion in a paragraph.

3. A walled garden has long been a symbol of virginity. The groom sings with joy of the maiden who has kept herself for their bridal union.

Read Song of Songs 4:12-16.

In verse 12, the term *sister* is one of endearment, not kinship.

4. The bride longs to be as close to the groom as the name seal that he wears on a cord about his neck, resting on his heart. She would be one with him—as he and his name are one.

Read Song of Songs 8:6-7.

Wisdom: Why do the Wicked Flourish?

The Book of Wisdom was written to strengthen the Jews' faith and to answer the old question, Why do the wicked flourish while the good continue to suffer? Its author is a scholarly Jew who lived in Alexandria, Egypt, around 100 B.C.E.

1. For the first time in the Bible, this sage says that life with God forever is the soul's destiny. Sin, not God, is responsible for the death of the spirit: ". . . God did not make death . . ." (1:13). And he adds that contrary to earlier teachings, the good are not necessarily rewarded on earth nor the wicked always punished.

Read Wisdom 1:12-16; 2:21-24; 3:1-5.

2. The author of Wisdom also rejects the belief that childlessness is a disgrace. The childless person can bear fruit in virtues that benefit everyone. Unfortunately, he does hold that the children of the wicked share their doom; whether he means the disasters that affect their lives or eternal doom is not clear. Early death, he holds, is not a punishment for sin but may even be an escape from future sin.

Read Wisdom 3:13-19; 4:7-11.

3. At the final judgment the wicked will see that their wealth and success are not rewardable in the arithmetic of eternal life. They will remember their mockery of the just ones and see that all the while *they themselves* were the fools.

Read Wisdom 5:3-14.

The resurrection of the body

The writer of Wisdom talks about eternal life and the soul's survival of death. This concept of the soul as separate from the life of the body indicates his exposure to Greek thought, and this author was the first to put Jewish teaching into Greek terms and language. Generally the Jews had seen the person as body-and-soul—a whole. Thus, up to this time, their conception of resurrection had more to do with restoring people to earthly life—as in the miracle by Elisha (2 Kings 4:32–37).

The writer of the Book of Wisdom talks about the soul and eternal life. *Above:* The butterfly has long been a symbol of the afterlife because the lowly caterpillar, entombed in its cocoon, bursts out transformed into a gorgeous creature capable of flight.

Sirach: Who Is Wisdom?

Jesus ben Sirach ran a school for scriptural study and Jewish wisdom in Alexandria, Egypt, and wrote between 200 and 175 B.C.E. He wanted to show his fellow Jews, who were confused by the philosophical questions of the Greeks, that true wisdom was found in the teachings of Israel. Sirach said that all wisdom came from God and that it had a feminine voice. Keeping the Commandments is the way to wisdom, he said, and his book is as full of wisdom for us as it was for the ancients.

Read Sirach 1:19–23; 2:1–6; 3:1–4; 4:1–5,8–10; 5:11–15; 6:8–12,14–17; 11:7–9; 24:1–8.

If you were to personify wisdom, would it be young or old? male or female? human or another animal? Create a written portrait of wisdom. Once you have thoroughly described wisdom, let it speak: what is its wisest saying?

In praise of wisdom

Chapter 24 is one of the greatest writings about wisdom in the Bible. Sirach says that wisdom came forth from the mouth of God to make her dwelling with Jacob's people. He is reminding the Jews, and us, that God's wisdom is far above the wisdom of the world.

Wisdom's testing

Wisdom tests us with difficulties. Times of difficulty can be seed times, times for growing strong.

A story is told of a man who saw a monarch butterfly struggling to get out of its cocoon. Wanting to help it, he took his penknife and carefully slit the cocoon to free the butterfly. To his astonishment, the butterfly gave a few flutters and died. Cutting it free was the worst thing the man could have done. The butterfly needed to struggle in order to strengthen its wings.

The Story Books: Encouraging Israel to Be Faithful

Unlike the stories of Jacob, Rebekah, David, Saul, Jonathan, and the rest, which take us through the history of Israel's calling to be God's people, the later tales are told to inspire courage and faith in times of trial.

The Book of Tobit is a wisdom tale like the story of Joseph and tells of a noble and faithful elder who remains steadfast in the face of disaster.

The Book of Judith tells of a courageous woman who defies all the stereotypical notions of "how women are supposed to be." Saving her people from the Assyrian army with wit and wisdom has made Judith a universal favorite, whether or not she is a fictional character.

The Book of Esther, on the other hand, is about a naturally timid woman—a queen—who risks her life to save her people from a wicked schemer who plans to slay them. Esther is a model for those who are not brave.

The Book of Daniel is listed as a prophetic book because of a prophetic vision of "the son of man," and it provides both high entertainment and heroic faith.

The Book of Jonah is a lesson for us as well as for the ancients to whom it was told—and it ends with a searching question that we are all required to answer, sooner or later.

Tobit: The Faithful Jew

The Book of Tobit was written by an unknown author about 200 B.C.E., to encourage faithful Jews to be righteous and patient during the difficult Seleucid period. The story is set around five hundred years earlier, in the Assyrian capital of Nineveh after the fall of the northern kingdom.

Tobit is a faithful Jew: Even after the northern kingdom broke away from Judah, Tobit journeyed south to worship in Jerusalem. In exile, he has kept the Law, tithed for the poor, and worshiped God. During the reign of Sennacherib, who vengefully executes many Jews, Tobit takes on the task of burying their bodies; when this becomes dangerous, he goes into hiding. Upon the death of the king, Tobit returns to Nineveh.

Read Tobit 1:1-22.

One day in the year of Tobit's return, another slain Jew is found, and Tobit buries him. That night as Tobit sleeps outside, bird droppings fall on his eyes, cataracts form, and soon he becomes blind. Thereafter he has to depend upon his wife for support. One day, when she returns from work with a goat for payment, Tobit crankily comments that it was probably stolen by her employers, and she turns on him in anger; now his *true* character is showing, she complains. Frustrated and ashamed, Tobit prays that God will take his life.

Read Tobit 2:1-14; 3:1,5-6.

The scene changes to the city of Ecbatana, in Media, where Sarah, the daughter of a man named Raguel, is being taunted by a maid. Sarah has been married seven times, but a jealous demon has killed each husband on the wedding night. Bewildered, Sarah has been so hard on her maids that one now suggests that she join her husbands! In despair Sarah wants to hang herself, but the thought of her father's grief deters her. Like Tobit, she prays that God will let her die.

Read Tobit 3:7-15.

On that very day, Tobit remembers some money he has left in the hands of a relative in Media and decides to send his son Tobiah to get it. He gives Tobiah the necessary document and bids him to find a trustworthy guide and companion and be off. A young man, really the angel Raphael, is sent to Tobiah by God. Tobit approves of Azariah—the angel's assumed name—and the two leave, accompanied by Tobiah's dog.

The story of faithful Tobit and his family is set in the time of the Assyrian conquests.
Above: A carving depicts a city in Israel falling to the Assyrians.

The Book of Tobit encourages devout Jews to righteousness and patience in the face of life's injuries. Tobit suffers blindness when bird droppings fall in his eyes. Later, the angel Raphael cures him with fish gall.

In Tobit, we see the model of a faithful Jew in ancient Israel. In writing, create a model of a faithful Christian today.

That night, when Tobiah catches a fish, Raphael tells him to save the heart, the liver, and the gallbladder, which possess wonderful powers. Raphael also tells Tobiah to ask for the hand of Sarah, his next of kin. Understandably, Tobiah is hesitant, but Raphael counsels him to marry her. On his wedding night, Tobiah is to throw the fish liver and heart on the coals that warm the room, and the demon will vanish.

Read Tobit 4:1-6,12-15,20-21; 5:1-22; 6:1-18.

Tobiah and Raphael reach Ecbatana and are welcomed by Raguel, but when Tobiah asks to marry Sarah, her father warns him about the husbands. Tobiah insists, the marriage takes place, and that night, when Tobiah puts the fish liver and heart on the coals in their bedroom, the demon departs. Needless to say, all goes well, and a great wedding feast is held. While the family celebrates, Raphael travels to reclaim Tobit's money from his kinsman.

Read Tobit 7:1-17; 8:1-21; 9:1-6.

At home, Tobit and Anna wait fearfully for their son, who has been away so long. Tobiah and Sarah set out at last, and as they near Tobit's home, Raphael tells Tobiah to keep the fish gallbladder ready in his hand. Anna sees them and runs to embrace her son, with blind Tobit stumbling after her. Young Tobiah smears the fish gall on Tobit's eyes, peels off the cataracts, and his sight is restored! The people of Nineveh marvel that Tobit can see again.

More celebration follows, and at last Tobit says that Azariah must have a reward. But the angel refuses the money. He reveals his identity and tells the family that the prayers of both Sarah and Tobit were heard and that he was sent to them by God. When they fall on their knees in fear, he bids them to rise and praise God—and disappears, while Tobit sings a song of praise to God.

Read Tobit 12:1-5,11-22.

The grateful dead

The writer of Tobit was familiar with the folk literature of his time, and the Book of Tobit shows traces of several ancient stories—among them one called "The Grateful Dead." This folktale tells how a young man buries a corpse in perilous circumstances and later obtains a bride with the help of a companion and protector, who is ultimately revealed as the spirit of the deceased.

Judith: Courage and Piety

The author of the Book of Judith was probably a Palestinian Jew who wrote sometime after 150 B.C.E., during the rule of the Hasmoneans. The story is set in the Persian period after the Babylonian exile, and the first sentence of the book contains a blooper. Nebuchadnezzar, the author says, is king of Assyria—when everyone knows that he was king of Babylon. It is so obviously wrong that we know that the author is teaching a lesson—not a history—in the manner of folk and hero legends. Judith may not have been a historical person, but she was a model of faith and courage, and that was what the Jews needed.

Holofernes, Nebuchadnezzar's general, marches his army to the borders of Israel and deals out such destruction on the way that nations surrender without a struggle. Earlier, the Israelites had refused to help Nebuchadnezzar in a war, so now he is going to punish them. The Jews in Jerusalem warn the border districts to post guards, fortify towns, and store food—and the city of Bethulia especially must defend the mountain passes where the Assyrians could enter.

Holofernes, wanting to know this enemy better, asks leaders of neighboring nations for information about the Israelites. An Ammonite named Achior says that as long as Israel does not disobey its God, it is invincible. Holofernes must not attack until they have sinned, or disaster will befall him.

Read Judith 1:1,7,11-12; 2:1,4-9,14-20,28; 3:1-4,9; 5:1-5,20-21.

Holofernes, furious at Achior, has him bound and left on the plain below Bethulia, where he will be executed when the town falls. The Bethulians find him, take him back to their city, listen to his report of Holofernes's plan, and give him asylum.

Holofernes moves his army to the plain for attack, but the Edomites point out that he now controls the springs for the city. Why not wait for the Bethulians to run out of water and die of thirst, and spare the lives of his men? Pleased, Holofernes has the army settle down for a little R and R while Bethulia slowly perishes.

In Bethulia, water is rationed, the inhabitants panic, and after thirty-four days the people denounce the elders for not surrendering—begging them to do so " 'this very day' " (7:28). But Uzziah, the chief elder, persuades them to wait five days longer. They will pray even harder, and then, if God does not answer, they will give themselves up.

Read Judith 6:1-21; 7:1-16,19-32.

Judith is everything a heroine should be—pious, disciplined, intelligent, and fearless. Hearing the elders' plan, she orders them to her home and berates them. They are laying down conditions for *God?* She is appalled. Surrender means that Israel will fall, Jerusalem and the Temple will be destroyed, and the people will be enslaved. This is a time for testing, not defeat!

But Uzziah reminds her that they must honor their vow to the people unless another solution can be found. Maybe she would pray for rain? Judith, who already has a plan, contemptuously ignores this suggestion and tells the elders that she and her maid will be at the city gate that night and want to pass through with no questions asked.

Alone again, she dons sackcloth, strews ashes upon herself, and prays that God will make her strong—to crush the enemy " 'by the hand of a woman' " (9:10).

Read Judith 8:1-36; 9:1-14.

Then Judith bathes and anoints her body with scented oils, arranges her hair, puts on rich clothing, and makes herself beautiful to captivate the enemy commander. Giving a sack of provisions to her maid, they set out for the city gate. When the elders see Judith, they are astonished by her beauty, ask God's blessing on her, and let the two women through the gate.

Judith and her maid go down the mountain to the plain, where they meet Assyrian soldiers, who ask their identity. Judith says that she is a Hebrew who is running away from Bethulia before it falls and that she has information for Holofernes about the mountain passes to use in his attack. The men, dazzled by her beauty, escort her to Holofernes, and when the general sees her, he too is astonished. Judith easily deceives him with her plan, saying that in order to help him, she must leave camp each evening to pray to her God. Holofernes's success depends upon attacking only after the Jews have sinned; otherwise he will be defeated. In prayer, God will tell her when the Jews have committed their crimes.

Holofernes is hopelessly befuddled by the sight of this enchanting woman and has a tent prepared for her. He invites her to a meal, but she graciously refuses food, saying that she can only eat her own—kosher—food. When Holofernes asks what she will eat when her food is gone, she answers that her supplies will doubtlessly last until her task is accomplished. Escorted to her tent, Judith sleeps until midnight, then rises, and with her maid goes out of the camp to pray. For three nights she does this, going to the springs, where she bathes and asks God to guide her.

Read Judith 10:1-23; 12:1-9.

After waiting impatiently for three days, Holofernes invites Judith to a banquet—after which he plans to seduce her. When she, as impatient as he, accepts, Holofernes is beside himself with expectation and celebrates so enthusiastically that he gets drunk and falls asleep. Once the servants withdraw, Holofernes's orderly closes the tent so that the love scene will be private—but not before Judith reminds the orderly that later she and her maid will go out for prayer.

Alone with the drunken Holofernes, Judith prays for strength, then takes his sword, grabs him by the hair, and strikes two blows with all her might, cutting off his head. She rolls his body off the bed, puts the head in her sack, summons her maid, and the two "go off to pray."

This time they walk until they reach Bethulia. At the gates, Judith shouts, "Our God is with us!" The people open the gates and call the elders, and Judith draws the head out of the bag as she thanks God that by the power of her beauty and without defilement, she has triumphed.

Read Judith 12:10-12,15-20; 13:1-20.

The head of Holofernes is hung from the city wall, and Judith tells the men to arm themselves at dawn and rush outside, pretending to attack. The Assyrians will run to get Holofernes, discover that he is dead and Judith is gone, and panic. This happens, and with a cry—" 'A single Hebrew woman has brought disgrace on the house of King Nebuchadnezzar' " (14:18)—the Assyrians flee. The Israelites follow them, slay many, loot the camp, and return with riches for the town and for Judith. The women of Israel dance and sing

Judith combines personality traits often referred to as feminine with others seen as masculine. Answer the following in writing:

- Do males and females have different qualities of mind, heart, and feelings? If so, list those that each gender possesses. If not, list some traits that are shared by both.

The fearless Judith prayed for strength to crush the enemies of her people—and then did so by slaying the Assyrian general.

in her honor, then all the people journey to Jerusalem to present the spoils at the Temple. Judith returns to Bethulia and lives to an honorable old age.

Read Judith 14:1–19; 15:1–13; 16:18–25.

A historical mirror

The author of Judith recalled Israel's history, when both Assyria and Babylon sent armies to commit deeds just as bloody as Holofernes's plans. His object was to remind the people that in the past, Israel had *not* trusted God, only its own schemes, and had fallen.

Kosher food

The word *kosher* means "fit" or "proper" in Hebrew. Kosher food is prepared according to Jewish dietary laws based on the Bible and later interpreted in the Talmud. To be kosher, meat must come from animals slaughtered and inspected by persons trained in these laws. And unless it is broiled, meat must be thoroughly salted and rinsed to remove any blood.

Esther: A Timid Queen Is Heroic

We do not know when the Book of Esther was written, but we do know that it had two purposes: to praise the goodness of God, who saved the Jews from annihilation, and to explain the origin of the feast called Purim. The festival celebrates the triumph of the Jewish queen Esther over the villain Haman, who plotted to slay all the Jews in Persia. The time of the story is the reign of King Xerxes I—called Ahasuerus—around 485 to 464 B.C.E., and the place is Susa, a Persian city where many Jews of the Dispersion settled. One such Jew, Mordecai, is the only historical figure in the book other than King Ahasuerus. Esther is fictional.

The story opens with a banquet that King Ahasuerus gives for the nobles of the land. On the seventh day, when the men are very drunk, he calls for the queen, Vashti, so that he may show off her beauty. Knowing that the men are all drunk, Vashti refuses to appear, and the king and the court are aghast. What should be done to such a queen?

Read Esther 1:1–22.

Sober again, the king deposes Vashti in order to save face and calls to the palace all the beautiful maidens of the realm. The one most pleasing to the king will take Vashti's place.

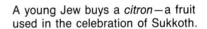
A young Jew buys a *citron*—a fruit used in the celebration of Sukkoth.

Modern Branches of Judaism

Judaism today has three main branches—Orthodox, Reform, and Conservative—all of which profess to be truly Jewish. Yet the branches differ from one another as much as do the Catholic, the Protestant, and the Eastern churches in Christianity.

Orthodox Judaism is the oldest and largest group within Judaism. Orthodox Judaism calls itself "Torah-true Judaism" because of its strict adherence to the Law of Moses. This traditional stance shapes its approach to theology, worship, morality, and festivals.

Within this Orthodox branch is a very conservative group known as the *Hasidim*, which developed in reaction to the scholarly forms of Judaism. Hasidim's founders preached that God is not to be found in researching the Hebrew Scriptures but rather in simple, heartfelt faith.

Reform Judaism arose from the desire to adapt to modern society. This liberal branch found many adherents in the United States, where Jewish people enjoyed greater freedom and acceptance than elsewhere. Reform Jews call their houses of worship "temples" rather than "synagogues" and have begun to ordain women rabbis. Although they believe that the Mosaic Law need not be followed literally, Reform Jews still hold to the belief in one God and to the need for high standards of morality.

Conservative Judaism lies between the strict Orthodox and the liberal Reform branches. Conservative Jews hold that conscience must be the final rule of life, and they cautiously apply the Jewish traditions to modern life. Frequently, Conservative Jews are involved in the professions and the arts, and their rabbis are leaders in secular life as well as within their congregations.

Mordecai sends his lovely cousin Esther to be a candidate, and he cautions her not to reveal her Jewish origins. When it is Esther's turn to visit the king, he is so struck with her beauty and simplicity that he chooses her above all the others to be his queen.

Read Esther 2:1-23.

The king appoints a man named Haman as prime minister, before whom all are to bow in passing, but Mordecai will not do so. Angry, Haman determines to punish not only this Jew but *all* Jews, and slyly he tells the king of a treasonous people in his kingdom who deserve to be slain. The king, without question, gives assent—thus Haman sets a date for the slaughter of all the Jews in Persia.

When Mordecai hears this news, he begs Esther to plead for her people before the king, but she says that to go to court without the king's summons is to risk death. Mordecai wryly points out that she will die, one way or another—what is to risk? Esther agrees, saying, " 'If I perish, I perish!' " (4:16). She fasts and prays, then adorns herself beautifully, and appears in the throne room shaking with fear. When Ahasuerus offers her his golden scepter, a sign of welcome, she faints—but finally explains that she wants the king and Haman to be her guests at dinner.

Read Esther 3:5-7; 4:1-16; 5:1-5.

After dining with the two men, the timid Esther hesitates to tell the king her purpose and instead asks them to return the following night, when she will explain.

The king retires but cannot sleep, and he calls his scribes to read aloud to him the history of his reign. Hearing that Mordecai once uncovered a plot to kill him, he discovers that Mordecai was never rewarded for this good deed and is determined to honor him. But at that moment Haman arrives, having built a gallows on which to hang Mordecai. Before Haman can speak to the king, Ahasuerus asks him what the king should do to honor a certain man. Thinking that *he himself* is the man, Haman dreams up an elaborate procession, and the king, pleased, says in effect, "Splendid—now go do it for Mordecai." Needless to say, it ruins Haman's day.

Read Esther 5:6-14; 6:1-14.

The next evening, the king and Haman are once again with Esther, and after dining she tells the king that one of his nobles wants to murder the queen and all her people. When, outraged, the king asks who, she points to Haman.

In the story of Esther, King Ahasuerus gives the evil minister Haman his signet ring, which bears a seal used to authenticate royal documents. Haman uses it to decree the slaughter of all the Jews in Persia. (See Esther 3:8-13.)

The king is wild, Haman grovels before Esther—and in the end it is Haman, not Mordecai, who hangs on the gallows. *Read Esther 7:1-10.*

A Persian version

In addition to its Jewish themes, the Book of Esther reveals traces of Persian folklore. A similar story, *The Thousand and One Nights,* tells of a king who is angry at the infidelity of a former wife. He weds a different maiden every day and has her beheaded the following morning. But the beautiful Scheherazade outwits him by telling an unfinished story every night so that he must wait another day for its ending. After a thousand and one nights, the king abandons his dreadful scheme because he now loves her. Both Esther and Scheherazade are bringers of salvation: Scheherazade to the maidens of her land, and Esther to her people.

Purim

The Jewish feast of Purim honors the courage of the gentle and beautiful Esther. It gets its name from the lot—the *pûr*—that Haman drew to determine the date of the slaughter of the Jews. Purim is one of the feasts that Jesus celebrated in the synagogue as a child, booing Haman and cheering Esther. Although not a profoundly religious feast, Purim is dear to Jews everywhere.

Daniel: A Nonviolent Hero

The Book of Daniel was probably written between 167 and 164 B.C.E. It combines early folktales with apocalyptic writing—a style using symbols and visions to show, in times of distress, "how it will turn out." The oppression of the Jews under Antiochus Epiphanes was such a time, and the book was written to encourage the oppressed Jews to have faith and persevere. The authors of Daniel were nonviolent Jews who disapproved of the Maccabees' violence and set forth the character Daniel's trust in God as the acceptable response to persecution.

1. When Nebuchadnezzar takes Jerusalem, among the Israelites exiled to Babylon are four young men of royal blood whose names—Daniel, Hananiah, Mishael, and Azariah—are changed to the Babylonian Belteshazzar, Shadrach, Meshach,

In our century, a "Haman" killed six million Jews and one million other Europeans. Who was he? Explain in writing how such crimes can evolve within a community or a country.

The Feast of Purim celebrates the courage of Esther and the downfall of Haman. Fun and melodrama accompany the reading of the Book of Esther, as children boo the villain and cheer the heroine.

and Abednego to show their adoption by the Babylonian king.

While training for royal service to Babylon, Daniel asks the king's chamberlain to substitute vegetables and water for their nonkosher food. The chamberlain hesitates lest it be bad for their health—and *his*, should they not survive—but after ten days, Daniel and his friends are healthier than any who sit at the royal table.

Nebuchadnezzar has a dream that his seers cannot interpret, but Daniel explains its meaning. A huge statue symbolizes the Babylonians, the Persians, and the Greeks—all oppressors of the Jews. A stone from a mountain dashes the statue to bits and itself grows into a mountain that fills the earth. The stone is the kingdom of God that one day will rule the nations. Nebuchadnezzar is so awed that he gives Daniel and his friends the highest positions in the realm.

Next, Nebuchadnezzar orders his court to worship a golden statue or be thrown into a fiery furnace. When Shadrach, Meshach, and Abednego refuse, they are cast into the flames, but inside the furnace the three walk calmly about, singing a canticle of praise to the LORD. The king, astounded, calls them out and finds them totally unharmed; not even their clothing is scorched. He then orders that whoever blasphemes the God of the Jews will be chopped to bits! He seems determined to put *someone* to death.

2. Belshazzar, the next Babylonian king mentioned in Daniel, gets drunk at a banquet and lets his friends toast pagan gods with vessels taken from the Jerusalem Temple. Suddenly he sees a hand that is writing three strange words on the wall. When his seers cannot interpret them, Daniel is called. The three words—*Mene, Tekel,* and *Peres*—have the following meanings: *Mene,* "His days are numbered"; *Tekel,* "He has been weighed on the scales of God and been found wanting"; and *Peres,* "His kingdom will end up in the hands of the Persians." That night Belshazzar is slain.

3. Darius—a fictional Persian king—puts Daniel in charge of the kingdom, which incites jealous officials to plot against him. They suggest a law forbidding anyone to pray to any god but the king, or they will be thrown to the lions. That very day, when Daniel prays to his God, his enemies report him. Darius tries to exempt Daniel but cannot find a way, and Daniel is thrown to the lions. The next morning, Darius is delighted to hear Daniel say that his God sent an angel to close the mouths of the lions. Thereupon the perpetrators

The story of Daniel in the lions' den ends with his accusers and their families suffering Daniel's punishment.

of Daniel's sentence are themselves and their families thrown to the lions.

4. Daniel's dreams symbolize prophetic events. In one dream, four powerful beasts—representing Israel's enemies— rise out of a boiling sea. But God condemns them and gives dominion to "one like a son of man" (7:13)—meaning human—whom all peoples and nations will one day serve. Christians see this promise kept in the coming of Christ, which is why the Book of Daniel is placed among the prophetic books.

The angel Gabriel tells Daniel that many of those who sleep in the dust of the earth shall arise; some will live forever. It is the first mention of resurrection in the Hebrew Scriptures.

Read Daniel 12:2-3.

5. Next comes a morality tale about Susanna, the beautiful wife of a wealthy Jew in Babylon. Two local judges, filled with lust for her, meet at her home and plot to catch her alone. When Susanna decides to bathe in her garden, she sends her maids to fetch fragrant oils and bids them to lock the gate. But the judges, hiding there, come out and demand that Susanna lie with them, or they will say that she has been with a young man. Susanna is dismayed but refuses the judges. When everyone believes their lie, Susanna is condemned to death for adultery. She prays, and the LORD inspires a young man named Daniel to cry out, " 'I will have no part in the death of this woman' " (13:46). Berating the people for condemning Susanna without question, he calls up the culprits and cleverly traps them with their own lies.

Read Daniel 13:1-64.

6. Several of the other stories in Daniel mock idol worship. In the first, a mini-mystery, the Persian king Cyrus asks Daniel why he does not worship the Babylonian god Bel— another name for Marduk. Daniel says that he worships only the living God. When Cyrus says that Bel is a living god who eats great quantities of food daily, Daniel laughs and says that Bel eats *nothing*. The king tells the priests of Bel that if Bel does not eat the food they offer, they shall die; if he does, Daniel shall die.

Anxiously, the priests vow that Bel eats the food and suggest that the king prove it. Quantities of flour, sheep, and wine are set in front of Bel, but before the king locks the door,

Daniel sifts ashes over the temple floor. That night the priests and their families come to the temple by secret access and devour the food. In the morning, the king triumphantly shows Daniel that the food is gone, but Daniel laughs and points to the footprints on the floor. The priests and their families are all executed.

Read Daniel 14:1-22.

7. Daniel destroys a dragon-god—a serpent—by feeding it cakes of tar, fat, and hair until it bursts. He taunts the people, and they furiously demand that he be thrown to the lions. He is—but at that moment far away in Judaea, the prophet Habakkuk, about to take food to the reapers in the fields, is plucked by the hair and carried to the lions' den. The lions are mesmerized, Daniel eats the food, and seven days later the king finds Daniel safe and sound. You can easily imagine what the king does to the men who planned Daniel's destruction.

Read Daniel 14:23-42.

Daniel and the belief in resurrection

Long before the time of the Book of Daniel, the Jews believed that the dead resided in *Sheol*—a shadowy, melancholy place where the spiritual remains of the dead roamed about aimlessly forever. Their neighbors the Egyptians believed in life after death, but it was life as it was before death—including food, drink, clothing, and even slaves. That the good go to be with God in a new and glorified life was a belief that first appeared sometime in the third century B.C.E.

The question arises, On what is the teaching of resurrection based? The answer is hope. Considering the growth over the centuries of Israel's knowledge of God's love and power, it became unreasonable—and unacceptable—to the Jews that God's love would end with death.

Jonah: A Narrow-minded and Vindictive Prophet

The Book of Jonah, only four chapters long, is the most humorous book in the Bible—which does not mean that it is not to be taken seriously. The book is fiction, its author unknown, and its setting the Assyrian Empire around 750

The fictional quality of the stories in Daniel does not prevent them from teaching helpful truths. Rewrite one of the Daniel stories into a modern parable.

Sometime in the third century B.C.E., there arose the belief that good people live with God in a glorified existence after death.
Above: A tomb of the kind used in ancient Israel

B.C.E.—although Jonah was written in the fifth century B.C.E. It is a parable addressed to some narrow-minded Jews who held that Israel alone was the object of God's mercy. It also spoke to their forgetfulness of God's call to bear witness to the nations, and today it speaks to Christians just as sharply, for all its humor.

God tells Jonah to go to Nineveh, the capital of Assyria, and warn its people that their wickedness is known and is about to be punished. To Jonah the Ninevites are filthy pagans, and he wants nothing to do with them. So instead of doing as God instructs, he buys passage on a ship bound for the other end of the earth, Tarshish—that is, present-day Gibraltar. We might say Timbuktu.

Not to be outdone, God sends a storm, and Jonah's ship begins to founder. The sailors pray to their gods and throw cargo overboard—but Jonah, apparently feeling no guilt, sleeps peacefully in the hold. Finally the captain awakens him and orders him to pray to *his* God, while the sailors draw lots to see who is to blame for the peril. The finger points to Jonah, and when they ask who he is, Jonah confesses that he is running away from God. What should they do? Jonah says that there is nothing to do but throw him overboard. The sailors, nice men, try first to row ashore, but when at last they throw Jonah into the sea, they ask his God—whom they now take seriously—to forgive them.

Read Jonah 1:1-16.

Jonah is swallowed by a fish, in whose belly he remains for three days and three nights. Strangely enough, he sings a psalm of thanksgiving—as though he remembers that God is a saving God—after which the fish belches him up on the shore.

Now God sends Jonah to Nineveh a second time, and this time he goes and delivers the message: " 'Forty days more and Nineveh shall be destroyed' " (3:4). When Jonah has proclaimed his message only one day, the people repent, and the king puts on sackcloth, calls for a fast even for the cattle and sheep, and tells everyone to call loudly to God for mercy. Upon hearing Nineveh repent, God decides not to destroy it after all.

Read Jonah 2:1-11; 3:1-10.

But even though God is pleased, Jonah is not. He throws God's mercy back in God's face. This was the reason he refused to go to Nineveh in the first place! He *knew* that God would be too kindhearted to the Assyrians. Furthermore,

> Have you ever "run away" from a difficult situation like Jonah did? Did running away work? Write down your story and include the consequences of your running away.

now Jonah will be called a false prophet, and people will never take God seriously again. Jonah says that he wants to die, and God asks, " 'Have you reason to be angry?' " (4:4).
Read Jonah 4:1–4.

Jonah leaves the city in a huff, goes to a hillside, builds himself a hut, and waits to see if God will yet wreck Nineveh. A gourd vine grows up beside the hut, keeping Jonah cool in its shade, and he is cheerful for the first time in days. But the next morning a worm gnaws the vine until it withers and dies. A hot east wind blows and the sun beats down, and once again Jonah cries out angrily, "I want to die!"

God asks Jonah, "Have you good reason to be angry about the plant?" And Jonah, feeling abused, says, "Yes, I have . . . enough reason to want to die!" Then God reminds Jonah that the gourd plant was not his, cost him nothing, and that he did not make it grow or die. Is the fact that it wilted *really* Jonah's reason for wanting to die? Or is it because God chose to show mercy to the city of Nineveh and its 120,000 people, " 'who cannot distinguish their right hand from their left' " (4:11)? And the book ends; we never hear Jonah's answer.
Read Jonah 4:5–11.

Skirting the mission

A story told by Fr. Vincent Donavan fits the astonishing response of the Ninevites to Jonah's announcement. Father Donavan had served many years in Africa with the Masai tribe of Kenya. His community had worked hard to build schools and clinics, to teach, serve health needs, and much more. Finally, he decided that he wanted to do nothing but *evangelize* the Masai—teach them about Jesus. When he went to tell his Masai friends, they asked him, "Why did you wait so long?"

A Final Word

At last you have finished your study of the Hebrew Scriptures. We hope that you have enjoyed meeting Israel's patriarchs and prophets, kings (good and bad), and heroic men and women—and found them not so very different from yourself. At their best, they are like us at our best; and at their worst, they remind us that we have the same capacity for mediocrity and sin, and for calling upon God's saving help. If their stories have become part of your reflections as you face your challenges, they have served their purpose. And if knowing them helps you understand the teaching of

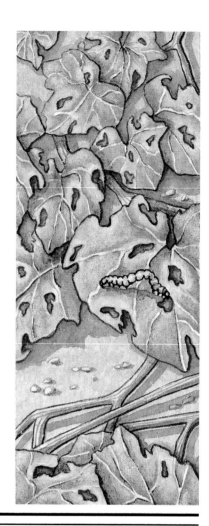

God asks the prophet Jonah why he is so upset about the death of a vine—but showed so little mercy toward the entire city of Nineveh. We never hear Jonah's answer.

Answer the following in writing:
● What do you think was Jonah's answer to God's question at the end of the Book of Jonah?

Jesus—which grew out of this saga of his people—then you are well-prepared to find ever-more power in the teaching of the Gospels.

We ask that God bless you richly with the enthusiasm that grows in those who learn to know and love the Scriptures, and we are grateful for having a small part in your journey.

For Review

1. What is the message of the Book of Job?

2. Who wrote the Psalms? When? Why were they written?

3. Explain the purpose of the Book of Proverbs.

4. What is Qoheleth's response to life's inconsistencies?

5. What is the subject of the Song of Songs?

6. What "first" is found in the Book of Wisdom?

7. According to Sirach, what was the way to wisdom?

8. Summarize the story of Tobit; tell how God answered both his prayers and Sarah's.

9. Retell briefly the story of Judith.

10. Why was the Book of Esther written? What Persian story does it reveal?

11. Summarize the mini-mystery in the Book of Daniel.

12. When did belief in resurrection first appear?

13. Retell the part of the Jonah story concerning the gourd plant.

Index

Pronunciation Key

ə	A schwa is used for very short vowels, for example, about, system, clarity, lemon, focus.	ō	obey, know	( )	Parentheses indicate that the sound symbolized between them is pronounced by some people but not by others.
a	mat, sad	ȯ	saw, caught		
ä	father, bother	oi	oil, boy		
ā	day, face	u̇	pull, book		
au̇	now, loud	ü	rule, spool		
e	end, met	zh	vision, treasure		
ē	seek, only	'	An accent mark follows a syllable that is stressed. Note that some foreign words require stress on all syllables and some have no accent mark at all.		
i	in, active				
ī	idea, buy				

C

Caesar, Julius, 222

Cain, 15, 27

Caleb \kā'-ləb\, 75, 77

Cambodia \kam-bōd'-ē-a\, 75

Canaan \kā'-nən\: aerial view of, 84; Egyptian control of, 87; Israelites' conquest of, 95–97; Israelites' entry into, 12; Moses' exploration of, 75, 77; as Promised Land, 11

Canaanites: alphabetic writing by, 155; Baal as god of, 146; cultural history of, 89

canon, 14

Canticle of Deborah, 99

canticles, 56, 157

capital punishment, 59

Carthage \kär'-thij\, 142

Catholic Worker Movement, 145

C.E. (of the common era), 10

Celts, 142

chaff, 107

Chaldeans \kal-dē'-ənz\, 190

chariots, 148, 185

charisma, 212

Chavín \chä-vēn'\, 119, 142

cherubim, 185–186

children, treatment of, 229

China: Chou \jō'\ dynasty, 142; Confucianism and Taoism, 210; first dictionary written, 119; picture writing system, 76; 2000–1700 B.C.E., 39; 1700–1250 B.C.E., 76; 1250–900 B.C.E., 119; 900–600 B.C.E., 142; 600–1 B.C.E., 210

Chronicler \krän'-i-k(ə-)lər\, the, 200

Chronicles, Books 1 and 2, 199–200

church, 75

circumcision, 33, 183

cleansing rite, 212

Commandments (Decalogue), the, 69, 82

concubines, 33

Confucianism \kən-fyü'-shə-niz-əm\, 210

Confucius \kən-fyü'-shəs\, 210

Conservative Judaism, 241

Consolation, Book of, 192–196

consonants, 155

Constitution, U.S., 69

contradictions in the Bible, 19, 21, 91

Corinthians \kə-rin'-thē-ənz\, First Letter to, 81

Court History of David, 113

covenant: Abram's with God, 33; Israel's with beasts and birds, 156; defined, 12; Noah's with God, 28

Covenant of Sinai, 16–17, 49; Israelites and, 11–12; Priestly Writer and, 17; renewal of, 96, 172; sealing of, 62–67

covenant of covenants, 62–63

covetousness, commandment against, 61

Creation, the, 15, 25–27; Sabbath and, 26

Crete, 39, 154

Croesus \krē'-səs\, 202

Crusades, the, 151

Cyrus \sī'-rəs\ the Persian, 192–194, 199, 202; conquest of Babylon by, 209; Daniel and, 245–246

Cyrus II, 202–203

D

Dagon \dā'-gon\, 100

Dan, brother of Joseph, 42

Dan, golden calf shrine at, 143, 201–202

Dan, tribe of, 101–103

Daniel, Book of, 18, 234, 243–246

Darius \də-rī'-əs\, 244

David: Absalom's death and, 131; anointed as king, 12, 117–118, 124–125; Bathsheba and, 128–129; children of, 130–131; in Chronicles, 200; death of, 133–134; empire of, 132; Goliath and, 117–118; as

king, 123–133; marriage to Abigail, 121–122; Meribbaal and, 127–128; and messianic promise, 127; as outlaw, 121–122; with the Philistines, 122–123; psalms attributed to, 16, 184, 225, 227; Ruth as ancestor of, 110; Saul's jealousy of, 120; unites Israel, 124–126

Day, Dorothy, 145

Day of Atonement, 71

Dead Sea Scrolls, 20

Deborah, 97, 98–99

Decalogue \dek'-ə-log\, 58

Delilah \də-lī'-lə\, 102

Demetrius \də-mē'-trē-əs\, 219

descendants of Abram, 32

Deuteronomists \d(y)üt-ə-rän'-ə-məsts\, 17; editing of Books of Samuel by, 113; on outdoor sanctuaries, 134; portrayal of David by, 200

Deuteronomy \d(y)üt-ə-rän'-ə-mē\, Book of, 81–84; first sermon, 81–82; second sermon, 82–84; third sermon, 84

Diaspora \dī-as'-p(ə-)rə\, 14

Diego, Juan, 166

Dispersion, the, 14, 141, 182–183; Jewish assimilation in foreign cities, 240; the Scriptures as letters from home, 15

divorce, 212

Donavan, Fr. Vincent, 248

donkey, 163

doubt, Abram's, 32

dragon, 191

dragon-god, 246

E

Ecbatana \ek-bat'-ən-ə\, 235–236

Ecclesiastes \ik-lē-zē-as'-tēz\, Book of, 16, 18, 229–230

Edict of Cyrus, 200–201

Edom \ēd'-əm\, 38, 132, 160, 214–215

G

L

Laban \lā'-bən\, 38, 40
Lamentations, Book of, 18, 171, 181, 184
Lao-tzu \laùd'-zü'\, 210
Last Supper, 54–55
latter prophets, 141
Law of Moses, 69
Lawrence, Saint, 179
laws in Deuteronomy, 84
Leah \lē'-ə\, 40
leprosy, 75
letters, the Scriptures as, 15
Levi, 69–70
levirate \lev'-ə-rət\ **law,** 84, 106, 109
Levites, 69–70, 212; Aaron's authority challenged by, 77; priestly role of, 74
Leviticus \li-vit 'i-kəs\, **Book of,** 69–73; Aaron and his sons, 72–73; holiness code, 72
Lincoln, Abraham, 118
lion's den, 244
Lo-ammi \lō-am'-mē\, 157
locusts, plague of, 153, 214
Lo-ruhama \lō-rü-hä'-mə\, 156–157
Lot, 34–35
Lourdes \lù(ə)rd(z)'\, 166
Luke, Gospel of, 35, 149, 225

M

Macbeth, 123
Maccabees \mak'-ə-bēz\, **Books 1 and 2,** 199, 215–220, 243
Maccabeus \mak-ə-bē'-əs\, **Judas,** 215, 217–220
magi \mā'-jī\, 80
Magnificat \mag-nif'-i-kat\, 114
major prophets, 18
Malachi \mal'-ə-kī\, 18, 160, 199, 204, 207–208
Manasseh \mə-nas'-ə\, 44, 46, 96, 99–100, 168–169, 172
manger scene, source of, 163
manna, 57, 91
Mara \mä'-rə\, 106

Marduk \mär'-dük\, 119, 191, 195, 202, 212
Mary, 114
Masai tribe of Kenya, 248
matriarchs, 11, 16
Mattathias \mat-ə-thī'-əs\, 217–218
Matthew, Gospel of, 80
Matthias \mə-thī'-əs\, 96
matzo, 55
Mayans \mī'-ənz\, 154
Media \mēd'-ē-ə\, 235
Melchizedek \mel-kiz'-ə-dek\, 32
Mene \mē'-nē\, 244
menorah, 218–219
mercy seat, 65
Meribbaal \mer-ə-bā'-əl\, 127–128, 131, 133
Meshach \mē'-shak\, 244
Messiah, the: of David's line, 113; Elijah prophesies, 149; Zechariah prophesies, 206–207
messianic promise, 127
mezuzah \mə-zùz'-ə\, 83
Micah \mī'-kə\, 18, 141, 158–159, 160, 175
Michal \mī'-kəl\, 130; as David's wife, 120, 122, 124–125; fate of, 126–127
Michelangelo, 130
Midas, King, 202
Midianites, 99–101
Midians \mid'-i-ənz\, 50
minor prophets, 18, 171
Miriam \mir'-ē-əm\, 56; and Aaron, 75; punishment of, 82
Mishael \mish'-ə-el\, 243
Moab \mō'-ab\, 79, 105; Moses' journey to, 81
Modein \mō'-din\, 217
monogamy as biblical ideal, 33
monotheism, 14, 210
Mordecai \mor'-də-kī\, 240, 242–243
Moresheth \mor'-ə-sheth\, 158
Mosaic Law, 69, 191, 241

Moses, 144; and Aaron and his sons, 72–73, 75; and bronze serpent, 78; and burning bush, 50–51; and Covenant of Sinai, 11–12, 62–67; crossing Sea of Reeds, 55–56; death of, 84; destroying tablets, 63–64; early life of, 49–50; fleeing Egypt, 19, 49–50, 55; and golden calf, 63–64; heroic stature of, 11–12; and Miriam and Aaron, 75; at Mount Sinai, 50–51, 57; and murmuring stories, 56–57; and Passover, 54–55; and Pharaoh, 51, 54, 55–56; protecting Israelite slave, 50; return to Egypt, 51; sermons of, in Deuteronomy, 81–84; and Ten Commandments, 58–59, 61–62; and water from rock, 78; Yahweh and, 64
Mount of Olives, 131
Mozart, 116
multiplication of loaves, 149
murder: commandment forbidding, 59; David guilty of, 129
murmuring stories: in Exodus, 56–57; in Numbers, 74–75

N

Naaman \nā'-mən\, 149–150
Nabal \nā'-bəl\, 121–122
Naboth's \nā'-boths\ **vineyard,** 146–147, 150
Nadab \nā'-dab\, 143
Nahum \nā'-(h)əm\, 18, 160, 171–172, 180–181
Naomi \nā-ō'-mē\, 105, 109–110
Naphtali \naf'-tə-lī\, 42, 98
Nathan, 127, 144; denunciation of David by, 129, 141; parable and prophecy of, 129; and Solomon's kingship, 133–134
Nazirite \naz '-ə-rīt\, 102–103

R

Ra \rä'\, 49, 51–53
Rachel: death of, 42; marriage of, 38, 40
Raguel \rə-gyü'-əl\, 235–236
Rahab \rā'-hab\, 88, 90, 91
rainbow, 28–29
Ramses \ram'-sēz\ II, 53
rape, 34, 129–130
Raphael \raf'-i-el\, 235–236
reaping, 107
Rebekah, 36–38
rebellion stories, 77
redemption, 71
red hair, symbolism of, 38
Reform Judaism, 241
Rehoboam \rē-(h)ə-bō'-əm\, 143, 159, 161
Reigns, Books of, 113
remnant, Israel as, 180
resurrection: atonement and, 71; Book of Daniel and, 246; in Book of Wisdom, 233
Reuben, 42, 44, 77
Revelation, Book of, 206
revenge, commandment forbidding, 59
ritual: in Leviticus, 69–73; Priestly Writer and, 17; religion reduced to, 152–153; sacrifice, 32
Roman Empire: compared with Assyrian Empire, 165; Jewish population in, 182–183; ruling Israel, 13, 220–221
Ruth, Book of, 87, 105–111

S

Sabbath, 26; commandment enforcing, 59; keeping of, 212
sacrifice, 71, 117. *See also* human sacrifice
sages, 10
saints, 148
Salem, 32

Salieri \säl-yer'-ē\, 116
salt pillars, 34–35
Salvadoran refugees, 96
Samaria \sə-mer'-ē-ə\, 141, 144, 153, 164, 185, 188, 201
Samaritans: hatred of Jews, 201–202; Jesus and the woman, 153
Samson, 97, 101–103
Samuel, 144; anointing David, 117–118; anointing Saul, 113; birth of, 114; God's call to, 114; as prophet, 115–116; rejecting Saul, 116–117, 141
Samuel, Books 1 and 2, 97, 113, 123–133
Sanballat \san-bal'-ət\, 211
sanctuary, 95
Sarah (daughter of Raguel), 235–236
Sarah (matriarch): and birth of Isaac, 35; name change to, 33; at visitation, 33–34
Sarai \sa(ə)r'-ī\, 32–33
Satan, 226
Saul \sol'\, 113; anointed king, 113, 116; David and, 117–118, 120–121; death of, 123–124; descendants of, 127; rise and fall of, 114–117; and witchcraft, 122–123
Scheherazade \shə-her-ə-zäd(-ə)'\, 243
scrolls: Dead Sea (Qumran) scrolls, 20; eaten by Ezekiel, 185–186; parchment, 11
Sea of Reeds, 55–56
Second Isaiah, 14, 18, 160–161, 171, 192–196, 204. *See also* First Isaiah; Third Isaiah
Second Vatican Council, 19–20
Seder \sād'-ər\, 54–55
Seleucid \sə-lü'-səd\ dynasty, 215–216, 218–220, 235

Semites \sem'-īts\, 31, 49; as pharaohs, 53
Sennacherib \sə-nak'-ə-rəb\, 235
Septuagint \sep-t(y)ü'-ə-jənt\, 182
septuaginta \sep-t(y)ü'-ə-jənt-ə\, 182
seraphim \ser'-ə-fim\, 166
serpent: in Genesis, 26; bronze, 78, 167–168
Servant Songs, 193–196
sexuality, 231–232; commandments against illicit, 59, 61
Shadrach \shad'-rak\, 243
Shakespeare, William, 123, 131
Shallum \shal'-əm\, 211
Shamash, 60
Sheba, queen of, 138
Shechem \shēk-əm\, 96
Sheep Gate, 209
Shema \shə-mä'\, 82
Sheol \shē-ōl'\, 246
shepherd allegory, 206–207
Sheshbazaar \shesh-baz'-ər\, 201
shofar \shō'-fär\, 91
Siddhārtha Gautama \sid-där'-tə-gaù'-tə-mə\, 210
Sidon \sīd'-n\, 144–145
Simchas Torah \sim-kə-stōr'-ə\, 6–7
Simeon \sim'-ē-ən\, 44
Simon, 217, 219–220
sin: in Creation story, 26–27; spread of, 27–29
Sinai \sī'-nī\, Mount, 16, 146; Israelites' arrival at, 57; Moses' calling at, 50
Sinai Peninsula, 58, 73
Sirach \sir'-ak\, Book of, 18
Sirach, Jesus ben, 233–234
Sisera \sis'-ər-ə\, 99
slaughter of the Innocents, 222
slavery, laws against, 62, 84
Socrates, 210
Sodom \säd'-əm\, 34–35, 188
sodomy, 34–35

Acknowledgments *(continued)*

The scriptural quotations in this book are from the New American Bible. Copyright © 1987 by the Confraternity of Christian Doctrine, Washington, D.C. All rights reserved.

The quotation on page 19 is from *The Dogmatic Constitution on Divine Revelation,* as printed in *Vatican Council II: The Conciliar and Post Conciliar Documents,* Austin Flannery, OP, general editor (Northport, NY: Costello Publishing Co., 1975), page 757.

The excerpt on page 23 is quoted in *Great Religions of the World,* by Sr. Loretta Pastva, SND (Winona, MN: Saint Mary's Press, 1986), page 170.

The quotation by Martin Buber on page 115 is from *The Writings of Martin Buber,* edited by Will Herberg (Cleveland: The World Publishing Co., 1956), page 296.

The poem on page 176 is from *Letters and Papers from Prison* (revised, enlarged edition), by Dietrich Bonhoeffer. Copyright © 1971 by SCM Press, Ltd. Reprinted with permission of Macmillan Publishing Company.

Photo Credits

Cover: Tom Nebbia (large photo), Richard Nowitz (inset)

Art Resource: page 130

The Bettmann Archive: page 124

The British Museum, courtesy of the trustees: page 165

Catholic News Service: pages 9, 75, 95, 145

Robert Echert: pages 14, 188, 196, 205, 228, 231 (right)

Editorial Development Associates: pages 110, 126, 128

Explorer: pages 33, 170, 194, 197

Robert Harding Picture Library: pages 39, 198, 223

Michael Holford: pages 53 (left), 119

Israel Department of Antiquities and Museums: page 185

Barry Iverson, copyright © 1987 by Time-Life Books, Inc., from the Time Frame series: page 89

Erich Lessing: pages 31, 58, 68, 85, 135, 151, 154, 168, 175, 190, 193, 202, 215, 221, 222

Pierre Mion, copyright © National Geographic Society: page 191

National Aeronautics and Space Administration: page 73

Tom Nebbia: pages 1, 24, 47, 80, 84, 86, 92, 111

Richard Nowitz: pages 2, 4, 6, 20 (left), 23, 40, 55, 91, 107 (left), 112, 139, 140, 163, 169, 173, 183, 213, 230 (left), 241, 246

The Oriental Institute of the University of Chicago: page 203

G. Dagli Orti: pages 52, 53 (right), 210, 216

Peabody Museum, Harvard University, photographed by Hillel Burger: page 142

Ann Purcell: page 147

Carl Purcell: page 19

Zev Radovan: pages 11, 34, 48, 67, 76, 83 (left), 104, 107 (right), 182, 224, 235, 243, 249

Religious News Service: pages 56, 176, 226

David Rubinger: page 122

Scala/Art Resource: page 155

Lorraine O. Schultz: pages 20 (right), 83 (right)

Service photographique de la Réunion des musées nationaux: page 60

James Shaffer: page 231 (left)

Kay Shaw: page 233

The Washington Post: page 230 (right)